Adolescent Literacy

Adolescent Literacy
Strategies for Content Comprehension in Inclusive Classrooms

edited by

Richard T. Boon, Ph.D.
The University of Sydney
Australia

and

Vicky G. Spencer, Ph.D.
George Mason University
Fairfax, Virginia

·P·A·U·L·H·
BROOKES
PUBLISHING CO ®

Baltimore • London • Sydney

Paul H. Brookes Publishing Co.
Post Office Box 10624
Baltimore, Maryland 21285-0624
USA

www.brookespublishing.com

Typeset by Integrated Publishing Solutions, Grand Rapids, Michigan.
Manufactured in the United States of America by
Sheridan Books, Inc., Chelsea, Michigan.

All examples in this book are composites. Any similarity to actual individuals or
circumstances is coincidental, and no implications should be inferred.

Cover photo © iStockphoto.com/Goldfaery.

Figures 2.1 and 7.1 clip art © 2012 Jupiterimages Corporation.

Library of Congress Cataloging-in-Publication Data

Adolescent literacy : strategies for content comprehension in inclusive classrooms / edited by Richard T. Boon,
Ph.D., and Vicky G. Spencer, Ph.D.
    pages   cm
    ISBN-13: 978-1-59857-220-9; ISBN-10: 1-59857-220-2
    1. Language arts (Secondary)   2. Content area reading.   3. Inclusive education.   I. Boon, Richard T.
    LB1631.A343786   2013
    428.4071'2–dc23   2012033680

British Library Cataloguing in Publication data are available from the British Library.

2016   2015   2014   2013   2012

10   9   8   7   6   5   4   3   2   1

Contents

About the Editors

Richard T. Boon, Ph.D., is a lecturer in the Faculty of Education and Social Work, Special & Inclusive Education program, at The University of Sydney, Australia. His research interests include cognitive strategy instruction, literacy, adolescent learners, content-area instruction, inclusion, and technology-based applications for students with disabilities. He has authored more than 50 publications, including peer-reviewed journal articles, book chapters, and national/international conference proceedings. In addition, he has made more than 100 presentations at local, state, regional, national, and international conferences. Currently, he serves as Co-editor of *Learning Disabilities: A Contemporary Journal* and Associate Editor of *Reading & Writing Quarterly: Overcoming Learning Difficulties.*

Vicky G. Spencer, Ph.D., is an associate professor in the Division of Special Education and disAbility Research at George Mason University in Fairfax, Virginia. She also coordinates the applied behavior analysis and the autism certificate programs. Her research interests include cognitive strategy instruction and international issues in special education, inclusion, and autism. She has authored or edited numerous research articles and published four books that address differentiated instruction and teaching in the inclusive classroom. Dr. Spencer is a Fulbright Scholar and works internationally to improve the identification of and education for children with disabilities.

About the Contributors

Sheila R. Alber-Morgan, Ph.D., Associate Professor of Special Education, The Ohio State University, A356 PAES Building 305 W. 17th Ave. Columbus, OH 43210. Dr. Alber-Morgan's research focuses on multitiered reading and writing interventions in inclusive classrooms and programming for generalized outcomes.

Alison G. Boardman, Ph.D., Assistant Research Professor, University of Colorado Boulder, School of Education, 247 UCB, Boulder, CO 80309. Dr. Boardman is an assistant research professor at the University of Colorado at Boulder. Currently, she is the co-principal investigator of a U.S. Department of Education–funded grant to study the schoolwide use of Collaborative Strategic Reading in urban middle schools. A former elementary and middle school special educator, she has extensive experience providing professional development to teachers to successfully teach comprehension strategies in their classrooms.

Randall Boone, Ph.D., Professor, University of Nevada, Las Vegas, College of Education, Department of Teaching and Learning, 4505 Maryland Parkway, Las Vegas, NV 89154-3005. Dr. Boone is a professor of educational technology at the University of Nevada, Las Vegas. His research interests involve digital text, instructional design, and evaluating software for students with disabilities. He served as co-editor of the *Journal of Special Education Technology* for 6 years and currently co-edits *Intervention in School and Clinic.*

Michelle M. Buehl, Ph.D., Associate Professor, George Mason University, 4400 University Drive, MSN 6D2, Fairfax, VA 22030. Dr. Buehl is an associate professor at George Mason University and affiliated with the Educational Psychology program in the College of Education and Human Development. Her research focuses on the role of student and teacher beliefs in relation to learning and motivation.

Stephen Ciullo, Ph.D., Assistant Professor, Texas State University, and Meadows Center for Preventing Educational Risk, College of Education, 601 University Drive, San Marcos, TX 78666. Dr. Ciullo is an assistant professor of Special Education at Texas State University and a researcher for the Meadows Center for Preventing Educational Risk. His current research involves interventions to enhance content-area learning and reading comprehension for students with learning disabilities and emotional or behavioral disorders.

Sally Valentino Drew, M.S., Assistant Professor, Central Connecticut State University, 1615 Stanley Street, New Britain, CT 06050. Ms. Drew is an assistant professor of teacher education at Central

Connecticut State University (CCSU) and university facilitator of a CCSU professional development school. Ms. Drew's research examines the intersection of clinical practice and teacher education, especially related to literacy instruction and struggling learners. She is a Ph.D. candidate at the University of Connecticut in the Department of Educational Psychology with a concentration in special education.

Nancy Johnson Emanuel, M.Ed., Department Supervisor of Special Education, Osbourn High School, Manassas City Public Schools, Manassas, VA 20110. Ms. Emanuel graduated from Bridgewater State College, Bridgewater, Massachusetts, with a B.A. in history and secondary education. She went on to serve in the U.S. Navy for 9 years as a Russian linguist and has taught at both the secondary and elementary levels of public education. She received her master's degree in special education from the University of Virginia and is currently a doctoral student in special education and education leadership at George Mason University in Fairfax, Virginia. Ms. Emanuel is the department supervisor for special education in Manassas City, Virginia.

Michael N. Faggella-Luby, Ph.D., Associate Professor, University of Connecticut, Department of Educational Psychology, Neag School of Education, 249 Glenbrook Road, Unit 2064, Storrs, CT 06269-2064. Dr. Faggella-Luby is also a research scientist at the Center for Behavioral Education and Research and an associate research scholar at the Center on Postsecondary Education and Disability. Dr. Faggella-Luby conducts research on critical components of reading comprehension instruction with academically diverse students.

Lindsay J. Flynn, Ph.D., Assistant Professor, University of North Carolina at Charlotte, 9201 University City Boulevard, Charlotte, NC 28223-0001. Dr. Flynn's current research interests include assessment and intervention of reading difficulties, responsiveness to intervention, and designing instruction for students at risk for and identified with learning disabilities.

Douglas Fuchs, Ph.D., Nicholas Hobbs Professor of Special Education and Human Development, Peabody College, Vanderbilt University, Department of Special Education, 110 Magnolia Circle, Room 417C, Nashville, TN 37203. Dr. Fuchs is a former classroom teacher, special educator, and school psychologist. He directed the Vanderbilt Kennedy Center Reading Clinic for 12 years. His current interests include reading and math disabilities, intensive instruction, service delivery options, urban education, and education policy.

Lynn S. Fuchs, Ph.D., Nicholas Hobbs Professor of Special Education and Human Development, Peabody College, Vanderbilt University, Department of Special Education, 110 Magnolia Circle, Room 417C, Nashville, TN 37203. Dr. Fuchs's research addresses teachers' use of classroom-based assessment information and instructional practices for improving reading and mathematics performance.

Meenakshi Gajria, Ph.D., Professor and Dean, St. Thomas Aquinas College, School of Education, 125 Route 340, Sparkill, NY 10976. Dr. Gajria received her Ph.D. in special education from Pennsylvania State University. Her research interests focus on strategies to promote reading comprehension for students with learning disabilities and instructional practices of teachers.

Kyle Higgins, Ph.D., Professor of Special Education, University of Nevada, Las Vegas, College of Education, Department of Educational and Clinical Studies, 4505 Maryland Parkway, Las Vegas, NV 89154-3014. Dr. Higgins's research interests involve digital text, evaluating software for students with disabilities, and the application of common core standards for students with disabilities. She served as co-editor of the *Journal of Special Education Technology* for 6 years and currently co-edits *Intervention in School and Clinic.*

Asha K. Jitendra, Ph.D., University of Minnesota, Department of Educational Psychology, 245 Education Sciences Building, 56 East River Road, Minneapolis, MN 55455. Dr. Jitendra received her Ph.D. in curriculum and instruction (special education) from the University of Oregon. She is the Rodney Wallace Professor for Advancement of Teaching and Learning at the University of Minnesota. Her research interests include academic and curricular strategies in mathematics and reading for students with learning disabilities, assessment practices to inform instruction, and instructional design and textbook analysis.

Laurice M. Joseph, Ph.D., Associate Professor, Director, School Psychology Program, The Ohio State University, 305 West 17th Ave., PAES Building, Room 460, Columbus, OH 43210. Dr. Joseph's research has involved examining the effectiveness and efficiency of literacy interventions.

Margaret E. King-Sears, Ph.D., Professor, George Mason University, 4400 University Drive, MS 1F2 Fairfax, VA 22030. Dr. King-Sears has researched and published about topics such as teaching students how to use self-management and teaching educators how to differentiate for inclusion while still ensuring students receive intensive specialized instruction for academics and social skills. Current research includes analyzing middle school content textbooks to determine features that promote students' effective learning from the texts. She is also examining how co-teachers interact when demonstrating new content to students, as well as students' perceptions of "who's in charge" during their co-taught classes.

Janette K. Klinger, Ph.D., Professor, University of Colorado at Boulder, School of Education, 249 UCB, Boulder, CO 80309. Dr. Klinger was a bilingual special education teacher for 10 years before completing her Ph.D. in reading and learning disabilities at the University of Miami. She has been developing and conducting research on Collaborative Strategic Reading for almost 20 years.

Joseph John Morgan, Ph.D., Assistant Professor, University of Nevada, Las Vegas, 4505 S. Maryland Parkway, Box 453014, Las Vegas, NV 89154. Dr. Morgan's research areas of interest are social skills instruction for students with behavioral disorders, academic achievement of students with high-incidence disabilities, and multicultural education.

Leila Richey, M.A., Doctoral Student, George Mason University, 4400 University Drive, Fairfax, VA 22030. Ms. Richey taught high school social studies in a large Northeast urban district prior to obtaining a master of arts degree in the reading specialist program at Teachers College, Columbia University. She is currently a doctorate student studying at George Mason University with a primary specialization in teacher education and secondary emphasis in literacy.

Colleen Klein Reutebuch, Ph.D., Research Associate, The University of Texas, The Meadows Center for Preventing Educational Risk, College of Education, 1 University Station D4900, SZB 228, Austin, TX 78712. Dr. Reutebuch has experience coordinating and managing large-scale research projects funded by the Institute of Education Sciences, as well as grants related to state and federally funded professional development and technical assistance in reading success initiatives.

Suzanne M. Robinson, Ph.D., Associate Professor, The University of Kansas, Department of Special Education, Joseph R. Pearson Hall, 1122 West Campus Rd., Room 544, Lawrence, KS 66045-3101. Dr. Robinson's work is focused on teacher preparation in special education for K–12 students with high-incidence disabilities and doctoral student preparation for those who will become professors of teacher education at universities and colleges. She has spent over 25 years working with schools, school districts, state and regional agencies, and professional organizations in school restructuring activities to promote academic achievement for struggling learners. Dr. Robinson's expertise is in collaboration (co-teaching, coaching, teaming) and evidence based academic instructional practices, with a focus on school restructuring through building responsive tiered student support structures.

Karla Scornavacco, Ph.D., Research Associate, University of Colorado Boulder, 249 UCB Boulder, CO 80309. Dr. Scornavacco specializes in teacher support and school capacity building for Collaborative Strategic Reading Colorado. Her research investigates the positioning and academic preparation of adolescents in high-poverty classrooms, with a focus on what it takes for schools and teachers to support students in becoming college-bound and college-successful readers and writers.

H. Lee Swanson, Ph.D., Distinguished Professor of Educational Psychology, University of California, Graduate School of Education, Riverside, CA, 92521. Dr. Swanson's research focuses on cognitive processes in children with learning disabilities.

Ana Taboada Barber, Ph.D., Assistant Professor, Literacy and Educational Psychology Programs, College of Education and Human Development, George Mason University, Thompson, Room 2506, 4400 University Drive, MS 4B3, Fairfax, VA 22030. Dr. Taboada Barber is a member of the education faculty at George Mason University. Dr. Taboada Barber's research focuses on the examination of classroom contexts that support reading engagement for monolingual and second language learners. She is currently the principal investigator of an Institute of Education Sciences grant that investigates some of these topics in young adolescents. Her research has been published in the *Journal of Educational Psychology, Reading Psychology, Reading and Writing: An Interdisciplinary Journal, Journal of Literacy Research,* and *Journal of Experimental Research.* She is a former classroom teacher and Fulbright Scholar.

Jessica R. Toste, Ph.D., Postdoctoral Research Fellow, Vanderbilt University, Department of Special Education, 110 Magnolia Circle, Room 401, Nashville, TN 37203. Dr. Toste is an elementary teacher and learning disabilities specialist. She is also an adjunct professor in the Department of Educational & Counseling Psychology at McGill University. Her research interests are related to school success and psychosocial functioning of youth at risk, with a particular interest in struggling readers.

Sharon Vaughn, Ph.D., H.E. Hartfelder/Southland Corp. Regents Chair in Human Development and Executive Director of the Meadows Center for Preventing Educational Risk, The University of Texas at Austin, College of Education SZB 228, 1 University Station D4900, Austin, TX 78712. Dr. Vaughn was Editor-in-Chief of the *Journal of Learning Disabilities* and Co-editor of *Learning Disabilities Research and Practice.* She is the recipient of the AERA SIG distinguished researcher award and The University of Texas Distinguished Faculty Award. She is the author of numerous books and research articles that address the reading and social outcomes of students with learning difficulties. She is currently Principal Investigator or Co-principal Investigator on several Institute of Education Sciences, National Institute of Child Health and Human Development, and U.S. Department of Education research grants investigating effective interventions for students with reading difficulties and students who are English language learners. She is the author of more than 10 books, 150 peer-reviewed research articles, and 50 chapters.

Yan Wei, M.A., Doctoral Student, University of Connecticut, Department of Educational Psychology, Neag School of Education, 249 Glenbrook Rd, Unit 2064, Storrs, CT 06269. Ms. Wei is also a graduate assistant at the Center for Behavioral Education and Research. Her research interest focuses on literacy instruction and motivation for struggling adolescent readers.

Foreword

Significantly less attention has been given by researchers, policy makers, and those involved in professional preparation to adolescents who struggle in learning than to their younger age counterparts. Most funding investments, for example, have been directed at younger students on the assumption that if intervention is provided at a young age, many learning difficulties would be minimized or avoided altogether in later years. However, research has shown that adolescents who struggle in learning demonstrate characteristics that are manifested in differing ways as development and setting demands change.

Although the goals for early identification and intervention are important and laudable, there is a potential danger in overemphasizing early treatment *at the expense of* interventions at later ages. That is, the calls for these early intervention efforts *may be* misinterpreted as implying that by intervening early, most of the problems presented by students will be taken care of and students will be placed on a path of academic success. Although this is certainly a desired outcome, this book underscores the fact that sizable numbers of individuals arrive at adolescence in need of being taught in ways that will enable them to successfully navigate the rigorous demands of secondary curriculum requirements.

The need for effective instructional and intervention strategies for older individuals is as great as, if not greater than, the need for interventions for younger children because of all the emotional overlays that generally emerge as individuals mature and continue to encounter significant failure. Each chapter in this book is written by leading scholars in the field of adolescent literacy. The information provided in the text about the unique learning characteristics and dispositions of struggling adolescent learners as well as the nature of the complex curriculum demands across subject matter disciplines provides a very informative backdrop against which to design and implement instruction.

This book is in a class of its own. Not only does it make a compelling case for the unique and very significant needs of struggling adolescent learners, but it does so in ways that other books on adolescent literacy do not. Specifically, many books on adolescent literacy are narrow in scope and limited to surface level overviews of a broad array of topics related to adolescent literacy. This book, on the other hand, provides detailed explanations of specific instructional strategies for enhancing the comprehension and performance of struggling older learners. Topics range from story-structure routines and graphic organizers to peer-mediated learning strategies and technology-based interventions. Each topic presents explicit explanations and protocols of how to plan, organize, and deliver instruction in general education classrooms and support environments. Each chapter is clearly organized and clearly written.

In light of the way that this book is structured, I am convinced that practitioners will find it to be one of the most valuable resources available to them for the following reasons:

- It is grounded in the empirical literature—hence, the instructional suggestions can be used with confidence of achieving favorable outcomes.

- It is principle based.

- It is comprehensive in scope, including a broad array of related resources for extended study of key topical areas.

- It provides clear, step-by-step instructions for how to implement and interpret various assessment protocols and how to link them to program plans and instructional routines.

I believe that this book will provide practitioners, researchers, and policy makers with the foundation that they will need to successfully create the kinds of environments and cultures of learning that will promote optimal academic, social, and employment success. Each chapter in this very readable book is written with passion, vivid examples, and numerous practical suggestions that can be readily implemented.

Donald D. Deshler, Ph.D.
Williamson Family Distinguished Professor of Special Education
Director, Center for Research on Learning
University of Kansas

Acknowledgments

We express our sincere gratitude and appreciation to the contributing authors for taking the time to share their expertise in the area of adolescent literacy and to further the education of those who work with students who struggle with reading comprehension in content areas. We also thank all of the students, teachers, administrators, and researchers we have worked with over the years who have taught us about providing effective instruction to meet the needs of *all* learners in the inclusive classroom. Finally, we sincerely thank Dr. Donald Deshler for writing the foreword to our book.

To our parents, William and Linda Boon and Herman and Bobbie Wilcox,
and our spouses, Julia and Steve,
for their continuous love and support in pursuing
our passion to improve the lives of individuals with disabilities

1 | Understanding Reading Comprehension

Challenges for Older Students with Reading Disabilities

Lindsay J. Flynn and H. Lee Swanson

Content area literacy is a critical component to academic success for adolescent students. For many years, however, significantly more attention has been paid to improving the reading skills of elementary school students, and neglecting the needs of older readers struggling with both basic reading skills and content knowledge acquisition. Not all students at risk for reading deficits receive intervention early in their literacy skill development, despite the fact that early intervention is a key component to remediating reading difficulties, and, in many cases, intervention is ineffective (Flynn, Zheng, & Swanson, 2012). This leaves a significant number of adolescent students with reading disabilities. Unfortunately, the problems associated with reading disabilities will continue to follow individuals beyond the K–12 education system and into adulthood. The impact of such reading deficits can be seen in all facets of adult life, including continued education, employment opportunities, daily living skills, and community involvement.

The demands of content area academics for older students are complex, challenging, and necessitate the integration of multiple skills. Older students are required to use numerous text materials to increase and demonstrate knowledge of varying content. Deficits associated with reading skills, including word identification, fluency, vocabulary, and comprehension, will not only affect an older reader's capacity to gain access to text, but also successfully master and demonstrate core academic skills. The skill set associated with text comprehension is of particular importance. Comprehension is viewed as the ultimate goal of reading. Adolescent readers, however, must do more than simply make meaning from the text they read. They must also connect prior knowledge to new information, identify key components and concepts related to the content area of focus, learn and use new vocabulary in novel situations, and employ strategies enabling them to gain access to and acquire content area knowledge.

Adolescents with reading disabilities must navigate the challenges involved in content knowledge acquisition paired with deficits in reading comprehension skill. The learning demands placed on these students exceed those experienced by their typically developing peers and add an element of difficulty to instruction as teachers must concurrently address content and comprehension within an environment already stretched tight on time. Addressing comprehension skills within content area instruction becomes complex as text structures vary widely across materials, language is often abstract and relies on knowledge of conceptual constructs (De Oliveira, 2010), unfamiliar vocabulary may hinder basic understanding (Hairrell et al., 2011), and older students with reading disabilities frequently have difficulty selecting and using appropriate comprehension strategies (Gersten, Fuchs, Williams, & Baker, 2001).

Some of the data discussed in this chapter are found in greater detail in the following resources: Swanson (2001); Swanson and Deshler (2003); Swanson and Hoskyn (1998, 2001).

Several factors contribute to poor comprehension in adolescent readers. The remainder of this chapter discusses the contributing factors, including problems at the word level, issues associated with fluency, challenges faced with content area vocabulary, the impact of a student's background knowledge, understanding of text structure, and organizational knowledge on comprehension, strategy use, and motivation. This discussion is followed by highlighting the key findings related to a meta-analysis of reading intervention research directed at the instructional practices for improving comprehension in older readers. The chapter concludes with a brief summary and recommendations for the direction educators and researchers should head to effectively address the challenges associated with reading comprehension skills of adolescents.

FACTORS CONTRIBUTING TO POOR COMPREHENSION

Multiple skills working in tandem are required to ensure successful comprehension of a given text. A deficit in any one of these skills may significantly affect a student's understanding of text and subsequent learning. It is important to understand the contribution that each of these skills has to comprehension because it will enable teachers to effectively select instructional methods at improving reading comprehension.

Word Level Problems

Word level reading skills are essential for students to gain access to texts and other materials containing information specific to content area learning. Unfortunately, merely identifying the words within their content text materials presents a major challenge for many struggling readers. Comprehension is an impossible feat without the ability to translate the letters on the page into recognizable words in language. Successful word level reading for older readers includes a wide array of skills associated with having phonological awareness, understanding morphology, and knowing the complexities affiliated with reading multisyllabic words.

Phonological Awareness   Phonological awareness encompasses the understanding that words are comprised of separate units of sound and letters or combinations of letters represent these same units of sound. The systematic and predictable relationships between spoken sounds and written letters are not transparent to students demonstrating deficits in phonological awareness. It is critical, however, that students develop a strong sense of phonological awareness given its high correlation to reading achievement (Adams, 1990; Bhat, Griffin, & Sindelar, 2003; Juel, 1988), including performance on tasks of comprehension.

Comprehension relies on accurately identifying the words within a given text. Students struggling at the word level expend significant cognitive resources decoding the text, which leaves limited capacity available to make meaning of the reading (LaBerge & Samuels, 1974). The fact that there are 44 sounds in the English language with only 26 letters available to represent the sounds increases the challenges faced by students struggling to make sense of reading individual words. Errors in word identification or inordinate amounts of time spent distinguishing letter–sound correspondences increase the likelihood that a struggling reader will experience comprehension deficits and low levels of achievement in core academic content areas.

Morphology   Despite the highly alphabetic nature of the English language, there are aspects of the writing system that require knowledge of more than letter–sound correspondences (Nagy, Berninger, & Abbott, 2006). Morphology involves studying the smallest units of meaning in words (morphemes) and breaking those units apart to decipher the meanings of new or unknown words (Ebbers & Denton, 2008). Understanding the meanings of word parts such as prefixes and suffixes can improve performance on tasks of reading comprehension (Nagy et al., 2006). This is important because morphemic knowledge is useful to determine word meanings as the words found in core academic content area texts become increasingly morphologically complex (Nagy & Anderson, 1984).

Understanding the morphology of complex words found in various texts is related to reading comprehension for adolescent students (Nagy et al., 2006). Students with lower levels of morphological understanding will be less adept at tapping this knowledge source and using morpheme meanings to aid in defining unknown words, which may leave significant deficits in understanding content area and informational texts. This not only affects comprehension of content text, but also impedes core academic learning and achievement. The impact of such learning and achievement gaps is far reaching and may inhibit future learning opportunities and successful transition to adult life.

Multisyllabic Word Reading

In addition to understanding the role morphology plays in identifying words, knowing syllable types and how to segment words into syllables increases word reading accuracy, which, in turn, is connected to reading comprehension. Although teaching the rules of syllabication to students seems to be an intuitive solution, research demonstrates that this has limited effects on improving word reading accuracy (O'Connor & Goodwin, 2011), and students often do not generalize this knowledge to reading tasks outside of syllabication instruction due to the complexity of the rules (Cunningham, 1998). When students are able to segment words into syllables using features of the word (e.g., vowels, prefixes, suffixes), however, they are able to more accurately blend the segments together to correctly identify the word (Bhattacharya & Ehri, 2004). In addition, reading multisyllabic words by dividing them into familiar word parts provides struggling older readers with a reasonable strategy for managing the reading of unknown, complex words (McCormick, 2007).

Fluency Problems

As noted with problems at the word level, slow, labored reading decreases a student's capacity to engage in the higher-order processes required for comprehending text (LaBerge & Samuels, 1974; Samuels, 1997). Reading fluency refers to the speed and accuracy with which an individual reads. It is typically measured in words read correct per minute, and research has demonstrated a clear connection between fluency and comprehension (Fuchs, Fuchs, Hosp, & Jenkins, 2001). It is important to note that this relationship is much better evidenced for younger readers than older readers. Regardless, it is essential for students to be both accurate and swift at the word reading level for fluency to be evident (Nathan & Stanovich, 1991).

The difficulty associated with increasing their reading rate is one significant issue older struggling readers face. Fluency growth rates decrease as students' grade levels increase, even with intensive intervention (Deno, Fuchs, Marston, & Shin, 2001; Fuchs, Fuchs, Hamlett, Walz, & Germann, 1993). Despite the decreased rate of fluency growth for older readers, studies implementing interventions designed to increase fluency have met some measure of success and increased the fluency scores of their participants (O'Connor & Goodwin, 2011). In addition, research shows gains in comprehension even when fluency growth was minimal (Fuchs, Fuchs, & Kazdan, 1999). Furthermore, there may be a decreased correlation between fluency and comprehension for older readers, which extends the possibility that addressing word level and vocabulary deficits may be more effective for improving the comprehension skills of older struggling readers.

Vocabulary Problems

Word level reading and fluency problems are just two aspects that affect reading comprehension for struggling older readers. Vocabulary knowledge is crucial for students to extract meaning from texts and other materials containing information specific to content area learning. Vocabulary is not merely important to reading comprehension but fundamental (Jitendra, Edwards, Sacks, & Jacobson, 2004). Comprehending text is incomplete without knowing word meanings. Successful vocabulary acquisition and comprehension of text for older readers is influenced by exposure to content-specific words, short- and long-term memory, and delivery of instruction.

Vocabulary Exposure   Exposure to word meanings through either direct or indirect experiences is strongly related to vocabulary knowledge (Rupley, 2005). It is theorized that the more experience students have reading text, the more developed their vocabularies (Stanovich, 1986). Research identified a correlation between vocabulary knowledge and comprehension skill. Students who struggle, however, tend to avoid reading (Baker, Simmons, & Kame'enui, 1998) and, thus, suffer the consequences of limited exposure to content-specific vocabulary, which inhibits further reading skill development, including skills associated with reading comprehension. In addition, struggling readers often select texts composed with lower vocabulary and comprehension demands, which further limits their opportunities to increase vocabulary knowledge and refine word level reading and comprehension skills (Cain & Oakhill, 2011).

It is critically important to note the disparity in vocabulary exposure between typical and struggling readers. Anderson, Wilson, and Fielding (1988) reported that typical readers read about 600,000 words per year, in stark contrast to the approximate 50,000 words per year for struggling readers. Typical readers are not exposed to just merely a greater volume of words, but the depth and quality of the vocabulary is vastly different (Cunningham & Stanovich, 1998). This leads to a domino effect of sorts. Struggling readers read fewer words of lesser complexity but still face the demands required in their content area text. With less developed vocabulary, however, the knowledge struggling readers bring to the task of making meaning from the materials they read reduces their level of understanding and further affects overall academic achievement.

Memory Deficits   In addition to lower levels of exposure to essential vocabulary, struggling older readers often deal with deficits in short- and long-term memory (Swanson & Sáez, 2003). A definite relation exists between memory and gaining vocabulary knowledge from print (Cain, Oakhill, & Lemmon, 2004; Daneman & Green, 1986). Maintaining new knowledge of word meanings in short-term memory as vocabulary is introduced is essential for comprehending text as it is read. Successful transfer of word meanings from short- to long-term memory and then eventual retrieval of that knowledge from long-term memory is critical to understanding text that repeatedly uses content-specific vocabulary as well as high-frequency vocabulary found across a variety of written materials. Increasing short- and long-term memory capacity is not a reasonable undertaking for a teacher working with students exhibiting limited vocabulary knowledge and impaired comprehension. Utilizing vocabulary instruction techniques that explicitly teach strategies addressing memory deficits, however, is a practical enhancement to instruction that may have a positive impact on vocabulary learning.

Vocabulary Instruction   Variations on mnemonic devices, which provide some measure of scaffolded support for students exhibiting memory deficits, have proven successful for struggling readers during vocabulary instruction (see O'Connor & Goodwin, 2011). Mnemonic devices are memory aids that typically link easily remembered verbal or auditory cues with information tied to specific words and concepts. Several studies that used keywords or word clues demonstrated positive outcomes for students exhibiting difficulty learning and remembering new vocabulary (e.g., Burns, Hodgson, Parker, & Fremont, 2011; Mastropieri, Scruggs, Levin, Gaffney, & McLoone, 1985; Veit, Scruggs, & Mastropieri, 1986). In addition to vocabulary learning, keyword word instruction can significantly affect the comprehension of text for older struggling readers (Burns et al., 2011; Mastropieri, Scruggs & Fulk, 1990).

Background, Text Structure, and Organizational Knowledge Problems

Vocabulary and background knowledge play significant roles in reading comprehension for older readers. In fact, background knowledge contributes more to comprehension than word reading and strategy use (Cromley & Azevedo, 2007). Unfortunately, readers struggling with comprehension often cannot understand the texts they read due to limited background knowledge (Gersten et al., 2001). Students need a framework within which to add new information and reformat existing knowledge. As the spiral of reading problems decreases the amount of text a student consumes, it is likely that struggling older readers are lacking prior experience with and exposure to the information presented in content area material as well as recreational text. This lack of exposure negatively affects comprehension because students have no foundation on which to build new learning and attach novel concepts to existing schema. This not only inhibits comprehension of reading material, but also affects overall academic achievement within the content areas.

In addition to background knowledge of content presented in text, knowledge of text structure is also a contributor to comprehension. Students with reading disabilities often have limited knowledge of both expository and narrative text structure (Gersten et al., 2001). This leads them to approach a variety of texts without purpose and retrieve information using less systematic organizational techniques (Gersten et al., 2001; Meyer, Brandt, & Bluth, 1980). Understanding the common formats under which texts are designed is an important reading skill because it enables the student to recall and organize information in a way that parallels the delivery of the content. This provides the reader with a template within which to construct an organized summary of the most important details and a framework for understanding. Incomplete understanding of material and misunderstanding the most important facts and details of a text are the result of limited knowledge of text structure.

How struggling students choose to organize the information they retrieve from text further affects comprehension. Arbitrary details often are deemed as some of the most important by older struggling readers because they lack not only knowledge of how the text is constructed, but also have limited skills in discriminating between key points and supporting information. Inappropriately selecting critical information is often characterized by recalling tangentially connected details and an inability to convey the overall message of a reading. In addition, even when taught to use various methods of organizing information from text, struggling readers often do not generalize these skills or strategies across content, text materials, and assessment measures (Kim, Vaughn, Wanzek, & Wei, 2009). Use of these tools may be incorrectly applied to various texts or students are unaware that organizational methods are applicable in multiple situations. Regardless, skill deficits in organizing information lead to decreased levels of understanding and lower levels of achievement.

Strategy Use Problems

Struggling older readers often are inconsistent with their use of a variety of comprehension strategies, as demonstrated by the use of organizational strategies. Gersten et al. (2001) noted that students with reading disabilities may not have a repertoire of strategies to employ in the event of a comprehension breakdown. In addition, they are often unaware of when to use a strategy they previously may have learned. Furthermore, struggling readers may ineffectively implement a given strategy with limited benefit to their comprehension of text. Finally, in some instances, struggling students are oblivious to the fact that they do not have a complete understanding of the content addressed in their reading materials and texts and, therefore, fail to employ a necessary strategy to aid in comprehension. Each of these potential roadblocks associated with strategy use compounds the problems struggling older readers face in making meaning from and connecting learning to the texts they need to comprehend.

Motivation Problems

Reading comprehension achievement is positively affected when, over time, students are actively engaged in text reading and motivated to understand (Guthrie & Wigfield, 2000). Unfortunately, older struggling readers are often less motivated to engage with and understand text. The impact of decreased motivation on comprehension is far reaching. Unmotivated students read less (Baker et al., 1998; Stanovich, 1986), which decreases their exposure to critical vocabulary and varied text genres and structure, as well as limits the amount of background knowledge they bring to the task of reading new content. Students lacking motivation often exhibit frustration and a potentially paralyzing expectation of failure (Gersten et al., 2001), which affects the way they approach reading activities and instruction tied to reading. This may, in turn, decrease the effectiveness of interventions designed to improve reading skills (Guthrie & Humenick, 2004) because students are not as engaged or easily give up as learning becomes more challenging. Finally, after having struggled with reading skills for an extended number of years, it is difficult to reverse the associated negative effects for older students. Despite the negative effects that lack of motivation has on comprehension for older struggling readers, research has demonstrated success with interventions designed to increase motivation in adolescent readers (see Guthrie & Humenick, 2004; O'Connor & Goodwin, 2011).

SYNTHESIS OF INTERVENTION RESEARCH TARGETING READING PROBLEMS

As indicated, reading comprehension difficulties are one of the most significant problems experienced by adolescents identified as struggling readers, especially those with learning disabilities. This is because reading comprehension underlies performance in the majority of academic content areas, as well as adjustments to most school activities. Several comprehensive descriptive and quantitative reviews of reading comprehension interventions for students with learning disabilities have been published (e.g., Berkeley, Scruggs & Mastropieri, 2010; Flynn et al., 2012; Gertsen et al., 2001; Kamil, 2003; Savage & Pompey, 2008; Scammacca et al., 2007; Wanzek, Wexler, Vaughn, & Ciullo, 2010). For example, Gersten et al. comprehensively reviewed several reading comprehension intervention studies for students with learning disabilities and concluded that systematic strategy instruction improves reading comprehension performance. Specific intervention suggestions were given related to the type of text used (e.g., narrative, expository) as well as some of the instructional issues to be considered in establishing generalization to content beyond where the instruction took place. This chapter complements some of their findings. In contrast to describing the individual interventions within studies, however, we primarily focus on findings from a meta-analysis of the literature.

Meta-analysis is a statistical reviewing technique that provides a quantitative summary of findings across an entire body of research. The results of individual studies are converted to a standardized metric or effect size (ES). The scores are then aggregated across the sample of studies to yield an overall estimate of ES. Particular attention is given to the magnitude of the ES. According to Cohen (1988), .80 is considered a large ES, .50 moderate, and .20 small.

Strategy Instruction Defined

In general, the majority of the literature on reading comprehension argues that students with learning disabilities underutilize access to information and knowledge unless they are explicitly prompted to use certain strategies. Students with learning disabilities, who have reading comprehension difficulties, are primarily seen as inefficient processors of information. Strategy instruction is viewed as providing a means to help students efficiently and accurately process text information. Strategy instruction within this context is broadly defined as a teaching method organized in such a manner as to solve a problem. The teaching method generally includes two or more goal-oriented tactics. A *tactic* reflects a single processing technique (e.g., elaboration) or a means of monitoring information (e.g., reducing information processing demands with prompts or cues). These tactics are usually mediated by the teacher, text, peers, and/or generated by the student. Several excellent examples of strategy models exist in the literature that focus on struggling readers (e.g., Berkeley, Mastropieri, & Scruggs, 2011; Block, Parris, Reed, Whitely, & Cleveland, 2009; Borkowski, Weyhing, & Carr, 1988; Bulgren, Deshler, Schumaker, & Lenz, 2000; Palincsar & Brown, 1984; Spencer & Manis, 2010). Earlier syntheses of the literature also outlined principles related to strategy instruction models (e.g., Levin, 1986; Swanson, 1993).

Determining Effective Instructional Components

The remainder of the chapter reviews some general instructional models, plus instructional components, found in the meta-analysis of intervention studies that positively influence reading comprehension outcomes. As a point of contrast, instructional models and components that improve word level reading are compared. We draw mainly on comprehensive meta-analyses of experimental interventions for adolescent students with learning disabilities (Swanson, 1999b, 2001; Swanson & Deshler, 2003; Swanson & Hoskyn, 1998). These studies using meta-analysis are the only ones to date that focus on outcomes in reading at the instructional component level (Suggate, 2010; see Flynn et al., 2012, for an update).

Uncovering key components of effective instruction was not an easy task because a distinction must be made between "what was taught" and "how it was taught." Our analyses did not focus on what was taught (e.g., content vocabulary words, teaching vowel sounds) but on how information was taught and sustained. Our rationale, quite simply, was that one cannot adequately assess what should be taught unless one can clearly identify how information should be taught, sustained, and retrieved. Testing what should or should not be taught (or, more appropriately, what information should or should not be emphasized) becomes a moot point unless these instructional components are identified and their influence on the effectiveness of reading instruction clearly delineated. Good information processing relies on the interplay between the knowledge base of the student, the nature of the content, and the context that constrains or activates learning (e.g., Pressley, 1991). Even when analyzing direct instruction models with explicit content variations (e.g., Necheochea & Swanson, 2004), how instructional activities (e.g., modeling, explicit practice) were delivered accounted for the majority of differences in the effectiveness of instruction and, therefore, serve as an important focus of analysis for designing effective reading comprehension instruction.

Determining effective instructional components across intervention studies is a difficult task because the instructional components identified in each study would be limited by the way they are described. Although the instructional components evaluated by Swanson and colleagues (Swanson & Deshler, 2003; Swanson & Hoskyn, 1998, 2001; Swanson, Hoskyn, & Lee, 1999) reflected components described from several comprehensive reviews of the instructional literature, the components coded for analysis may not have matched the components emphasized by the primary authors. In addition, descriptions of the same teaching practice may vary considerably by authors of different theoretical orientations, thereby introducing additional complexity in the coding procedure. This issue has been addressed in previous studies (e.g., Swanson, 1999b; Swanson & Hoskyn, 1998, 2001) by using multiple examples for each component category, using several terms that share key concepts, creating hierarchical (categories within categories) and overlapping (allowing various degrees of overlap) categories and coding by representation rather than the absolute quantity of statements within a category (see Swanson, 1999b). Nevertheless, there are studies in the synthesis in which it was difficult to match the authors' general instructional model and/or the label of the instructional components to what actually was reported (see Swanson & Hoskyn, 1998).

Characterizing Instructional Approaches

Despite the difficulties encountered in determining the instructional components characterizing effective reading comprehension programs, we found that higher ESs emerge for a combined strategy instruction and direct instruction approach when compared with the other instructional approaches (e.g., Swanson, 1999b; Swanson & Hoskyn, 1998). Distinctions between strategy instructional approaches and direct instruction are sometimes subtle, creating difficulties in clearly analyzing the two approaches. Lovett et al. (1994), however, provided a clear comparison in their study of both approaches. For example, both strategy intervention models and direct instruction included a graduated sequence of steps with multiple opportunities for overlearning the content and reading skills. In addition, both instructional models included cumulative review routines, mass practice, and teaching of all component skills to mastery criterion.

Students learned sound units with the strategy model, with additional discussion given to metacognitive issues such as strategy implementation, strategy choice, and self-monitoring. Clear discussions were given to students about: 1) why a strategy facilitates word recognition, 2) how to apply the strategy, and 3) how to check to see if the strategy is working.

The direct instruction condition followed the same procedures as strategy instruction except for two variations: 1) direct instruction focused on subskills (sound units, such as letter sounds, or linguistic units, e.g. *mat-cat-hat*) and 2) discussion of processes and use of general rules was minimized. Thus, focus is what appears to separate the two instructional models. The strategy program focused on processes or global skills for a general approach to reading, whereas a direct instruction model focused on word level reading.

Strategy instructional models and direct instruction treatments may be distinguished by the unit of information (i.e., direct instruction focuses primarily on isolated skills, whereas strategy instruction focuses primarily on rules) and processing perspective (i.e., direct instruction is characterized as a bottom-up processing approach, whereas strategy instruction as a top-down processing approach). Of course, other distinctions are less subtle. For example, strategy instruction programs focus on instructional components that emphasize advanced organizers (providing students with a type of mental scaffolding on which to build new understanding); organization (directing students to stop from time to time to assess their understanding); elaboration (thinking about the material to be learned in a way that connects the material to information or ideas already in their mind); generative learning (making sense of what they are learning by summarizing the information); general study strategies (underlining, notetaking, summarizing, having students generate questions, outlining, and working in pairs to summarize sections of materials); thinking about and controlling one's thinking process (metacognition); and attributions (evaluating the effectiveness of a strategy). In contrast, direct instruction emphasizes fast-paced, well-sequenced, and highly focused lessons. The lessons usually occur in small groups of students who are given several opportunities to respond and receive feedback about accuracy and responses. There is overlap in the two approaches. This is important because it may account for some confusion in differentiating between the two models. Strategy instruction and direct instruction models overlap in at least two ways. First, both models (in one form or another) assume that effective methods of instruction include 1) a daily review, 2) a statement of an instructional objective, 3) teacher presentation of new material, 4) guided practice, 5) independent practice, and 6) a formative evaluation. Second, both strategy instruction and direct instruction follow a sequence of events, such as the following:

1. State the learning objectives and orient the students to the content they will be learning and the performance expectations.

2. Review the skills necessary to understand the concept.

3. Present the information, give examples, and demonstrate the concepts/materials.

4. Pose questions (probes) to students, assess their level of understanding, and correct misconceptions.

5. Provide group instruction and independent practice. Give students an opportunity to demonstrate new skills and learn the new information on their own.

6. Assess performance and provide feedback. Review the independent work and give a quiz. Give feedback for correct answers and reteach skills if answers are incorrect.

7. Provide distributed practice and review.

We consider this overlap as reflecting a "common instruction core." This was important in our earlier meta-analysis (Swanson, 1999b) because it allowed us to check on the unique contribution of specific instructional components to enhance performance outcomes after this common instruction core has been considered.

Three Important Findings

The following important findings are based on the previous discussion. First, the majority of studies in the domain of reading comprehension that used experimental measures met Cohen's (1988) criterion of .80 as a substantial finding. The magnitudes of ESs in reading comprehension were significantly higher on experimental (researcher-developed) measures (ES = .81) when compared with norm-referenced measures (ES = .45). Although the magnitude of ESs related to word level reading were smaller in magnitude, they were more stable across experimental and standardized measures (ES = .53 versus .62). More important, we found that a combined strategy instruction and direct instruction model was the most effective procedure for remediating reading comprehension deficits. The combined model yielded high ES instructional effects (ES = 1.15) that exceeded Cohen's .80 criteria for a substantive finding in the domain of reading comprehension. The model included small-group instruction and emphasized attributions and teacher modeling of processing steps to perform a task. The instructional components that the combined model shared with a direct instructional model were activities related to explicit practice, sequencing, segmentation of information, and one-to-one instruction.

Second, only a few instructional components uniquely increased the intervention effectiveness, regardless of the instruction model (e.g., strategy, direct, a combination). The key instructional components (as stated in the treatment conditions) for reading comprehension that contributed unique differences to the effectiveness of instruction were as follows:

- *Directed response/questioning:* Instruction included dialectic or Socratic teaching, the teacher directing students to ask questions, and the teacher and student or students engaging in reciprocal dialogue.

- *Control difficulty or processing demands of task:* Instruction included short activities, level of difficulty controlled, the teacher providing necessary assistance, the teacher providing simplified demonstration, tasks sequenced from easy to difficult, and/or task analysis.

- *Elaboration:* Instruction included additional information or explanation about concepts, procedures, or steps and/or redundant text or repetition within text.

- *Modeling by the teacher of steps:* Instruction included the teacher demonstrating processes and/or steps the students are to follow to solve the problem.

- *Small-group instruction:* Instruction was provided in a small group and/or verbal interaction occurring in a small group with students and/or the teacher.

- *Strategy cues:* Instruction included reminders to use strategies or multisteps, the use of think-aloud models, and/or the teacher presenting the benefits of strategy use or procedures.

The important instructional components for word level reading that emerged from our analyses were as follows:

- *Sequencing:* Instruction included breaking down the task, fading of prompts or cues, sequencing short activities, and/or using step-by-step prompts.

- *Segmentation:* Instruction included breaking down the targeted skill into smaller units, breaking into component parts, and segmenting and/or synthesizing components parts.

- *Advanced organizers:* Instruction included directing students to look over material prior to instruction, directing students to focus on particular information, providing prior information about task, and/or the teacher stating objectives of instruction prior to commencing.

The importance of these findings is that only a few components from a broad array of instructional activities enhance treatment outcomes.

Finally, only two components contributed to reading comprehension beyond the common instructional core. In our analyses, all those components related to the common core were entered into our regression model. We then determined if any additional instructional component added significantly to differences in the effectiveness of the model beyond the instructional core. We found no component entered significantly contributed to the instructional core in the area of word level reading. That was not the case for reading comprehension, however. Strategy cuing and small-group interactive instruction contributed significantly to differences to the effects on reading comprehension beyond the instructional core model.

CONCLUSION

We have described the factors contributing to poor comprehension for older readers and briefly highlighted some important findings across studies that have included reading comprehension as an outcome measure. We conclude that there are instructional models that can improve comprehension skills, despite the devastating effect comprehension difficulties have on adolescent achievement. Specifically, combined strategy and direct instruction models for adolescents who struggle in reading do make a significant contribution to treatment outcomes in reading comprehension. In contrast, direct instruction is the preferred means of enhancing word level reading. We also find, however, that some instructional components are more important than others in making reading comprehension instructional practices more effective, and those components differ from those that improve word level reading skills.

REFERENCES

Adams, M.J. (1990). *Beginning to read: Thinking and learning about print.* Cambridge, MA: The MIT Press.

Anderson, R.C., Wilson, P.T., & Fielding, L.G. (1988). Growth in reading and how children spend their time outside of school. *Reading Research Quarterly, 13,* 285–303.

Baker, S.K., Simmons, D.C., & Kame'enui, E.J. (1998). Vocabulary acquisition: Research bases. In D.C. Simmons & E.J. Kame'enui (Eds.), *What research tells us about children with diverse learning needs: Bases and basics* (pp. 183–218). Mahwah, NJ: Lawrence Erlbaum Associates.

Berkeley, S., Mastropieri, M.A., & Scruggs, T.E. (2011). Reading comprehension strategy instruction and attribution retraining for secondary students with learning and other mild disabilities. *Journal of Learning Disabilities, 44*(1), 18–32.

Berkeley, S., Scruggs, T.E., & Mastropieri, M.A. (2010). Reading comprehension instruction for students with learning disabilities, 1995–2006: A meta-analysis. *Remedial and Special Education, 31*(6), 423–436.

Bhat, P., Griffin, C.C., & Sindelar, P.T. (2003). Phonological awareness instruction for middle school students with learning disabilities. *Learning Disability Quarterly, 26,* 73–87.

Bhattacharya, A., & Ehri, L. (2004). Graphosyllabic analysis helps adolescent struggling readers read and spell words. *Journal of Learning Disabilities, 37,* 331–348.

Block, C.C., Parris, S.R., Reed, K.L., Whitely, C.S., & Cleveland, M.D. (2009). Instructional approaches that significantly increase reading comprehension. *Journal of Educational Psychology, 101,* 262–281.

Borkowski, J.G., Weyhing, R.S., & Carr, M. (1988). Effects of attributional retraining on strategy-based reading comprehension in learning-disabled students. *Journal of Educational Psychology, 80,* 46–53.

Bulgren, J., Deshler, D.D., Schumaker, J.B., & Lenz, B.K. (2000). The use of and effectiveness of analogical instruction in diverse secondary content classrooms. *Journal of Educational Psychology, 92,* 426–441.

Burns, M.K., Hodgson, J., Parker, D.C., & Fremont, K. (2011). Comparison of the effectiveness and efficiency of text previewing and preteaching keywords as small-group reading comprehension strategies with middle-school students. *Literacy Research and Instruction, 50,* 241–252.

Cain, K., & Oakhill, J. (2011). Matthew effects in young readers: Reading comprehension and reading experience aid vocabulary development. *Journal of Learning Disabilities, 44*(5), 431–443.

Cain, K., Oakhill, J., & Lemmon, K. (2004). Individual differences in the inferences of word meanings from context: The influence of reading comprehension, vocabulary knowledge, and memory capacity. *Journal of Educational Psychology, 90,* 671–681.

Cohen, J. (1988). *Statistical power analysis for the behavioral sciences* (2nd ed.). New York, NY: Academic Press.

Cromley, J.G., & Azevedo, R. (2007). Testing and refining the direct and inferential model of reading comprehension. *Journal of Educational Psychology, 99*(2), 311–325.

Cunningham, A.E., & Stanovich, K.E. (1998). What reading does for the mind. *American Educator, 22,* 8–15.

Cunningham, P.M. (1998). The multisyllabic word dilemma: Helping students build meaning, spell, and read "big" words. *Reading and Writing Quarterly, 14,* 189–218.

Daneman, M., & Green, I. (1986). Individual differences in comprehending and producing words in context. *Journal of Memory and Language, 25,* 1–18.

Deno, S.L., Fuchs, L.S., Marston, D., & Shin, J. (2001). Using curriculum-based measurement to establish growth standards for students with disabilities. *School Psychology Review, 30,* 507–524.

De Oliveira, L.C. (2010). Nouns in history: Packing information, expanding explanations, and structuring reasoning. *The History Teacher, 43*(2), 191–203.

Ebbers, S.M., & Denton, C.A. (2008). A root awakening: Vocabulary instruction for older students with reading difficulties. *Learning Disabilities Research and Practice, 23*(2), 90–102.

Edmonds, M.S., Vaughn, S., Wexler, J., Reutebuch, C., Cable, A., Tackett, K.K. (2009). A synthesis of reading interventions and effects on reading comprehension outcomes for older struggling readers. *Review of Educational Research, 79*(1), 262–300.

Flynn, L.J., Zheng, X., & Swanson, H.L. (2012). Instructing struggling older readers: A selective meta-analysis of intervention research. *Learning Disabilities Research and Practice, 27*(1), 21–32.

Fuchs, L.S., Fuchs, D., Hamlett, C.L., Walz, L., & Germann, G. (1993). Formative evaluation of academic progress: How much growth can we expect? *School Psychology Review, 22,* 27–49.

Fuchs, L.S., Fuchs, D., Hosp, M.K., & Jenkins, J.R. (2001). Oral reading fluency as an indicator of reading competence: A theoretical, empirical, and historical analysis. *Scientific Studies of Reading, 5*(3), 239–256.

Fuchs, L.S., Fuchs, D., & Kazdan, S. (1999). Effects of peer-assisted learning strategies on high school students with serious reading problems. *Remedial and Special Education, 20,* 309–318.

Gersten, R., Fuchs, L.S., Williams, J.P., & Baker, S. (2001). Teaching reading comprehension strategies to students with learning disabilities: A review of research. *Review of Educational Research, 71*(2), 279–320.

Guthrie, J.T., & Humenick, N.M. (2004). Motivating students to read: Evidence for classroom practices that increase reading motivation and achievement. In P. McCardle & V. Chhabra (Eds.), *The voice of evidence in reading research* (pp. 329–354). Baltimore, MD: Paul H. Brookes Publishing Co.

Guthrie, J.T., & Wigfield, A. (2000). Engagement and motivation in reading. In M.L. Kamil & P.B. Mosenthal (Eds.), *Handbook of reading research* (Vol. 3, pp. 403–422). Mahwah, NJ: Lawrence Erlbaum Associates.

Hairrell, A., Simmons, D., Swanson, E., Edmonds, M., Vaughn, S., & Rupley, W.H. (2011). Translating vocabulary research to social studies instruction: Before, during, and after text-reading strategies. *Intervention in School and Clinic, 46*(4), 204–210.

Jitendra, A.K., Edwards, L.L., Sacks, G., & Jacobson, L.A. (2004). What research says about vocabulary instruction for students with learning disabilities. *Exceptional Children, 70*(3), 299–322.

Juel, C. (1988). Learning to read and write: A longitudinal study of fifty-four children from first through fourth grade. *Journal of Educational Psychology, 80,* 437–447.

Kamil, M.L. (2003). *Adolescents and literacy: Reading for the 21st century.* New York, NY: Alliance for Excellent Education, Carnegie Foundation.

Kim, A., Vaughn, S., Wanzek, J., & Wei, S. (2009). Graphic organizers and their effects on the reading comprehension of students with LD: A synthesis of research. *Journal of Learning Disabilities, 37*(2), 105–118.

LaBerge, D., & Samuels, S.J. (1974). Toward a theory of automatic information processing in reading. *Cognitive Psychology, 6*(2), 293–323.

Levin, J. (1986). Four cognitive principles of learning strategy instruction. *Educational Psychologist, 21,* 3–17.

Lovett, M.W., Borden, S.L., DeLuca, T., Lacerenza, L., Benson, N.J., & Brackstone, D. (1994). Treating the core deficits of developmental dyslexia: Evidence of transfer of learning after phonologically and strategy-based reading training programs. *Developmental Psychology, 30,* 805–822.

Mastropieri, M.A., Scruggs, T.E., & Fulk, J.M. (1990). Teaching abstract vocabulary with the keyword method: Effects on recall and comprehension. *Journal of Learning Disabilities, 23*(2), 92–96.

Mastropieri, M.A., Scruggs, T.E., Levin, J.R., Gaffney, J., & McLoone, B. (1985). Mnemonic vocabulary instruction for learning disabled students. *Learning Disability Quarterly, 8*(1), 57–63.

McCormick, S. (2007). *Instructing students who have literacy problems* (5th ed.). Upper Saddle River, NJ: Pearson Prentice Hall.

Meyer, B.J.F., Brandt, D.M., & Bluth, G.J. (1980). Use of top-level structure in text: Key for reading comprehension of ninth-grade students. *Reading Research Quarterly, 16,* 72–103.

Nagy, W., & Anderson, R.C. (1984). The number of printed words in printed school English. *Reading Research Quarterly, 19*(3), 304–330.

Nagy, W., Berninger, W.W., & Abbott, R.D. (2006). Contributions of morphology beyond phonology to literacy outcomes of upper elementary and middle-school students. *Journal of Educational Psychology, 98*(1), 134–147.

Nathan, R.G., & Stanovich, K.E. (1991). The causes and consequences of differences in reading fluency. *Theory Into Practice, 30*(3), 176–184.

National Reading Panel. (2000). *Report of the National Reading Panel* (NIH Publication No. 00-4754). Washington, DC: U.S. Government Printing Office.

Necheochea, D., & Swanson, H.L. (2004). The role of reading intervention research in the identification of children with reading disabilities: A meta-analysis of the literature funded by NICHD. In T. Scruggs & M. Mastropieri (Eds.), *Advances in learning and behavioral disabilities* (Vol. 16, pp. 205–222). Oxford, UK: Elsevier Science LTD.

O'Connor, R.E., & Goodwin, V. (2011). Teaching older students to read. In R.E. O'Connor & P. Vadasy (Eds.), *Handbook of reading interventions* (pp. 380–411). New York, NY: Guilford Press.

Palincsar, A.S., & Brown, A.L. (1984). Reciprocal teaching of comprehension: Fostering and comprehension monitoring activities. *Cognition and Instruction, 1,* 117–175.

Pressley, M. (1991). Can learning disabled children become good information processors? How can we find out? In L. Feagans, E. Short, & L. Meltzer (Eds.), *Subtypes of learning disabilities* (pp. 137–162). Mahwah, NJ: Lawrence Erlbaum Associates.

Rupley, W.H. (2005). Vocabulary knowledge: Its contribution to reading growth and development. *Reading and Writing Quarterly, 21,* 203–207.

Samuels, S.J. (1997). The importance of automaticity for developing expertise in reading. *Reading and Writing Quarterly, 13*(2), 107–122.

Savage, R., & Pompey, Y. (2008). What does the evidence really say about effective literacy teaching? *Educational and Child Psychology, 25*(3), 21–30.

Scammacca, N., Roberts, G., Vaughn, S., Edmonds, M., Wexler, J., Reutebuch, C.K. (2007). *Interventions for adolescent struggling readers: A meta-analysis with implications for practice.* Portsmouth, NH: RMC Research Corporation, Center on Instruction.

Spencer, S.A., & Manis, F.R. (2010). The effects of a fluency intervention program on the fluency and comprehension outcomes of middle-school students with severe reading deficits. *Learning Disabilities Research and Practice, 25*(2), 76–86.

Stanovich, K.E. (1986). Matthew effects in reading: Some consequences of individual differences in the acquisition of literacy. *Reading Research Quarterly, 21*(4), 360–407.

Suggate, S.P. (2010). Why what we teach depends on when: Grade and reading intervention modality moderate effect size. *Developmental Psychology, 46*(6), 1556–1579.

Swanson, H.L. (1993). Principles and procedures in strategy use. In L. Meltzer (Ed.), *Strategy assessment and instruction for students with learning disabilities* (pp. 61–92). Austin, TX: PRO-ED.

Swanson, H.L. (1999a). Instructional components that predict treatment outcomes for students with learning disabilities: Support for a combined strategy and direct instruction model. *Learning Disabilities Research and Practice, 14,* 129–140.

Swanson, H.L. (1999b). Reading research for students with LD: A meta-analysis of intervention outcomes. *Journal of Learning Disabilities, 32,* 504–532.

Swanson, H.L. (2001). Research on interventions for adolescents with learning disabilities: Meta-analysis of outcomes related to higher-order processing. *Elementary School Journal, 101*(3), 331–348.

Swanson, H.L., & Deshler, D. (2003). Instructing adolescents with learning disabilities: Converting a meta-analysis to practice. *Journal of Learning Disabilities, 36*(2), 124–135.

Swanson, H.L., & Hoskyn, M. (1998). A synthesis of experimental intervention literature for students with learning disabilities: A meta-analysis of treatment outcomes. *Review of Educational Research, 68,* 271–321.

Swanson, H.L. & Hoskyn, M. (2001). Instructing adolescents with learning disabilities: A component and composite analysis. *Learning Disabilities Research and Practice, 16*(2), 103–112.

Swanson, H.L., Hoskyn, M., & Lee, C. (1999). *Interventions for students with learning disabilities: A meta-analysis of treatment outcomes.* New York, NY: Guilford Press.

Swanson, H.L., & Sáez, L. (2003). Memory deficits in children and adults with learning disabilities. In H.L. Swanson, K.R. Harris, & S. Graham (Eds.), *Handbook of learning disabilities* (pp. 182–198). New York, NY: Guilford Press.

Torgeson, J.K., & Kail, R.J., Jr. (1980). Memory processes in exceptional children. In B.K. Keogh (Ed.), *Advances in special education: Basic constructs and theoretical orientations* (Vol. 1, pp. 55–99). Greenwich, CT: JAI Press.

U.S. Department of Education, Institute of Education Sciences, National Assessment of Educational Progress, National Center for Education Statistics. (2005). *The nation's report card, reading.* Washington, DC: Author. Available at http://nces.ed.gov/nationsreportcard/

Vaughn, S., Klingner, J.K., Swanson, E.A., Boardman, A.G., Roberts, G., Mohammed, S.S., et al. (2011). Efficacy of collaborative strategic reading with middle school students. *American Educational Research Journal, 48*(4), 938–964.

Veit, D.T., Scruggs, T.E., & Mastropieri, M.A. (1986). Extended mnemonic instruction with learning disabled students. *Journal of Educational Psychology, 78*(4), 300–308.

Wanzek, J., Wexler, J., Vaughn, S., & Ciullo, S. (2010). Reading interventions for struggling readers in the upper elementary grades: A synthesis of 20 years of research. *Reading and Writing: An Interdisciplinary Journal, 23*(8), 889–912.

2 ‖ Promoting Comprehension and Motivation to Read in the Middle School Social Studies Classroom

Examples from a Research-Based Curriculum

Ana Taboada Barber, Leila Richey, and Michelle M. Buehl

Students are motivated to read when they express interest in their reading, feel excited about the content they are reading, share it with others, or think it is worthwhile for school success and beyond. Motivation to read is a multidimensional construct that refers to students' values, beliefs, affects, and goals related to reading (Guthrie & Wigfield, 2000). Motivation to read has been found to increase reading comprehension by enhancing attention, perseverance, and effort (Guthrie & Wigfield, 1999; Wang & Guthrie, 2004). Furthermore, highly motivated children read three times as much outside of school as their less motivated peers (Wigfield & Guthrie, 1997), and motivation to read significantly predicts reading amount and reading comprehension after statistically controlling for prior reading achievement and prior topic knowledge (Guthrie & Wigfield, 1999).

Although many educators see the importance of students' motivation to read, it is not always clear how to foster reading motivation in the classroom, especially in the middle and high school grades when students are faced with making the transition from learning to read (K–3) to reading to learn (Grades 4–12). Reading to learn requires numerous academic concepts and modes of reasoning that are discipline specific because each academic discipline or content area assumes specific kinds of background knowledge about how to read texts in that area (Lee & Spratley, 2010). Young adolescents suffer a decline in motivation in their transition to middle school because of the challenges arising from this shift, the less personalized structure of middle school, and the cognitive and physical changes brought by adolescence (Anderman, Maehr, & Midgley, 1999). Longitudinal studies have noted specific declines in the level of students' competence beliefs and intrinsic motivation to read (Jacobs, Lanza, Osgood, Eccles, & Wigfield, 2002). In addition, descriptive studies depict adolescents as resistant readers (Bintz, 1993; Reeves, 2004). Resistant readers are not necessarily passive, but, rather reluctant readers who choose not to read school-related texts (Hamston & Love, 2003) or who appear to lack a connection between their lives, experiences, and world knowledge and their school reading (Alvermann & Moore, 1991; Ivey & Broaddus, 2001). This trend is especially noticeable in the social studies domain in which students perceive their learning as boring, with little relevance or value to their lives (Almarza, 2001; Brophy, 2009).

In addition to reluctant readers, struggling readers are also common to the middle school classroom. Struggling readers lack the skills of fluent readers, read below grade level, and generally struggle with multiple components of reading, such as word recognition, vocabulary, and comprehension. Language minority students comprise a large number of struggling readers in

---

The research reported here was supported by the Institute of Education Sciences, U.S. Department of Education, through Grant R305A100297 to George Mason University. The opinions expressed are those of the authors and do not represent views of the Institute or the U.S. Department of Education.

the secondary school (August & Shanahan, 2006). Although language minority students speak more than 400 languages at home, about 80% of them are Spanish speakers (Kindler, 2002). The academic development of language minority students is low overall (Lee, Grigg, & Donahue, 2007) and, in particular, in English literacy and comprehension (August & Shanahan, 2006). Language minority students in middle school and high school struggle with reading because of the challenges presented by academic texts, lack or limited content area knowledge, and, often times, underdeveloped oral language and vocabulary that can negatively affect their academic achievement. Both native English speakers and language minority students who are struggling readers present additional motivational challenges in that they may be lacking the skills to read the required content and doubt their ability to succeed in the classroom, which can contribute to behavior problems and further alienation from the content and reading. Thus, there is a need to address the content area literacy for middle school students in a way that promotes both students' content area comprehension and their motivation to read in the content area. Literacy researchers' focus often tends to be on the enjoyment, fun, or pleasure of reading when they discuss motivation practices to enhance literacy instruction. Teachers must address the essential content while concurrently offering supports for reading comprehension and motivation to read because of the demands placed on schools and teachers to meet specific content standards.

We are developing a research-based curriculum for content area literacy to provide teachers with concrete practices to support students' reading comprehension and motivation to read. The United States History for Engaged Reading (USHER) is designed to address middle school U.S. history. We specifically chose to focus on middle school history given the limited research in this domain that bridges across cognitive and motivational practices. First, this chapter describes the broader framework for USHER. Then, the case of Mrs. Finn's sixth-grade class and her implementation of a portion of the USHER curriculum is presented. The chapter's focus is only on one aspect of motivation to read—students' self-efficacy beliefs for reading—and two comprehension strategies—identifying the main idea and forming text-based questions. After presenting Mrs. Finn's case, self-efficacy is discussed as a construct and is drawn from Mrs. Finn's teaching to elaborate on how teachers can support students' self-efficacy for reading. Next, the focus is on student text-based questioning, a comprehension strategy that attends to both cognitive and motivational dimensions of reading. To substantiate the impact of USHER instruction, the chapter concludes with data on the history comprehension and reading self-efficacy of sixth-grade students of diverse reading and language skills who participated in 7 weeks of USHER instruction.

THE NOTION OF VALUE FOR HISTORY READING: THE USHER FRAMEWORK

History is not a discipline that is naturally motivating or enticing to all learners as documented in the literature and by many teachers. Brophy noted, "History and social studies educators have long recognized that most K–12 students do not enjoy history as much as other school subjects, and many complain that it is boring and irrelevant" (2009, p. 3). Although some students are easily engaged by and curious about history, these dispositions may not naturally generalize to the majority of middle schoolers.

Our goal when we conceived USHER did not consist of increasing multiple dimensions of motivation for learning history in general. Rather, our goal was less ambitious and more focused. We wanted to increase student motivation and engagement for *reading* in history. In order to get students to become more engaged in reading expository texts in history, we saw the need to provide alternative books to the textbook so that all learners could develop and improve their text comprehension and motivation for history reading. In part, USHER was inspired by the first author's work on the reading engagement model developed by Guthrie and colleagues (Guthrie & Wigfield, 2000; Guthrie et al., 2004) that successfully integrated motivation and cognitive supports for science instruction in the elementary grades. In addition, USHER relies on the principle that for students to appreciate the value of history learning, curriculum developers and teachers "need to first create good reasons to learn each knowledge network we teach, and second, develop the network in such a way that students can appreciate its value" (Brophy, 2009, p. 7). Students need to be afforded opportunities to focus on big ideas that anchor knowledge networks in order for them to value learning history, and they also need activities designed to apply these big ideas (Brophy, 2009).

Social studies state standards were our starting point for developing big ideas in USHER. USHER lessons are developed on the basis of the broad, guiding, essential questions that define each unit. We use these content standards to select authentic texts that provide the breadth and depth not normally encountered in textbook treatment of history standards. We then articulate and develop the goals for comprehension (i.e., cognitive strategies, special vocabulary) and supports for reading motivation (e.g., self-efficacy, relevance for reading). These become the instructional tools used for applying, discussing, and analyzing the big ideas captured in the content standards. That is, it is through the specificity of digging into text, asking questions, finding main ideas, and responding to cognitive strategies in oral and written formats that teachers lead students to build knowledge networks over time and develop the reading comprehension strategies they need to sustain engaged reading over time. Thus, the content standards and related essential questions provide students with a reason for reading history texts—one dimension of students' motivation to read. In addition, students often complete a project at the end of each unit or set of related units that requires them to integrate and display the knowledge they have gained from reading (e.g., newspaper article on a presidential campaign, museum exhibit on westward expansion). These unit-culminating projects provide a further reason for reading and integrate knowledge across texts. Yet, other aspects of motivation to read also need to be addressed. As previously noted, we specifically focus on supporting students' reading self-efficacy beliefs—one motivation practice that is repeatedly addressed within and across USHER lessons.

SUPPORTING READING COMPREHENSION AND READING SELF-EFFICACY IN HISTORY: MRS. FINN'S CLASS

Mrs. Finn's sixth-grade class is making the transition to a unit on European exploration of the new world that will be the focus of social studies instruction for the next 2 weeks. Mrs. Finn's class is demographically similar to many American urban and suburban classrooms: approximately 40% of students are language minority students of varied English proficiency, about 20% are reading above grade level, and the remaining 40% are English native speakers who read on or below grade level. Mrs. Finn is in her sixth year as a language arts and social studies teacher. She is teaching U.S. history by following the state social studies standards and learning how to integrate literacy practices into history by participating in USHER.

The lessons in USHER are developed in part on the guided release of the responsibility model (Pearson & Gallagher, 1983). The teacher models the reading strategy with the class (modeling) and provides opportunities to practice it with the whole class (guided practice) before students work in small groups (individual practice). The teacher rotates among the small groups and provides specific scaffolds for students' strategy use, motivation, and knowledge development. Because the teacher scaffolds students' individual strategy use and helps them process a variety of increasingly challenging texts on their own, this small-group focused reading component in USHER can be likened to guided reading as defined by Fountas and Pinnell (2001). Furthermore, books for guided reading in USHER are leveled at above, below, or on grade level to lead individual students to use comprehension strategies toward mastery and independent use.

Prior to the current unit on European exploration, Mrs. Finn's class studied American Indian tribes for about 10 days. Students read books that were below and above grade level that discussed the Inuit, the Iroquois, the Pueblos, and the Lakota. Students spent time reading about each of these tribes in-depth by using two comprehension strategies—activating background knowledge by using text features and identifying the main idea for single and multiple paragraphs. Students now are ready to learn about the European exploration of America and then delve into the next unit on the cultural and economic interactions between European explorers and the American

Indians. The social studies standards for the unit are captured by guiding questions: Why did the European countries compete for power in North America? What obstacles and challenges did the explorers face? What regions of North America were explored by France, England, and Spain? What were the accomplishments of the exploration? These questions are posted on the board and classroom walls during USHER lessons. Teachers and students refer to these questions daily to guide their reading and knowledge building from text.

All of the sixth-grade students in Mrs. Finn's class are reading *Explorers of the Americas* (Sandler, 2005) for the European exploration unit, a trade book that is below grade level and focuses on several groups of European explorers (i.e., class book). *Sieur de La Salle* (Zronik, 2006) and *Samuel de Champlain* (Morganelli, 2006) will be used for guided reading instruction during the European explorers unit. The guided reading books provide more specific information on these explorers' lives, voyages, challenges, and missions when exploring North America. As previously noted, these books were selected because they address specific content standards. In addition, the books are leveled to meet the needs of the students in the group. The texts also contain numerous text features and are visually appealing.

Mrs. Finn uses *Explorers of the Americas* on the first day of the unit to introduce and model the two comprehension strategies that are the focus for this 10-day unit—identifying the main idea and student text-based questioning. Specifically, Mrs. Finn first engages the students in a brief discussion of the importance of asking questions. She emphasizes how asking questions helps individuals learn about new ideas and clarify ideas that are hard to understand. She then proceeds to use a paragraph to model identifying the main idea and supporting details, a strategy used extensively in the previous unit. This time, however, Mrs. Finn points to the importance of asking questions and uses a think-aloud procedure to model asking a question based on the main idea that she identified.

USHER includes a mnemonic called *R.I.C.H.* (*r*ead, *i*dentify the main idea and supporting details, *c*reate a question, *h*ow to answer your question) to help students focus on content and comprehension processes simultaneously (see Figure 2.1). Mrs. Finn first ensures that students have clear purposes for using each comprehension strategy. Students are ready to go through the steps in *R.I.C.H.* once the class has established the purposes for finding the main idea—to know what is important and what is not, to organize what we need to remember, and to remember important ideas—and for text-based questioning—to better understand what we read, to find out more information, and to have fun finding answers. Mrs. Finn spends time with the whole class modeling and practicing the *R.I.C.H.* mnemonic using *Explorers of the Americas*. Students are also guided to write text-based questions on sticky notes as they read. They place the notes on a classroom "parking lot," a wall poster where student questions are posted for all to see.

Students learn about questioning levels after they have practiced the *R.I.C.H.* mnemonic and successfully can use it. Specifically, they learn to differentiate questions that ask about facts, or yes/no answers (Level 1), explanation questions (Level 2), questions probing for specific knowledge (Level 3), and questions that ask about relationships among ideas across books and topics (Level 4). A questioning poster and a handout are used as references for students to understand that different question levels lead to simpler or more complex answers.

On subsequent days, Mrs. Finn has students work in small groups using the guided reading books. She ensures that students follow *R.I.C.H.* by having a class poster as well as individual student copies of the mnemonic. Students fluctuate between using *R.I.C.H.* while reading and entering their main ideas, supporting details, and text-based questions on individual student strategy charts, which provide students and the teacher with written outputs of their comprehension strategies.

While scaffolding students' use of strategies in small groups, Mrs. Finn notices that some students in one group are caught in the mechanics of *R.I.C.H.* but are failing to appropriately identify the main ideas of the paragraphs. She sees the need to redirect students to the process of identifying the main idea discussed in the American Indian unit. She encourages the students in the group to think about the following: What is the most general statement? Is there one general

Becoming *R.I.C.H.* in Knowledge

*R*ead the passage or chapter.

*I*dentify the main idea and supporting details.

*C*reate a question about the main idea or details.

*H*ow can you answer that question?

Figure 2.1. *R.I.C.H.* mnemonic.

idea repeated, hinted at, or emphasized? Is this idea always stated in the paragraph? Or, do you sometimes need to read across lines to find it? The group returns to the text, discusses what the most general idea is and how the supporting details point to this idea, and records them on their charts. Mrs. Finn listens and praises those ideas correctly identified. Before she leaves the group she asks students to back main ideas and supporting details up by pointing to where they are in the text. She shares with Beth that she did a good job of finding main ideas and backing them up with details.

Before the bell for recess rings, Mrs. Finn draws the whole class's attention to the guiding questions posted on the wall. "Which of these guiding questions have we answered through our reading today?" When Luis responds that the American Indians' way of life did not make them immune from certain diseases that the European explorers brought, Mrs. Finn takes the opportunity to state, "That is very good Luis. I really like how you connect what you've just read to what we learned about American Indians last week. And your use of the word *immune* is good. Can you explain what it means?"

Mrs. Finn goes on to say, "That idea will become particularly important in our next unit when we explore the interactions between the American Indians and the European explorers. Yet, it does not really get at why the explorers came to America or what they faced when they got here. Who found some information related to today's guiding questions?" Maria responds that she learned about the challenges faced by Sieur de La Salle when exploring what is now Quebec, and Tyler discusses with some surprise the many fights between the Spaniards and the Aztecs. Mrs. Finn writes this information on chart paper under the corresponding guiding question and places Maria's and Tyler's names next to their respective statements.

The students will continue reading about Sieur de La Salle and Samuel de Champlain the next day and asking questions to guide their reading. Ultimately, the students will use the knowledge they gain about the European explorers to create a group newspaper that highlights the voyages from France, England, Spain, and the Netherlands.

SELF-EFFICACY FOR READING

Self-efficacy beliefs are defined as one's perceived capabilities for learning or performing actions to attain designated performances (Bandura, 1986, 1997). Self-efficacy for reading refers to students' own perceptions of their reading capabilities, which would encompass students' perceptions of their competence to perform the skills and components involved in the act of reading (e.g., word decoding, identifying main ideas, inferencing, reading fluently). Being successful or experiencing difficulties on any of these reading skills will influence how students view their reading capabilities. When a student expresses self-doubt about his or her capability to read orally in front of classmates, then he or she expresses low self-efficacy for oral, fluent reading. Yet, when a student expresses that he or she feels he or she learns a lot by reading social studies books, then the student expresses his or her competence and a belief that he or she can learn from reading.

We chose to focus on self-efficacy for reading in USHER in general and in this chapter because of its importance for reading motivation and performance, its specificity, and the multiple ways it can be operationalized in the classroom. Numerous studies have demonstrated that self-efficacy beliefs are related to students' choices, effort, and performance. Reading self-efficacy relates to students' reading comprehension, what and when they choose to read, and the effort they expend on reading (e.g., Guthrie & Wigfield, 1999). Thus, we view reading self-efficacy beliefs as an important aspect of motivation to read that must be addressed to promote prolonged, engaged reading, particularly with struggling or resistant readers.

It is also important to recognize that self-efficacy as a motivational construct is best conceptualized as being domain or task specific. That is, students not only vary in their level of self-efficacy beliefs across domains (e.g., students may feel more efficacious about learning in science than in social studies), but they also may feel more or less efficacious about tasks within a domain. For instance, a student may believe that he or she can learn about history by watching a class video but have doubts about the extent he or she can learn by reading a history book. Thus, there is a need to promote students' sense of competence for the specific tasks involved in reading in the content area.

Fortunately, teachers and parents can structure curricular and social experiences to aid the development of adolescents' self-efficacy (Schunk & Meece, 2006). Students develop their self-efficacy beliefs from various sources of information (Bandura, 1997; Usher & Pajares, 2006). Some of these come from previous performances and the perceptions rooted in these performances. That is, if a student views a performance as a success, then he or she is likely to feel more efficacious about the task, compared with an instance in which he or she was not successful. Students also get information about their self-efficacy beliefs by watching others experience success or difficulty and by the verbal and nonverbal messages they receive from their families, peers, and teachers (Bandura, 1997; Usher & Pajares, 2006). Self-efficacy is enhanced when children are encouraged to achieve, when they are exposed to positive academic and social models, and when they are taught and shown strategies and behaviors that they can use to overcome difficulties (Schunk & Meece, 2006).

Instructional Contexts to Support Reading Self-Efficacy

How can teachers improve students' self-efficacy for reading? Some instructional conditions that foster self-efficacy among adolescents include the provision of: 1) proximal and specific learning goals, 2) opportunities for successful experiences, 3) instruction on learning strategies, 4) appropriate attributional feedback and praise to indicate progress, and 5) social models, particularly peer models (Schunk, 1995). We see each of these reflected in Mrs. Finn's instruction.

Proximal and Specific Learning Goals   Mrs. Finn is setting purposes for reading by using content goals when she posts the unit guiding questions for all to see and refers to them at the beginning and end of class. These are proximal goals because even if students cannot answer the guiding questions fully by the end of a lesson (due to their breadth), their partial answers are written down on wall charts and will be revisited by the end of the unit. Mrs. Finn also writes the students' names next to their contributions. This promotes students' sense of competence and improvement by providing a written and visible record of their progress toward achieving the goal.

Opportunities for Success   Personal mastery experiences are a powerful source of self-efficacy information (Bandura, 1986; Usher & Pajares, 2006). Thus, teachers can promote students' sense of self-efficacy for reading by providing opportunities for them to be successful. We see this at work in various ways within Mrs. Finn's class. For instance, as she makes the transition to teaching text-based questioning, Mrs. Finn starts by building on a strategy the students have already used extensively—identifying the main idea and supporting details. This allows students to see how the new learning builds on what they already know and supports their sense of self-efficacy for the task (Schunk & Meece, 2006). In addition, using leveled texts based on the students' reading provides a means for all students to gain access to the information and be successful in reading and mastering the content. Moreover, having students work in small groups allows Mrs. Finn to provide the specific scaffolding needed to help each group experience success.

Strategy Instruction It is necessary for students to improve their skills and become more competent in order for them to feel more confident in their reading capabilities. Thus, strategy instruction is an important component of supporting students' reading self-efficacy beliefs. Mrs. Finn provides specific instruction on reading strategies that will help students comprehend history texts. As part of this instruction, Mrs. Finn models the process of identifying the main idea and makes her thinking transparent to students through a think-aloud, which allows students to observe and participate in her thinking about using the strategy. In addition, when Mrs. Finn discusses how the strategy helps her understand the text, students develop a deeper understanding of how such a strategy contributes to their text comprehension. Furthermore, using *R.I.C.H.* provides students with the specific steps they need to successfully implement the questioning strategy. Mrs. Finn also provides students with numerous opportunities to practice the strategies and further develop their reading abilities. For instance, repeating the steps of main idea identification in small groups and with texts that are at students' reading levels allows students to develop confidence in their abilities to become better at finding main ideas in text.

Attributional Feedback and Praise Strategy practice alone is not enough. Even if a student is becoming a more capable reader through strategy use, it is essential that he or she recognize the improvements and feel more competent about his or her strategy use and reading comprehension. Teachers can play an important role here by providing specific, attributional feedback. Attribution theorists assume that people naturally search for an understanding of why events occur, especially when the outcome of an event is important or unexpected (Moeller & Koeller, 1999; Weiner, 1992). Thus, the student who expects to do well on a test but failed will try to answer the question, "Why did I do poorly on that test?" People's perceptions of the causes of outcomes are referred to as *causal attributions*. Ability ("I did well because I am smart," "I did poorly because I am dumb") and effort ("I did/did not do well because I did/did not study;" Weiner, 1992) are the most common attributions for performance outcomes. Effort is often viewed as an internal cause that is under the control of the individual, whereas ability is seen as an internal cause that the individual cannot control.

Many studies have shown that students who have a history of poor performance are more likely to attribute success to external causes beyond their control (e.g., easy task or question, luck) and failure to a lack of ability compared with students who have a history of good performance (Marsh, 1984; Vlahovic-Stetic, Vidovic, & Arambasic, 1999). Such attributions are not adaptive for students' future learning and motivation. Thus, it is essential to foster attributions that are accurate when working with students who are struggling readers and suggest pathways for future success. Specifically, it is more effective when students attribute both successful and unsuccessful outcomes to factors that they can control in future performance. Teachers can promote such attributions by providing specific attributional feedback.

Attributional feedback consists of direct statements given to students about their effort and competencies (Alderman, 2008; Stipek, 2004). Attributional feedback can affect students' judgments and perceptions of their competencies and efficacy. Broadly speaking, the goal is to lead students to believe that they are able to succeed if they try (effort) and that when they fail it is because they were not trying hard enough, they need more practice, or they were not using the appropriate strategy. This approach is likely to have students attribute their performance to internal and controllable factors. Therefore, teachers that attribute failure to low effort or an ineffective strategy (e.g., "I do not think you were really paying attention to your reading") communicate a belief in the student's ability to succeed with sufficient effort (Schunk & Carbonari, 1984). Teachers' feedback suggesting that a student performed poorly even though he or she tried hard (e.g., "Don't worry, you did the best you could do") may appear supportive, but it can unintentionally reinforce a student's doubts about his or her competence and abilities. Thus, it is important to keep in mind that students may feel confused and discouraged if the teacher suggests that their poor performance is due to poor effort when, in fact, students may have put forth substantial effort (Stipek, 2004).

In the same fashion, teachers should not attribute student success to effort unless the teacher is confident that the student put forth effort. If students perform well on a task, then it may not be due to the effort expended but, rather, to an easy task. If this is the case, then it would be better for the teacher to provide more challenging tasks to the students (Schunk, 1989).

Several researchers prefer strategy over effort attributions because of these possible misinterpretations (Hattie, Biggs, & Purdie, 1996; Pressley, El-Dinary, Marks, Brown, & Stein, 1992). Having teachers comment on the strategy students use, or suggesting that they try a different one, provides recognition for student effort and concrete, constructive feedback. Schunk (1989) pointed out that encouraging the use of different strategies can enhance feelings of self-efficacy by giving students a perception of control over outcomes. For example, Mrs. Finn indicated to her students how and when they used a strategy well when she provided corrective feedback on main ideas, had students substantiate these with text information, and praised the students for correctly identifying a main idea.

There are also times when students make mistakes or their skills are not improving. Offering praise when it is not deserved is not effective. Instead, teachers can provide supports for reading efficacy and comprehension by giving specific feedback about students' use of strategies. For example, when Mrs. Finn noticed that students misidentified the main ideas in a few passages, she was able to shape students' thinking by using corrective questions (e.g., What is the most general statement? Is there one general idea repeated, hinted at, or emphasized? Is this idea always stated in the paragraph?) and by clarifying where students went wrong. This may involve encouraging students to explain their reasoning so the teacher can help identify the problem. If teachers understand the strategies (e.g., the purpose and steps for identifying the main idea), then they can break down the process and foster student competence for the steps involved. Teachers can create contexts to support student efficacy for cognitive strategy use by helping students recognize when they are using strategies well and when the process is breaking down so they can connect the use of the strategy to improved reading and understanding.

Social Models Students' vicarious experiences have also been identified as a source of self-efficacy information (Bandura, 1986; Usher & Pajares, 2006). A student will develop a sense of his or her own competence at a task by observing others succeeding or failing at the task. Mrs. Finn models different reading comprehension strategies at various points during the USHER lessons. Although this provides students insight into how to use the strategy, it only offers minimal support for students' sense of reading self-efficacy as students often view the teacher as a mastery model (i.e., someone who has expertise and can easily accomplish the task). Instead, it is Mrs. Finn's use of other students in the class as peer models that is more likely to have an affect on the self-efficacy of other students in the class, particularly if students see themselves as similar to the peer models. When Luis, Maria, and Tyler were praised for successfully identifying important information from the text, other students may have taken note of their success. In addition, Beth may have served as a coping peer model for the other members of her group in that she initially struggled with identifying the main idea but was able to do so after teacher scaffolding and additional work with the strategy. Seeing other students work through a problem can help a student recognize that errors are a part of the learning process and can be overcome with effort and additional strategy use.

Self-efficacy for reading is an important aspect of students' motivation to read that teachers can support through specific classroom practices. Moreover, adolescents with cognitive maturity have a much more differentiated view of their abilities and interpret and integrate multiple sources of information about their competencies better than younger children (Eccles, Wigfield, & Schiefele, 1998). There tends to be a stronger relation between performance feedback and competence beliefs for adolescents than for younger children. In addition, strategy instruction is an important aspect of supporting students' self-efficacy beliefs. Student text-based questioning is one reading comprehension strategy that lends itself particularly well to supporting both students' reading comprehension and their sense of reading self-efficacy. The following section discusses this strategy in the larger context of questioning research and in the specific framework of USHER.

STUDENT TEXT-BASED QUESTIONING: COGNITIVE AND MOTIVATIONAL DIMENSIONS

The study of questioning as a learning strategy goes back to the 1980s when Dillon (1988) differentiated between two main contexts for questioning in classrooms: 1) recitation, which follows the traditional IRE format (i.e., teacher *i*nitiates with a question, a student *r*esponds, and the teacher again takes up a turn and *e*valuates) in which students answer questions that have one correct answer and speak only to the teacher, and 2) discussion, which consists of posing an open-ended question that is subject to multiple answers in which students speak to one another (not just to the teacher) and both answer and pose questions. Our work in USHER underscores the importance of students' and teachers' understanding the difference between these two contexts and teachers establishing rules or procedures to follow in each context. The guiding questions seek to integrate information within a unit of study in social studies. They are posed by the teacher, but they are far from the IRE format because they do not limit answers to a correct or incorrect simple statement. Rather, they focus on the learning goals derived from social studies state standards and provide students (and teachers) with overall, unitwide objectives for reading and learning. Student text-based questions, however, let teachers get behind student thinking by having students pose questions that focus on facts, concepts, and/or relationships in history while reading trade books. Guiding and student text-based questions foster discussion about history concepts and facts.

Studies on questioning provide evidence of the benefits that teaching question types (e.g., inferential versus literal, information gathering versus application, high versus low) across content domains has on generating new knowledge, stimulating further inquiry, increasing text comprehension, and monitoring understanding (e.g., Chin & Chia, 2004; Chin & Osborne, 2008; Davey & McBride,1986; Taboada & Guthrie, 2006). In addition to these cognitive benefits, student questioning supports student motivation by allowing students to be active in their learning (Chin & Kayalvizhi, 2005), pursue their interests, and have some control over their reading (Taboada & Guthrie, 2006). In addition, student-generated questions support students' novel ideas (Chin & Osborne, 2008; Therrien, Wickstrom, & Jones, 2006) and foster self-efficacy by providing opportunities for students to articulate what they do and do not understand (Therrien et al., 2006).

The majority of research in the 2000s focused on applying the strategy of student-generated questions in the science classroom (Chin & Chia, 2004; Chin & Osborne, 2008; Taboada & Guthrie, 2006). A few studies, however, explored student questioning in the teaching of social studies in general (Bulgren, Marquis, Lenz, Deshler, & Schumaker, 2011) and of history in particular (e.g., Logtenburg, van Boxtel, & van Hout Walters, 2010; Van Drie & van Boxtel, 2008). For instance, Logtenburg et al. proposed that asking history-related questions (e.g., descriptive, comparative, explanative, evaluative) is an important component of historical reasoning. They investigated the impact of three types of introductory texts on the industrial revolution on student interest and text-based questions for Dutch students in high school. Findings revealed that the type of introductory text had a significant effect on the level of student interest and type of questions asked. Narrative and problematizing texts (e.g., presenting ambiguity between past and present) elicited higher interest and more emotive questions (e.g., indignation, astonishment, anger) than expository texts (Logtenburg et al., 2010). Studies such as this contributed to better understanding of the question types that students can spontaneously generate in the domain of history. They also emphasized the challenges of having students pose text-based questions for expository texts in history. Although students can significantly benefit from historical fiction and biographical texts, reading and learning history necessitates using expository texts and cannot rely on narrative texts alone. The teaching of text-based questioning for expository texts in USHER may contribute to fill this gap in the questioning literature.

STUDENT TEXT-BASED QUESTIONING IN USHER:
A STRATEGY TO SUPPORT COMPREHENSION AND READING MOTIVATION

Walsh and Sattes expressed that quality questions have one main purpose: "To engage students in interactions with their teachers and peers around the content under study so as to increase student understanding and mastery of learning goals" (2011, p. 16). Although the authors alluded to teacher questions, the teaching of student-generated questions can follow the same goal. Quality questioning should not be limited to factual information that can be memorized. Rather, it is a dynamic process through which a teacher should guide students to engage in cognitive and metacognitive thinking. Instruction of student questioning in USHER refers to students asking or writing self-initiated questions about the content of the text before and during reading to help them understand the text and topic.

Mrs. Finn has three goals when teaching text-based questions. She aims to: 1) make students aware of the purpose and value of posing their own text-based questions, 2) encourage all of her students to ask questions about the main ideas in the text being read, and 3) make students think about the four question levels proposed in USHER (see Figure 2.2). Mrs. Finn first makes sure students become comfortable with main idea identification in order to scaffold these goals appropriately. *R.I.C.H.* has helped with that process, and the time spent reading and finding paragraph main ideas during guided reading has served to clinch this strategy. Mrs. Finn then presents examples and counterexamples of the four questioning levels. She ensures that students understand that factual or yes/no questions (Level 1) are necessary in history because, "Without facts, we won't have stories to tell. History is made of facts." But she also clearly establishes the difference between facts and conceptual explanations (Level 2). She asks students to think of a Level 1 question. Maria volunteers, "What did the French trade with the North Americans?" They discuss what the answer to the question can be and decide that a list of (factual) information on the resources traded between these groups qualifies the question for Level 1. Juan volunteers a Level 2 question: "What were the Spanish explorers like compared with the French explorers?" Again, a discussion ensues about the nature of the answer—a compare and contrast explanation. "Clearly a Level 2 question," Mrs. Finn praises Juan. They continue to focus on Level 3 questions and get into a lively discussion of what constitutes background knowledge contained within the question. Tyler and others point to sentences in the text that helped them form the question, "Why would France want to find the route to Asia?" and agree that France's attempts to find this route constitutes the background knowledge expressed in the question. In subsequent days, Mrs. Finn spends sufficient time letting students integrate information across texts and content from the previous unit on American Indians with European explorers. This information serves as the basis to get students to think of how to form questions that ask about patterns of relationships (Level 4). Beth's group proudly shares their text-based question: "How did the challenges encountered by Alvar Nuñez Cabeza de Vaca and Hernando de Soto change what happened next?" Quite a bit of reading across books helped with framing this question. Mrs. Finn asks Beth and her group why that would be a Level 4 question. Students elaborate on the need to integrate information across books. Mrs. Finn congratulates them and records some of these questions in the classroom poster under the appropriate question level.

How does text-based questioning support self-efficacy for reading? First, students set personal goals for reading when they ask their own text-based questions and, thus, are self-directed in their pursuit of knowledge (Taboada & Guthrie, 2006). Some sense of self-direction or control of what or how to learn within an established curriculum provides students with the opportunity to set goals and assess their competence in trying to achieve those goals. Monitoring that trajectory by recording their questions and identifying the level of each question can contribute to students' sense of reading efficacy as well. Second, using levels allows students to assess their own questioning ability. They can use "hangers" or labels to self-rate their own thinking about text. With sufficient and appropriate teacher feedback, students can reflect on their questions and polish the quality of their questions to chart their journey toward mastery. This is not to say that Level 1

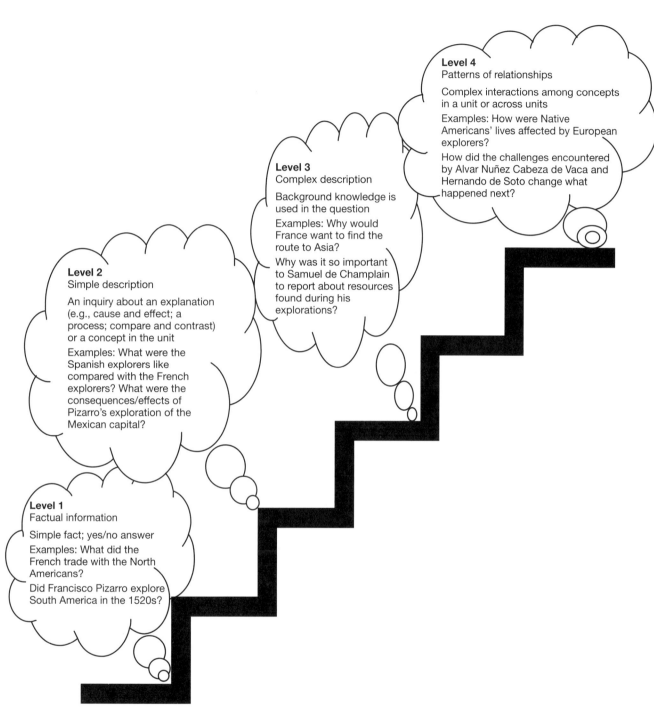

Figure 2.2. Text-based questioning.

questions should be discarded in the pursuit of higher-level questions. Rather, it tells students that Level 1 questions are the foundation for other types of questions that they can ask as they read text and build their knowledge of the topic. Third, students can reflect on their own questions as they listen to their peers' questions and benefit from teacher feedback to their peers to focus their attention on their own performance (i.e., use of peer modeling to support self-efficacy).

READING SELF-EFFICACY: EVIDENCE FROM USHER INSTRUCTION

We examined the impact of USHER on students' self-efficacy for reading during the 2010–2011 school year. Ten social studies teachers participated in USHER and implemented instruction during 7 weeks in the Spring of 2011. Each teacher taught one to two classes of sixth-grade students. Participants included 427 students—219 were identified as English native speakers and 208 were identified as language minority students based on school records (e.g., language other than English spoken at home). Spanish was the most common language spoken at home for the language minority students (i.e., 83% of the language minority students).

USHER adaptations for language minority students during the 2010–2011 school year consisted of trade books below grade level and incidental teaching of vocabulary present in the trade books. We were interested in examining history reading comprehension and reading self-efficacy, among other variables. History reading comprehension was assessed with four passages with eight multiple choice items per passage (i.e., 32 items total) that were each administered before and after USHER was implemented with the sixth-grade students. The passages ranged from 512 to 627 words and none of the content was addressed as part of sixth-grade USHER implementation. One passage was below grade level (i.e., Issues that Divided a Nation), one was above grade level (i.e., Age of Inventions), and two were on grade level (i.e., Water-Powered Mills, Battle of Antietam), according to the Flesch Kincaid reading index. Items consisted of literal and inferential comprehension and some history-specific vocabulary.

Students' general sense of reading self-efficacy was assessed using 13 items adapted from Shell, Colvin, and Bruning (1995) to assess students' perceptions of their ability to read. Students responded to each item by writing a number that best described how sure they could perform a series of reading related tasks on a scale from 0 (*cannot do at all*) to 100 (*completely certain I can do*). The items are continuations of an anchor question ("How sure are you that you can. . .") that include "recognize letters," "read a school book," "understand the main idea of a paragraph," and "think of what you know before you read."

Findings indicated that both language minority and English native speaking students increased in their history reading comprehension and reading self-efficacy over the 7 weeks of implementation. The improvement on history reading comprehension is important for at least three reasons. First, this finding provides evidence that USHER is working as intended. That is, students increased in their history reading comprehension after participating in the social studies lessons that included explicit strategy instruction and support for reading motivation. Second, and more important, the assessment of history comprehension consisted of topics in history that were new to the students and not taught during USHER implementation, which provides some measure of transfer of comprehension skills. Third, the increase in history comprehension was found for both language groups, indicating that USHER practices and differentiation of text levels may be addressing the comprehension needs of language minority students.

This indicates that students were more confident about their reading capabilities after the USHER lessons. Therefore, we have reasons to believe that this positive change may be due to using specific teacher praise and corrective feedback as well as the opportunities created by the modeling and scaffolding of comprehension strategies during USHER.

CONCLUSION

Motivation researchers have studied self-efficacy for decades. Research in self-efficacy beliefs has taken place in both constrained experimental contexts as well as in real classroom situations. A lot has been learned in both contexts about the dynamics of motivation in both elementary school children and adolescents. In addition, effective teachers are probably intuitively using many motivational and self-efficacy strategies in their teaching. When literacy researchers discuss motivation practices to enhance literacy instruction, however, the focus tends to be on the enjoyment, fun, or pleasure of reading. Although these dimensions of motivation require attention and are important to instill in every classroom, the type of reading associated with these motivations is not always conducive to the sustained learning that leads to the cognitive benefits and satisfactions associated with most history curricular objectives. Our work in USHER attempts to bridge some of this gap—help teachers instill motivational and cognitive practices that will lead students to deep, focused, and engaged reading of expository history texts. Self-efficacy for reading is one motivational practice that can assist teachers and students toward that goal.

REFERENCES

Alderman, M.K. (2008). *Motivation for achievement: Possibilities for teaching and learning* (3rd ed.). New York, NY: Taylor and Francis.

Almarza, D. (2001). Contexts shaping minority language students' perceptions of American history. *Journal of Social Studies Research, 25*, 4–22.

Alvermann, D.E., & Moore, D.W. (1991). Secondary school reading. In R. Barr, M.L. Kamil, P. Mosenthal, & P.D. Pearson (Eds.), *Handbook of reading research* (Vol. 2, pp. 951–983). New York, NY: Longman.

Anderman, E.M., Maehr, M.L., & Midgley, C. (1999). Declining motivation after the transition to middle-school: Schools can make a difference. *Journal of Research and Development in Education, 32*(5), 131–147.

August, D.L., & Shanahan, T. (Eds.). (2006). *Developing literacy in a second language: Report of the national literacy panel on language-minority children and youth.* Mahwah, NJ: Lawrence Erlbaum Associates.

Bandura, A. (1986). The explanatory and predictive scope of self-efficacy theory. *Journal of Social and Clinical Psychology, 4*, 359–373.

Bandura, A. (1997). *Self-efficacy: The exercise of control.* New York, NY: Freeman.

Bintz, W.P. (1993). Resistant readers in secondary education: Some insights and implications. *Journal of Reading, 36*(8), 604–615.

Brophy, J. (2009, April). *History aims and student motivation: Reducing the gap.* Paper presented at the annual meeting of the American Educational Association, San Diego, CA.

Bulgren, J., Marquis, J.G., Lenz, K., Deshler, D.D., & Schumaker, J.B. (2011). The effectiveness of a question-exploration routine for enhancing the content learning of secondary students. *Journal of Educational Psychology, 103*(3), 578–593.

Chin, C., & Chia, L.G. (2004). Problem-based learning: Using students' questions to drive knowledge construction. *Science Education, 88*(5), 707–727.

Chin, C., & Kayalvizhi, G. (2005). What do pupils think of open science investigations? A study of Singaporean primary 6 pupils. *Educational Research, 47*(1), 107–126.

Chin, C., & Osborne, J. (2008). Students' questions: A potential resource for teaching and learning science. *Studies in Science Education, 44*(1), 1–39.

Davey, B., & McBride, S. (1986). Effects of question-generation training on reading comprehension. *Journal of Educational Psychology, 78*(4), 256–262.

Dillon, J.T. (1988). *Questioning and teaching: A manual of practice.* London, England: Croom Helm.

Eccles, J.S., Wigfield, A., & Schiefele, U. (1998). Motivation to succeed. In W. Damon (Series Ed.) & N. Eisenberg (Vol. Ed.), *Handbook of child psychology* (5th ed., Vol. 3, pp. 1017–1095). New York, NY: Wiley.

Fountas, I.C., & Pinnell, G.S. (2001). *Guiding reading and writers.* Westport, CT: Heinnemann.

Guthrie, J.T., & Wigfield, A. (1999). How motivation fits into a science of reading. *Scientific Studies of Reading, 3*(3), 199–207.

Guthrie, J.T., & Wigfield, A. (2000). Engagement and motivation in reading. In M.L. Kamil & P.B. Mosenthal (Eds.), *Handbook of reading research* (Vol. 3, pp. 403–422). Mahwah, NJ: Lawrence Erlbaum Associates.

Guthrie, J.T., Wigfield, A., Barbosa, P., Perencevich, K.C., Taboada, A., Davis, M.H., . . . Tonks, S. (2004). Increasing reading comprehension and engagement through Concept-Oriented Reading Instruction. *Journal of Educational Psychology, 96*(3), 403–423.

Hamston, J., & Love, K. (2003). Reading relationships: Parents, boys, and reading as cultural practice. *Australian Journal of Language and Literacy, 26*(3), 44–57.

Hattie, J., Biggs, J., & Purdie, N. (1996). Effects of learning skills interventions on student learning: A meta-analysis. *Review of Educational Research, 66*(2), 99–136.

Ivey, G., & Broaddus, K. (2001). "Just plain reading": A survey of what makes students want to read in middle school classrooms. *Reading Research Quarterly, 36*(4), 350–377.

Jacobs, J.E., Lanza, S., Osgood, D.W., Eccles, J.S., & Wigfield, A. (2002). Changes in children's self-competence and values: Gender and domain differences across grades one through twelve. *Child Development, 73*, 509–527.

Kindler, A. (2002). *Survey of the states' limited English proficient students and available educational programs and services: 2000–2001 summary report*. Washington, DC: National Clearinghouse for English Language Acquisition.

Lee, C.D., & Spratley, A. (2010). *Reading in the disciplines: The challenges of adolescent literacy*. New York, NY: Carnegie Corporation.

Lee, J., Grigg, W.S., & Donahue, P.L. (2007). *The nation's report card: Reading 2007: National assessment of educational progress at grades 4 and 8* (NCES No. 2007-496). Washington, DC: National Center for Education Statistics, Institute of Education Sciences, U.S. Department of Education. Retrieved from http://nationsreportcard.gov/reading_2007

Logtenburg, A., van Boxtel, C., & van Hout Walters, B. (2010). Stimulating situational interest and student questioning through three types of historical introductory texts. *European Journal of Psychology of Education, 26*, 179–198.

Marsh, H. (1984). Relations among dimensions of self-attribution, dimensions of self-concept and academic achievement. *Journal of Educational Psychology, 76*, 3–32.

Moeller, J., & Koeller, O. (1999). Spontaneous cognitions following academic test results. *Journal of Experimental Education, 67*(2), 150–164.

Morganelli, A. (2006). *Samuel de Champlain from New Franc to Cape Cod*. New York, NY: Crabtree Publishing.

Pearson, P.D., & Gallagher, M.C. (1983). The instruction of reading comprehension. *Contemporary Educational Psychology, 8*, 317–344.

Pressley, M., El-Dinary, P.B., Marks, M.B., Brown, R., & Stein, S. (1992). Good strategy instruction is motivating and interesting. In K.A Reddinger, S. Hiddi, & A. Krapp (Eds.), *The role of interest in learning and development* (pp. 333–358). Mahwah, NJ: Lawrence Erlbaum Associates.

Reeves, A.R. (2004). *Adolescents talk about reading: Exploring resistance to and engagement with text*. Newark, DE: International Reading Association.

Sandler, M. (2005). *Explorers of the Americas*. Pelham, NY: Benchmark Education Company.

Schunk, D.H. (1982). Effects of effort attributional feedback on children's perceived self-efficacy and achievement. *Educational Psychology, 74*, 548–556.

Schunk, D.H. (1989). Self-efficacy and cognitive skill learning. In C. Ames & R. Ames (Eds.), *Research on motivation in education: Goals and cognitions* (Vol. 3, pp. 13–44). San Diego, CA: Academic Press.

Schunk, D.H. (1995). Self-efficacy and education and instruction. In J.E. Maddox (Ed.), *Self-efficacy, adaptation, and adjustment: Theory, research and practice* (pp. 281–303). New York, NY: Plenum Press.

Schunk, D.H., & Carbonari, J. (1984). Self-efficacy models. In J.D. Matarazzo, J.A. Herd, N. Miller, & S.M. Weiss (Eds.), *Behavioral health: A handbook of health enhancement and disease prevention* (pp. 230–247). New York, NY: Wiley.

Schunk, D.H., & Meece, J.L. (2006). Self-efficacy development in adolescence. In F. Pajares & T. Urdan (Eds.), *Self-efficacy beliefs of adolescents* (pp. 71–96). Charlotte, NC: Information Age Publishing.

Shell, D.F., Colvin, C., & Bruning, R.H. (1995). Self-efficacy, attributions, and outcome expectancy mechanisms in reading and writing achievement: Grade-level and achievement-level differences. *Journal of Educational Psychology, 87*, 386–398.

Stipek, D. (2004). *Engaging schools: Fostering high school students' motivation to learn*. Washington, DC: National Academies Press.

Taboada, A., Buehl, M., Kidd, J.K., & Sturtevant, E. (2010). *Fostering reading engagement in English-monolingual students and English language learners through a history curriculum*. Fairfax, VA: George Mason University.

Taboada, A., & Guthrie, J.T. (2006). Contributions of student questioning and prior knowledge to construction of knowledge from reading information text. *Journal of Literacy Research, 38*, 1–35.

Taboada, A., Guthrie, J.T., & McRae, A. (2008). Building engaging classrooms. In R. Fink & S.J. Samuels (Eds.), *Inspiring success: Reading interest and motivation in an age of high-stakes testing*. Newark, DE: International Reading Association.

Therrien, W.J., Wickstrom, K., & Jones, K. (2006). Effect of a combined repeated reading and question generation intervention on reading achievement. *Learning Disabilities Research and Practice, 21*(2), 89–97.

Usher, E.L., & Pajares, F. (2006). Sources of self-efficacy and self-regulatory efficacy beliefs of entering middle school students. *Contemporary Educational Psychology, 31*, 125–141.

Van Drie, J., & van Boxtel, C. (2008). Historical reasoning: Towards a framework for analyzing students' reasoning about the past. *Educational Psychology Review, 20*(2), 87–110.

Vlahovic-Stetic, V., Vidovic, V., & Arambasic, L. (1999). Motivational characteristics in mathematical achievement: A study of gifted high-achieving, gifted underachieving and non-gifted pupils. *High Ability Studies, 10*, 37–49.

Walsh, J.A., & Sattes, B.D. (2011). *Thinking through quality questioning: Deepening student engagement*. Thousand Oaks, CA: Corwin.

Wang, J.H., & Guthrie, J.T. (2004). Modeling the effects of intrinsic motivation, extrinsic motivation, amount of reading, and past reading achievement on text comprehension between U.S. and Chinese students. *Reading Research Quarterly, 39*(2), 162–186.

Weiner, B. (1992). *Human motivation: Metaphors, theories, and research.* Thousand Oaks, CA: Sage Publications.

Wigfield, A., & Guthrie, J.T. (1997). Motivation for reading: Individual, home, textual, and classroom perspective. *Educational Psychologist, 32*(2), 57–135.

Zronik, J.P. (2006). *Sieur de La Salle.* New York, NY: Crabtree Publishing.

3 Disciplinary Literacy

Suzanne M. Robinson

All students progress in literacy development by learning basic decoding, fluency, and vocabulary skills and acquiring comprehension strategies. Students continue applying all of the reading skills they have learned to specific knowledge domains, adding more sophisticated strategies to develop a deeper understanding of specific topics within disciplines. Reading instruction in elementary school focuses on developing proficient and fluent application of basic reading skills and increasing attention and instructional time spent on general comprehension skills (identifying main ideas and meanings, answering and asking questions, connecting text to prior knowledge, and predicting or inferring connections).

Adolescent students in secondary school are expected to apply reading skills to learn disciplinary content. They must use a range of strategies (e.g., vocabulary knowledge, general knowledge of topics and text structures, a variety of comprehension strategies, knowing what to do when comprehension breaks down, monitoring their progress toward understanding) in a variety of content areas that include English literature, history, geography, social studies, and different domains of science and mathematics. Students typically move among these disciplines on a daily or, certainly, weekly basis. In addition, the bar is set high due to Race to the Top and Common Core State Standards, and the expectation is that students will leave high school proficient in all realms of literacy so that they are ready for college or a career. A common belief is if young students learn to fluently decode and develop basic comprehension of a large number of frequently used words (common vocabulary) and text (general comprehension strategies), then they will naturally apply the general strategies they learned in earlier grades in more sophisticated ways as they are introduced to complex content and reading material. For example, children in elementary grades learn words such as *is, red, dog,* and *car.* Knowing these words will serve readers well. They will continue to see these words in text over their life in books, newspapers, instructional materials, and so forth. Learning within disciplines, however, will require students to learn vocabulary that is used in more constrained and specific contexts. Words such as *rhombus, mitosis, photosynthesis,* or *tundra* are found in discipline-specific texts and are useful to learning concepts within the discipline, but are not commonly used outside of that context. So, the vocabulary learning strategies the children used to master simple words (e.g., repetition by sight, frequent use and reuse, recognition across settings) might not serve them well when faced with content-specific vocabulary. The vocabulary, as well as the text structure, becomes more specific and constrained in its use within disciplines. Likewise, comprehension development moves from general to specialized. Complex and challenging mathematics texts, science texts, social science texts, and literature are organized differently as determined by the knowledge structures of each discipline, and this structure is often invisible to the casual reader. All students need specialized sets of strategies to develop advanced disciplinary literacy. The strategies need to be directed toward understanding ways of organizing, combining, and interpreting information that is discipline specific. One can see how these specialized skills might be difficult for many typical students to acquire and necessitate explicit instruction. The challenge is even greater for students with reading deficits; they need to continue to learn basic reading skills as well as general comprehension strategies and content-specific strategies if they are to be successful. Unless literacy instruction changes, it is unlikely that all students will meet the increasingly high literacy standards of the 21st century.

This chapter focuses on the topic of disciplinary literacy and how to assist all students in developing skills to become proficient learners of content. It includes descriptions of needed literacy instruction and how to further disciplinary literacy in inclusive schools.

This chapter does the following:

- Describes the context of literacy demands and literacy development for students with and without disabilities, with a focus on adolescent learners because disciplinary literacy is the focus of most secondary classrooms.

- Defines and illustrates what is entailed to comprehend texts within and across academic disciplines.

- Examines the research about general and discipline-specific reading comprehension.

- Identifies instructional strategies and approaches that assist all readers in developing reading skills that contribute to disciplinary literacy competence.

LITERACY PROFICIENCY OF STUDENTS IN SECONDARY SCHOOLS: THE CONTEXT FOR IMPROVING THE INSTRUCTIONAL LANDSCAPE

Following the Reading First initiative (U.S. Department of Education, 2008), efforts to overhaul primary school literacy programs led to modest improvements in reading as demonstrated by the National Assessment of Educational Progress (NAEP) (http://nces.ed.gov/nationsreportcard/). The average reading score for 9-year-olds was higher in 2008 than in all previous assessment years, increasing 4 points since 2004 and 12 points in comparison with 1971 (U.S. Department of Education, 2011). It appeared that the initiative to focus federal research dollars on early reading and the emphasis on applying the subsequent research findings to practice was working. Thus, policy makers, researchers, and various think tanks interested in adolescent literacy used a similar, albeit scaled down strategy, to address poor literacy outcomes of many older students. The strategy has not resulted in meaningful outcomes as of yet because of the challenges of implementing school-wide or targeted change in secondary schools and the typical time frame (5–7 years) before change reflects impact. According to the NAEP, although the average score for 13-year-olds in 2008 was higher than in 2004 and 1971, it was not significantly different from the scores in some assessment years in between. The average reading score for 17-year-olds followed the same relatively flat pattern as that of 13-year-olds (U.S. Department of Education, 2011). In practical terms, two thirds of adolescent students lack the reading skills necessary to succeed in disciplinary study; 70% of eighth graders perform at or below the basic level in reading comprehension (Lee, Griggs, & Donahue, 2007).

The complexity of improving disciplinary literacy is even more challenging than one might conclude after reviewing the data previously reported. It will require more than improved instruction and enacting what we know; it will also require understanding that the end goal of more ambitious and higher standards demanding advanced literacy is a very real need to address the societal and economic demands of the United States in the 21st century. The literacy landscape is changing. The demands of a knowledge-based economy and preparation for the type of jobs this economy entails requires individuals with very sophisticated literacy skills. No longer are there sufficient numbers of blue-collar jobs that provide an adequate livelihood for individuals, regardless of low literacy levels. As a matter of fact, the 2009 NAEP reading framework changed to respond to increasing literacy demands and now calls for two types of text on the assessment—literary texts (e.g., fiction, literary nonfiction, poetry) and informational text (e.g., exposition, argumentation and persuasive text, procedural text and documents). Vocabulary is assessed within these two types of texts. This 2009 reading framework is the conceptual base for and illustrates the content of the NAEP (National Assessment Governing Board, 2006).

It is telling, and arguably outdated, that the discussion of literacy and adolescents has focused on whether literacy instruction is necessarily the purview of secondary education beyond remedial support for those without basic reading and writing skills. Unfortunately, a course in reading in the content areas is frequently the extent of literacy preparation for secondary teachers. Secondary educators commonly maintain a generalist notion of literacy learning—the first line of defense is to "inoculate" students at a young age by ensuring success in basic literacy skills. Then, minimal literacy instruction should be needed by high school. Most secondary teachers also adhere to the belief that exposure to content instruction supported by general reading strategies should prove sufficient to develop high levels of disciplinary literacy. The NAEP data do not support this interpretation, and the changing economic/career contexts and related high-level literacy demands argue that challenges for students and adults are increasing. In response to the changing literacy environment of the 21st century, some researchers (Shanahan & Shanahan, 2012) recommended a tri-part conceptualization of literacy development that includes basic skill development, general comprehension strategy development, and specialized, discipline-specific approaches to literacy as a framework for providing literacy instruction so that all students develop a deep understanding and a way of thinking about each discipline's knowledge base.

Reports by various researchers and groups provided direction for those attempting to incorporate the available adolescent reading research into comprehensive, schoolwide practices that promise to improve the literacy outcomes for secondary school students. *Reading Next: A Vision for Action and Research in Middle and High School Literacy* (Alliance for Excellent Education, 2004), the federally funded Center on Instruction's (COI; 2010) *Academic Literacy Instruction for Adolescents: A Guidance Document from the Center on Instruction, Improving Adolescent Literacy: Effective Classroom and Intervention Practices* (U.S. Department of Education, 2008), and the Carnegie Corporation's (2010) series, *Time to Act: An Agenda for Advancing Adolescent Literacy for College and Career Success* are some reports that provided consistent and compelling guidelines about what must happen in literacy instruction to improve secondary student outcomes. These recommendations included teach vocabulary explicitly; use direct, explicit comprehension strategy instruction; discuss and interpret text meaning; increase the amount and quality of open, sustained discussion of content; teach essential content; increase student motivation and engagement in literacy learning; and provide qualified specialists for intensive, individualized interventions. To elaborate further on the last point, other researchers (e.g., Faggella-Luby & Deshler, 2008; Scruggs, Mastropieri, Berkeley & Gratz, 2011 reported improved outcomes for struggling readers with learning disabilities by providing increasingly intensive intervention through tiered support. Other recommendations for this population of students drawn from the reports included: 1) reinforcing core content literacy practices introduced elsewhere, 2) cuing students to activate prior knowledge and generic reading strategies, and 3) teaching content-specific vocabulary and strategies. Collaboration among education professionals within a school is necessary to enact the suggestions/recommendations.

Shanahan and Shanahan (2012) provided a conceptualization for literacy development that encompasses a progression from basic skills through increasingly more sophisticated and discipline-focused reading approaches (see Figure 3.1). This framework is instructive to the educator trying to choose an appropriate focus for students with varying instructional needs. It identifies three distinctly different foci for literacy instruction needed in schools and needed to differing degrees by students with novice to expert literacy skills profiles. The focus of instruction for students with a novice profile is on decoding, word study, knowledge of high-frequency words, and basic text structure that underlie virtually all reading tasks. For example, students develop a sight word vocabulary of common words, basic decoding strategies of single and multisyllabic words, and the "rules" of text (e.g., directionality, primacy of text over visuals, the role of punctuation, story structure versus simple expository text) (Shanahan & Shanahan, 2012). Instruction for students facing intermediate literacy demands (generic and somewhat simple comprehension tasks) includes generic comprehension strategies, learning common and multiple meanings for words, and basic fluency in reading different kinds of text. Students at this level of complexity learn the

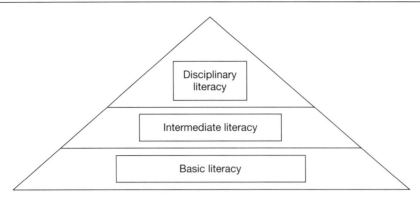

Figure 3.1. The increasing specialization of literacy development. (From Shanahan, T. & Shanahan, C. [2012]. Teaching disciplinary literacy to adolescents: Rethinking content-area literacy. In J. Ippolito, J.L. Steele, & J.F. Samson [Eds.], *Adolescent literacy* [p. 44]. Cambridge, MA: Harvard Educational Review; reprinted by permission.)

highly effective general comprehension strategies of asking questions, making predictions, testing hypotheses, summarizing, monitoring understanding, and deploying fix-it strategies (e.g., rereading) (Lee & Spratley, 2010). Readers focusing on disciplinary learning are required to employ expert and specific disciplinary approaches to understand and organize knowledge; their strategies become specialized to history, science, mathematics, literature, or other subject matter. For example, reading history requires the student to intuit the author's biases and perspective. The text is not read as "truth"; instead, understanding history requires reading multiple sources to develop understanding of reality from differing points of view while determining the missing pieces of the picture or historical record. As another example, reading mathematics requires the student to understand symbols and words that have both specific and general meanings (e.g., *prime*). Mathematicians report a process of close reading to determine accuracy or error in the processes described and conclusions drawn (Shanahan & Shanahan, 2012).

Comprehension within and Across Academic Disciplines

The process of comprehending text is extraordinarily complex. Early reading comprehension research focused on discrete skills such as finding the main idea and identifying answers to questions that required identifying facts or making inferences. Now there is greater appreciation and understanding of the constructive nature of comprehension; readers piece together understanding through the act of reading and these same readers draw from a deep well of prior knowledge that includes words, word forms, word families, sentence structure, text structure or genres, and topics (Lee & Spratley, 2010). Furthermore, goals for reading and motivation play a role in a reader's comprehension monitoring (Kosanovich, Reed, & Miller, 2010).

The context of secondary schools increases the complexity of reading comprehension across the disciplines when one thinks about the demands placed on each individual student. It is as though students take a journey every day to multiple foreign countries with unique cultures and each with its own "language" as they move from the "country" of science to those of literature, mathematics, history, and more.

Learning in the Disciplines

Students are expected to develop expertise in each discipline. Experts understand a discipline in specific ways (Bransford, Brown, & Cocking, 1999). First, they understand that the domain of knowledge under examination has a specific organization structure for knowledge—there is a system for organizing the ideas and concepts, there is a set of investigative methods used in the domain that helps the learner develop and deepen understanding, and there is a schema that helps one determine what information is more important and less important to understanding. Second, experts in a discipline develop habits of mind that characterize creative and high-level thinking in the knowledge domain. Third, experts in a domain develop a sophisticated and ever-changing schematic of the major concepts of the discipline that allow them to easily incorporate new learning and reorganize what is known to accommodate new information. Finally, experts develop the ability to use what is known beyond the context in which it was acquired to push at the boundaries of their understanding and investigate new possibilities as they reconcile potential conflicts between past understanding and new ways of thinking. Each discipline has its own discourse patterns and ways of thinking, believing, acting, and communicating that is reflected in disciplinary texts and in conversation and comprehension of that discipline (Moje & Lewis, 2007). Different knowledge structures are applied to disciplinary text and are often so embedded and implicit in the ways that knowledge is organized and understood that it is hidden from the novice learner and not revealed until students are explicitly taught the domain's "ways of knowing." Some common knowledge structures that may apply follow.

- Hierarchical: some ideas are subordinate to others.

- Linear: ideas or events are arranged in a specific order (e.g., steps in a process, chronological order).

- Cyclical: ideas are arranged in a recursive process or flow chart.

- Clusters: related concepts are organized in groups.

Literacy Demands in History   Some key concepts implicit to students thinking like historians include understanding the importance of the concept of time in dividing historical periods, which often run into each other and overlap, and understanding that change occurs gradually and with an evolutionary process. Even though the conversation might focus on events or a series of events, events are both exemplars and unique simultaneously. Furthermore, historical thinking requires empathy—taking the perspective of individuals in the context of past institutions, social practices, or in light of how people of that time saw things and the circumstances surrounding them. Historical thinking requires analyzing the source of evidence (e.g., photographs, artifacts, paintings, documents) and understanding the different points of view reflected in available evidence, as well as inferring points of view and evidence that might be missing.

Literacy Demands in Science   Thinking like a scientist requires different habits of mind. Order is a big idea in science. A hierarchy exists within the knowledge base; some knowledge is subordinate to other ideas. Linearity and/or cyclical organization of knowledge are important to scientific thought. Some ideas or events follow a specific order, whereas others (or the same information) are organized and thought about recursively. Taxonomies, or nested relationships of information, are reflected throughout the scientific knowledge base.

Literacy Demands in Mathematics   Mathematicians traverse the landscape and intersections of mathematical concepts, procedural knowledge of calculation, and procedural knowledge about problem solving. The standards of the National Council of Teachers of Mathematics refer to mathematics as a language and a form of communication. They encourage teachers to use literature in which mathematical problem solving is incorporated as a way to help students understand how the conceptual is connected to calculation. Mathematics literacy instruction often focuses on mastering a mathematics textbook with its examples, notations, definitions, margin notes, and more (Lee & Spratley, 2010). This type of instruction, however, does not necessarily lead to conceptual understanding. A unique challenge to mathematics literacy is a mythology based on the misperceptions that: 1) mathematics is about learning to compute, 2) mathematics is about "following rules" to guarantee correct answers, and 3) some people have the ability to "do math" and some do not (Fuson, Kalchman, & Bransford, 2005, pp. 220–221). These preconceptions complicate improving mathematics literacy instruction.

Literacy Demands in the English Language Arts   The discipline of English language arts encompasses a variety of text categories (narrative and expository) as well as composition. Each of the text categories and compositional styles has its own unique features. For example, fiction story grammar includes characters (particularly a protagonist who encounters a problem-solving situation), plot, and other consistently evident literary components (setting, theme, rising action, resolution). Each fictional form has its own specific conventions (e.g., screenplay, mystery story, play, poem) that the expert must learn. Then, expository text follows other structures and conventions (e.g., description, persuasive, compare and contrast, explanation), and students must apply specific organizational structures to these types of text to comprehend them at a high level. Different ways of thinking are required and applied in English language arts when compared with the other disciplines. Yet, often, it is the belief of educators that literacy is developed in this context. The task for all teachers is to explicitly teach students the necessary discipline-specific approaches to reading and thinking to develop disciplinary expertise.

Research About What Experts Do When Reading in the Disciplines

The skills needed for advanced disciplinary literacy are more sophisticated but less generalizable. They are most likely harder to teach and learn, are applied to difficult text, and do not have frequent parallels in oral language use. Content, not reading strategies, is the focus of teachers in advanced disciplinary learning. Yet, clearly, specialized skills and strategies are required. Shanahan and Shanahan (2012) reported findings from a study in which experts in disciplines were asked to reflect aloud on the literacy strategies they used while reading. The findings in this study are informative in thinking about needed instruction for novices.

Historians emphasized understanding sources and the conditional nature of truth in the reporting of events after they have occurred and often where the author was not present. A historian reported when reading about an account of Abraham Lincoln written by an author:

> I saw, oh. . . I don't know him very well, but he is part of a right-wing group of southern conservatives who is a secessionist. I'm not sure that the best model for thinking about Lincoln as a president is one that comes from a racist. So I have my critical eyes up a little bit, so it's a bit of a stretch to be friendly to, so I wanted to make sure to read it fairly. (Shanahan & Shanahan, 2012, p. 50)

This example shows how historians view documents reporting past events and as representing particular points of view and positioning. The reader must intuit the internal states, motivations, and situational context of the authors when viewing primary source material such as diaries, letters, newspaper articles, paintings, cartoons, and photographs. It can be argued that developing this critical lens and nuance is a requirement for citizenship in a democracy. Schools often teach students history as a chronology of events, however, and social, political, and economic descriptions as a master narrative not to be questioned (Lee & Spratley, 2010).

Scientists were found to move from text to diagrams, charts, or mathematical formulas in a recursive process. In their study of disciplinary experts talking about their literacy practices, Shanahan and Shanahan recorded the following description of a chemist's thinking:

> They give you the structure, the structure of the sensor is given, so I was looking at the picture as I was reading and I tried to relate what was in the picture to what they were saying about how mercury binds to one part of the molecule. (2012, p. 49)

Lee and Spratley (2010) noted that the abstracts, section headings, figures, tables, diagrams, photographs, endnotes, and so forth provide direction to the skilled reader and help him or her make predictions and know what to look for while reading. Vocabulary is understood in specific ways in science reading as well. Words used in general ways take on precise technical meanings (e.g., an invisible gas called water vapor), syntax guides the reader's understanding (e.g., animals that eat plants, herbivores, may be found. . .), and the use of Latin or Greek roots or words is frequent (e.g., "domesticated dogs referred to as canines belong to the kingdom of animalia, the phylum of chordate, the order of carnivore, and the family of canidae") (Lee & Spratley, 2010).

Shanahan and Shanahan (2012) found theoretical mathematicians noted that close reading and rereading was essential to their approaching mathematical text. One mathematician said, "I try to determine whether it [the solution to the problem] is correct. That's the important criteria, and it's by no means assumed. It would be unusual to read a paper like this and not find something incorrect" (2012, p. 51). They also noted, like the scientists who were questioned, that symbols were "vocabulary" and that words have both general and specific meanings. The mathematicians were adamant that the specific mathematical meanings of vocabulary needed to be memorized and automatic for comprehension to be fluent.

It is easier to make the case that strategies for reading literature are taught in English language arts classes. The genres introduced are limited, however, perhaps more so in low-track classes than in advanced placement courses and are often rewritten for students with limited basic reading skills. High-level literary works try to capture and reflect human experience. Readers must integrate different frameworks to comprehend the text—using prior knowledge across domains of knowledge to construct context and unstated fact, understanding psychological states that are universal while having individual manifestations, and knowing the text structure and frameworks of a range of genre (e.g., science fiction, myth, mystery, magical realism) that provide rules for the author and, thus, guide the presentation.

LITERACY INSTRUCTION FOR INCLUSIVE CLASSROOMS: WHAT ALL STUDENTS NEED

Research on various aspects of reading instruction can be applied to thinking about literacy development of students in inclusive schools. One must address basic literacy needs of students (basic decoding and multisyllabic word reading with fluency), develop the increasing sophistication with which students apply comprehension strategies to a variety of text, and teach strategic and specific approaches to unpacking high-level disciplinary text in order to be inclusive. Furthermore, teachers must be cognizant of learner variability in each class they teach; there will almost always be the full range of student needs represented in most classes. This next section addresses literacy instruction as it applies to advancing disciplinary learning in inclusive schools.

Basic Literacy Skills

Some students will lack basic literacy skills in decoding and sight vocabulary at grade level. Their reading will lack sufficient fluency and place them at a reading level significantly below typical peers and compromise their comprehension. These students will need targeted intervention to improve their basic literacy and general comprehension skills. They will still be included in content classes, however, and will need exposure and instruction to disciplinary literacy strategies. Although this type of literacy instruction is not the focus of this chapter, it is a part of literacy programs that must be included in inclusive schools. Comprehensive literacy programming is described in the final section of this chapter. Teachers in the disciplines need to consider the variability of their students' literacy proficiency when planning instruction. Teachers' repertoire of instructional practices should include those that improve mastery of discipline-specific content for all students.

Vocabulary Development in Content Classes

Students differ significantly in vocabulary development opportunities outside of school. Hart and Risley (1995) found that by the time children from low socioeconomic backgrounds were 3 years old, their parents had said fewer different words in their cumulative monthly vocabularies than the children in the most economically advantaged families during the same period. The differences in vocabulary growth in the 2 groups of 3-year-olds were striking: 8 words a day (3,000 new words a year) for those in advantaged circumstances in contrast to 2 words a day (700 new words in a year) for those children of disadvantage. Because vocabulary size at the end of first grade predicts comprehension 10 years later when direct, explicit instruction and planned vocabulary enrichment are not part of the instructional equation (Baumann & Kame'enui, 2004), planned vocabulary instruction that is provided by all teachers and includes both academic/mature and discipline-specific words is needed to address learner variability. The outcome is predictable and discouraging when a lack of opportunity both inside and outside of school persists.

Vocabulary development practices that address needs of students regardless of level of reading proficiency include rich and varied oral and print language experiences, instruction in individual words with multiple exposures to the words in a variety of forms, word learning strategies, and word consciousness or interest in vocabulary (Graves, 2006; Kosanovich et al., 2010). Some examples of how this might occur in content classes follow.

Beck, McKeown, and Kucan (2002, 2008) discussed the importance of a vocabulary rich environment. Their discussion of Tier 1, Tier 2 and Tier 3 words is helpful to the teacher trying to determine what words accord instructional attention. Tier 1 words are common and frequent (e.g., *clock, happy, water, food, car*) and do not warrant instructional time except in the case of English language learners (ELLs). Tier 2 words are the focus of a vocabulary rich environment and are used by mature language users (e.g., *coincidence, absurd, inevitable*). Use of Tier 2 words should be modeled in the classroom and implicitly or explicitly taught. Students should be encouraged to practice using vocabulary they are exposed to implicitly or explicitly. Adolescents will encounter 10,000 or more new words each year (Nagy, Berninger, & Abbott, 2006). Most of those will be multisyllabic and occur in discipline-specific text. If a student is an average reader, then he or she might be exposed to as many as 10 million words a year. If the student is a struggling reader, then he or she may be exposed to 60,000 words. Exposure to vocabulary results in indirect learning of 5%–20% of new words through context; 5%–20% adds up if one has been exposed to many words. If a student is not reading much, or not engaged in meaningful conversations with new vocabulary, then learning from context is not efficient enough. Explicit instruction will result in a minimum of 1,000–5,000 new words learned in a year (at a rate of 25–100 words a week).

Explicit teaching of Tier 2 and Tier 3 words may take a variety of forms. Word study, or learning word families, and morphemic analysis help all students systematically expand their vocabulary. More advanced readers use a variety of strategies to decode and figure out the meanings of new words. They see a new word (e.g., *minatory*) and determine how to pronounce it through analogy (it looks like *miniature* or *factory*), phonics or syllabication rules (closed syllables typically have a short vowel sound), and morphemes (prefixes, suffixes, or roots: *tory* is a suffix often added to a noun or verb and turns the word into an adjective). They guess at its meaning by word family or by knowing the meaning of common morphemes (derives from the Latin *menatorius*, meaning "menace"). There are approximately 86,000 word families in the English language, so teaching within a word family context amplifies instruction provided. Research has validated the efficacy of strategies such as word mapping (Harris, Schumaker, & Deshler, 2008), which provide students with a systematic process for putting these advanced word study strategies together. Students use the LINCS strategy (Ellis, 2000) to learn new words and definitions through creating verbal and visual memory links between new words, familiar words, and their meanings. Both of these strategies are proven to provide results for students regardless of literacy level (Ellis, 2000; Harris et al., 2008).

Skilled readers also use context to understand unfamiliar words (Nagy, 1988; Nagy & Scott, 2000). Although a strategy of limited utility (its highly dependent on surrounding text that provides definitional clues) (Beck et al., 2002), proficient readers are like good detectives—they see the clues and use them when provided. Others (Baumann et al., 2002) found that when students combined morphemic and contextual analysis as a strategy, it produced more powerful effects than using each strategy by itself.

Word consciousness, or developing an interest in and enjoyment of words, is critical to increased vocabulary learning outcomes for all students. It provides motivation for student participation in explicit and implicit vocabulary learning strategies. Although the research supporting word consciousness is qualitative or correlational (Anderson, 2003; Nagy, 2007), it makes instructional sense to provide the context for self-directed and self-monitored learning. Motivation is key when students are challenged with Tier 3 words that are discipline specific and have specific and limited utility. Learning the "language of mathematics," the "language of Shakespeare," and "the language of the scientist" is part of disciplinary literacy. Each discipline's teacher can challenge students to master the vocabulary of the discipline. Some examples exist, however, of schoolwide approaches to vocabulary development that support inclusive education. Word Generation (Lawrence, Snow, & White, 2009) is a program to assist students to learn and use Tier 2 and 3 words across disciplines systematically through critical conversations and academic writing. It is a research-based vocabulary program for middle school students designed to teach advanced vocabulary through collaboration across language arts, mathematics, science, and social studies classes systematically. The program employs several strategies (focusing on academic vocabulary; reading and talking about high-interest, current, and socially relevant national conversations; and collaborating/planning across faculty) to ensure that students learn words in a variety of contexts.

Learning both sophisticated general vocabulary (Tier 2) and discipline-specific vocabulary (Tier 3) is critical to advancing disciplinary literacy. Students need rich and varied oral and print language experiences and instruction in individual words and word learning strategies.

COMPREHENSION DEVELOPMENT IN CONTENT CLASSES

Comprehension is the process of simultaneously extracting and constructing meaning from text (Snow, 2002). Good instruction in comprehension must occur before, during, and after reading. It must include explicit teaching of strategies, classroom interactions that support the understanding of disciplinary knowledge and text, instruction in the skills and strategies used by experts (discipline-specific approaches), sensitivity to students' varied reading levels, and the provision of text that allows all students' sufficient levels of fluency to apply comprehension strategies. Instruction in disciplinary comprehension should occur in context because students must combine strategic comprehension techniques to the "ways of knowing" within a discipline (text structure, conventions, disciplinary ways of writing).

> Although we may highlight or focus on one strategy at a time to help clarify and make the strategy explicit, we need to ensure that our students know that strategies don't happen in isolation. We use them automatically, interchangeably, and usually, we use more than one at a time. (Children's Learning Institute, 2009, p. 27)

The following is an example taken from an account by Conley.

> Ms. Gunnings has identified that her students are to understand pollution as a scientific phenomenon with potentially devastating natural and social implications. They are to use scientific reasoning to develop an informed critical stance about pollution, including understanding ways that scientific information can be manipulated for different purposes. She engages the students' personal experiences with pollution, using media coverage of current events, issues with the community, articles from *Newsweek* magazine, research reports, political speeches about global warming, media about China's struggle with pollution prior to the Olympics, etc. Ms. Gunnings selects this range of text resources in order to provide discrepant points of view; students will need to compare reports with prior knowledge and make comparisons, evaluate claims and form conclusions about causes, consequences, and potential ways to address pollution.
>
> Ms. Gunnings views a graphic organizer as the ideal tool to support students' inquiry and cross-text comparisons. The organizer is continually consulted by Ms. Gunnings to demonstrate how to make initial claims and interrogate texts. Ms. Gunnings deliberately sets out to teach students how to use a graphic organizer as a cognitive tool to develop and organize their thinking. She names the cognitive strategy: "We are going to use a graphic organizer to record your observations." She provides her students with a brief explanation for how the strategy is useful for learning: "Graphic organizers are a way of picturing what you know. You can make a graphic organizer to think about

what you already know and when you are learning something new you can change what you think. I'll show you how." Ms. Gunnings models. . . encourages students to ask questions. . . transfers responsibility for the new strategy to her students. . . [they engage] in paired discussions with partners. . . At one point, a student volunteers that a number of people believe some kinds of pollution are not real, as with global warming from carbon emissions, or even air or water pollution. The class decides to add a category entitled "Pollution: Myth or Reality?" to the organizer. This category is extremely important as Ms. Gunnings engages her students in the competing points of view in the texts she selected. (2012, pp. 89–90)

Comprehension instruction is best when it is both explicit and contextualized. Strategies that support all students, regardless of reading level, include: 1) activating and engaging prior knowledge, 2) asking questions, 3) answering questions, 4) monitoring comprehension, 5) summarizing and paraphrasing, 6) recognizing text structure, and 7) using semantic and graphic organizers (IES Best Practice Guide on Adolescent Literacy, 2008; Kosanovich et al., 2010). Each will be discussed separately, but the preceding example sets the strategies into a disciplinary context where they are used together and flexibly.

Activating and engaging prior knowledge of students is intended to provide scaffolding hooks for new information. Vygotsky (1978), an early cognitive scientist, theorized that individuals' potential for developing new and more difficult conceptual understanding at every moment in time was constrained by what they already knew. If a teacher scaffolded new learning, knowing the outer boundaries of students' understanding, then new and deeper mental capacity could be systematically developed. He called this the zone of proximal development. Understanding about identifying prior knowledge, building prior knowledge, and activating and engaging prior knowledge and its essential role in comprehension development has grown from these early theoretical underpinnings. When considering learner variability, prior experience can mitigate vocabulary and content deficits in creating a cognitive geography for new learning to reside. Despite consensus on the importance of connecting new learning to what is known by students, there is a lack of evidence on the best methods for doing so. Nevertheless, most prereading strategies studied encourage students to make connections to personal experience in systematic ways. Some found if information about ideas in a passage were discussed prior to reading, then students understood narrative and expository texts better than when they had less structured conversation about their personal experiences (Dole, Valencia, Greer, & Wardrop, 1991). For example, researchers at the Vaughn Gross Center at The University of Texas at Austin (2009) found an anticipation reaction guide provided helpful structure to students when asked to reflect on existing understanding and incorporate what they already knew with new learning. Other researchers (Pressley et al., 1992) found it helped learning when students made statements of understanding prior to reading, then had to justify or change their statements after reading. The available evidence seems to point to the value of structured prereading activities that draw on existing understanding and personal experience. Given the variety of backgrounds that 21st-century students come from and their unique life experiences, this will be a critical component of disciplinary literacy instruction in the inclusive school.

Answering and asking questions are two important comprehension strategies to use independent of one another; it is not intuitive to students that sophisticated and expert comprehenders use them in combination and use this combination to monitor their level of understanding. The question-answer relationship (QAR) developed by Raphael (1986) is one strategy that has proven to help students understand question asking and answering at a metacognitive and cognitive level. QAR guides students to think about text, their prior knowledge, and author intent through learning four categories of relationships expressed within questions—right there, think and search, on my own, and author and me. This process and these labels provide the teacher and students vocabulary to explicitly discuss how the self-questioning process helps the reader/learner extract and construct understanding.

Asking self-questions is crucial to independently monitoring comprehension. Generating questions about text and content engages readers and motivates them to think beyond the teacher's

Question Exploration Guide

① What is the critical question?
What is the algorithm and an associated acronym for multiplying binomials?

② What are the key terms and explanations?

Algorithm	A set of steps for performing a math operation
Binomial	A mathematical expression comprised of two terms joined by a plus sign (+) or a minus sign (–)
Acronym	A word formed by the first letters of different words

③ What are the supporting questions and answers?

What is Step 1?	F = Multiply the first terms in each binomial $(2x - y)(3x + 2y)$ $2x * 3x = 6x^2$
What is Step 2?	O = Multiply the outside terms in each binomial $(2x - y)(3x + 2y)$ $2x * 2y = 4xy$
What is Step 3?	I = Multiply the inside terms in each binomial $(2x - y)(3x + 2y)$ $-y * 3x = -3xy$
What is Step 4?	L = Multiply the last terms in each binomial $(2x - y)(3x + 2y)$ $-y * 2y = -2y^2$
What is Step 5?	S = Set up and summarize the answer. $6x^2 + (4xy - 3xy) - 2y^2 = 6x^2 + xy - 2y^2$

④ What is the main idea answer?   The algorithm contains five steps involving multiplying the terms in a sequence and summarizing the answer. FOILS is an acronym that can be used to remember the steps.

⑤ How can we use the main idea again?   Solve this new problem using the FOILS algorithm: $(3x + 4y)(2x + 2y)$

⑥ Is there an overall idea? Is there a real-world use?   Explain how the FOILS acronym helps you as a learner. Create your own memory device for another math algorithm.

Figure 3.2. Example of using steps in a procedure. (From The University of Kansas Center for Research on Learning [2002]. *Content enhancement presentations* [CD-ROM]. Lawrence, KS: The University of Kansas; reprinted by permission.)

purposes (National Institute of Child Health and Human Development, 2000). Self-generated questions that require an examination of similarities and differences, causes and consequences, or relationships to other questions and alternative answers promotes the higher level critical thinking that advanced disciplinary literacy entails. Students can generate questions before, during, and after reading. They should explain how their answers changed throughout the reading process. Students' comprehension increased when they were required to follow a three-step process of asking a question, searching for the answer, and explaining their findings to peers (Anderson, West, Beck, MacDonnell, & Frisbie, 1997). Some researchers found students increased comprehension when asked to "wrap up what they read by generating questions a good teacher would ask" (Vaughn, Klingner, & Bryant, 2001), whereas others (Taboada & Guthrie, 2006) found self-questioning improved comprehension in both low and high readers in history. The question exploration routine strategy proved successful in assisting students to unpack questions and provided them with a systematic and explicit process for doing so (Bulgren, Deshler, & Lenz, 2007; Bulgren, Marquis, Lenz, Schumaker, & Deshler, 2009). This strategy requires students to identify key vocabulary, generate subquestions to a main question, locate information, answer subquestions, construct leveled answers to the subquestions, and create main ideas (see Figures 3.2 and 3.3). They use a graphic organizer to assist them in explicitly following this question and answer construction process. If students are to develop high levels of disciplinary literacy, then they need opportunities to practice using comprehension strategies as experts do—strategies combined with fluency and proficiency.

Question Exploration Guide

① What is the critical question?
  Why is a four-chambered heart two pumps in one?

② What are the key terms and explanations?
Chamber	An enclosed space
Heart	A muscle that pumps blood to the lungs through the body
Pump	A device for moving liquid from one place to another

③ What are the supporting questions and answers?
  A. What are the four chambers?

  What is the function of
  B. The right atrium?
  C. The right ventricle?
  D. The left atrium?
  E. The left ventricle?

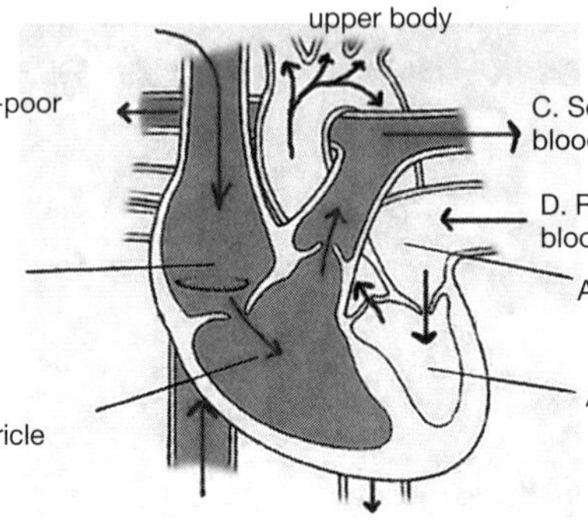

B. Receives oxygen-poor blood from head and upper body

E. Sends oxygen-rich blood to head and upper body

C. Sends oxygen-poor blood to lung

C. Sends oxygen-poor blood to lung

D. Receives oxygen-rich blood from lung

A. Right atrium

A. Left atrium

A. Left ventricle

A. Right ventricle

B. Receives oxygen-poor blood from head and upper body

E. Sends oxygen-rich blood to head and upper body

④ What is the main idea answer?   The right side of the heart pumps oxygen-poor blood to the lungs, and the lungs pump oxygen-rich blood through the body. (The right side is one pump; the left side is the second pump [2 pumps].)

⑤ How can we use the main idea again?   Why do the walls of the left ventricle have to be thicker than the walls of the right ventricle?

⑥ Is there an overall idea? Is there a real-world use?   If a person smokes, which pump is most affected and why?

Figure 3.3. Example of a sketch. (From The University of Kansas Center for Research on Learning [2002]. *Content enhancement presentations* [CD-ROM]. Lawrence, KS: The University of Kansas; reprinted by permission.)

Summarizing and paraphrasing are general comprehension strategies that are often used together. Readers must synthesize information across a breadth of content and identify critical information when they summarize. Paraphrasing requires the reader to transform text into their own words; this requires access to one's vocabulary and prior knowledge stores. Both strategies require critical and higher order thinking, thus are applicable to disciplinary literacy. Researchers note how these strategies are applied somewhat differently in various disciplines. Summarizing in literacy text often takes the form of retelling or restating the events of the passage (Klingner, Vaughn, & Boardman, 2007). Organizational patterns or text structure govern the selection of critical content when reading informational text (Goldman & Rakestraw, 2000).

Monitoring comprehension is critical when reading for new information and understanding. The reader must recognize when he or she does not understand and change strategies to improve comprehension. He or she might need to reread a section or review the table of contents. The student might preview questions to be answered or review an assignment description to focus his or her attention on reading for critical content. The National Reading Panel (National Institute of Child Health and Human Development, 2000) found the greatest research support for teaching more than one strategy for monitoring comprehension and for students to use strategies in combination.

In addition to the strategies previously listed, considerable research supports reciprocal teaching, which is a multiple strategy approach (Brown & Palincsar, 1984; Hattie, 2010) (see Chapter 9). The students and teacher practice questioning, clarifying, summarizing, and predicting in reciprocal teaching by going back and forth between themselves on strategy application to reading passages. The teacher models the process first, then alternates with students until students in pairs can take turns guiding each other through the text while fluently using these strategies. Teacher modeling is critical to students developing effective self-monitoring skills because it provides the explicit example of an invisible mental process (Almasi, 2003).

Modeling can be used when the teacher comes to a difficult passage, regardless of the strategy being taught. The teacher might say something such as, "This doesn't make sense to me. Maybe I'd better reread. Oh, here is a sentence I didn't pay close attention to and need to." Or, "I'm confused. Maybe if I stop, look at the diagram, and talk myself through it, it will help me understand this section." Although time consuming, teacher modeling provides explicit instruction in both monitoring comprehension and how a particular strategy is helpful (or not) with specific text or uncovering particular ways of understanding.

Recognizing text structure is an important skill for students to learn because the different disciplines adhere to various formats or styles in presenting text. Experts within a field use that specific style to help readers identify key information and make connections among ideas (Honig, Diamond, & Gutlohn, 2008). Students need to learn the cues within text that signal its structure—how information is organized, what is important, how information is connected or related, and how to anticipate what is to come. If the reader understands the structure, then he or she can organize his or her thinking to assist in constructing comprehension. Features such as the title, chapter index, illustrations, bold print, and dialogue are commonly used in fiction. The title, table of contents, the index, photographs, captions, diagrams, the glossary, citations and references, and headings and subtitles all signal the text structure in nonfiction. The more knowledge a reader has about what these signals convey, the more they assist comprehension.

Students also need to understand that some text is unfriendly. It is commonly believed that textbooks select and synthesize information but then present it in an easier form. In the attempt to create short texts with simple sentences, however, key features that structure information and convey meaning are often lost. Relational words, explanatory clauses, or paragraphs are omitted to shorten the text. Novice or struggling readers do not have enough structural knowledge to fill in the missing pieces (Lee & Spratley, 2010).

Using semantic and graphic organizers is a proven practice for scaffolding cognitive and metacognitive strategies (Armbruster, Lehr, & Osborn, 2001). It makes the thinking process, which is invisible and often confusing to the novice or struggling learner, explicit. Graphic organizers often are used in conjunction with instruction on text structure or story grammar (Onachukwu, Boon, Fore, & Bender, 2007; Scheiwe, Fore, Burke, & Boon, 2007; Stagliano & Boon, 2009; Stone, Boon, Fore, & Bender, 2008). They are also used to help students summarize text. They help students visualize the underlying structure of ideas or relationships among concepts (see Chapter 5).

INCLUSIVE SCHOOLS: ORGANIZING TO ADDRESS THE FULL RANGE OF LITERACY NEEDS

Inclusive schools are organized with the knowledge that their students present diverse learning profiles at every age and some will require significant scaffolding, accommodations, or modifications to gain access to challenging content, regardless of the standards, benchmarks, and outcomes students are expected to reach. Teachers need to know that students will vary in their proficiency of basic literacy skills (decoding, fluency, and basic word and text comprehension), intermediate literacy skills (generic comprehension strategies, common word meanings, and increased fluency), and disciplinary literacy skills (literacy skills specialized to history, science, mathematics, literature, or other subject matter), regardless of the students' age or grade level. Therefore, teachers in inclusive schools need to know how to engage diverse learners by ensuring that their instructional repertoire includes skills to address needs across the progression. Table 3.1

Table 3.1.   Teaching both generic and discipline-specific reading strategies

Generic reading strategies	Discipline-specific reading strategies
Preread.	Build specialized vocabulary.
Set goals.	Learn to deconstruct complex sentences.
Think about what one already knows.	Build prior knowledge.
Ask questions.	Pose discipline-relevant questions.
Make predictions.	Use knowledge of text structures and genres to predict main and subordinate ideas.
Test predictions against the text.	Compare claims and propositions across texts.
Reread.	Map graphic (and mathematical) representations against explanations in the text.
Summarize.	Use norms for reasoning within the discipline (i.e., what counts as evidence) to evaluate claims.
Monitor comprehension.	Confirm accuracy of comprehension for specific text that was read.

From Lee, C.D., & Spratley, A. (2010). *Reading in the disciplines: The challenges of adolescent literacy* (p. 16). New York: Carnegie Corporation of New York; reprinted by permission. For a free downloadable copy of this report, please go to http://www.carnegie.org

provides an example of what teachers need to think about in providing instruction for students at different levels of literacy proficiency (also see Figure 3.4). Some students will need instruction along all tiers and support that is coordinated through the programs that a school offers.

It is unrealistic to believe that each teacher in every instructional context will address all student literacy needs, however skilled the teacher is in planning a universally designed instructional setting (CAST, 2012), developing a range of literacy skills in a developmentally appropriate manner, or having the disposition necessary to invest in literacy instruction while challenged to teach to high standards and advanced disciplinary content. Inclusive schools must be organized to provide coordinated and collaborative support and programs to meet the needs of diverse learners. Teacher responsibilities in an inclusive school are discussed in the following two sections as well as examples of how schools might provide the needed programs.

EVERY TEACHER'S RESPONSIBILITY: TEACHING GENERIC AND DISCIPLINARY READING STRATEGIES IN TANDEM

All teachers teach literacy in an inclusive school. Teachers must abandon the belief that students learn to read in the primary grades and then read to learn from upper elementary through secondary school. In fact, there is no clear demarcation or transition from learning literacy skills to applying literacy skills. Instead, teachers must think about student literacy development as a progression, with skills at any level of the progression becoming more fluent and generalizable throughout one's reading experiences. Teachers must understand that although students learn basic literacy skills, comprehension strategies, and specialized disciplinary techniques, they never truly exit any skill development area and need continued opportunities to practice in a variety of settings with feedback. Thus, all teachers are teachers of literacy, regardless of learner profile (advanced to struggling) and level (elementary through secondary). Lee and Spratley (2010, p.16) noted that teachers in successful content area classrooms organize instruction in routine ways that

- Reinforce conceptions of reading as a meaning-making process
- Provide guided support for making sense while students are engaged in acts of reading
- Shift responsibility for thinking and making sense of texts to students themselves through guided supports in both small- and whole-group work
- Sequence discipline-specific inquiry tasks and the reading of a range of discipline-focused texts in ways that build knowledge and dispositions over time
- Focus classroom talk on how students make sense of texts and how they use what they learn from texts to carry out discipline-specific thinking tasks or what Michaels and colleagues call accountable talk (Michaels, O'Connor, Hall, & Resnick, 2002)
- Provide consistent supports so that students experience success and develop or reinforce their sense of efficacy as readers as well as individuals who value the practices of the disciplines as these are instantiated in authentic classroom tasks (Lee, 2010)

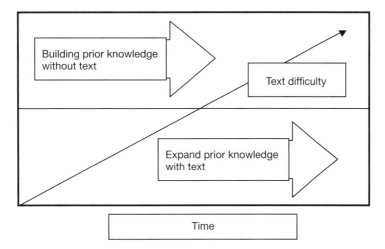

Figure 3.4. Balancing difficult text and alternative forms of prior knowledge development.

Table 3.2 provides an example of how teachers might think about their instruction to support both general and disciplinary-specific literacy instruction.

Whole School Frameworks and Programs Supporting Literacy Development

Tiered support programs or response to intervention (RTI) provide a framework for organizing systematic and coordinated instructional support programs that can support a progression of literacy development. They provide a schoolwide structure for differentiating instruction and responding to learner diversity.

The Content Literacy Continuum:
An Example Framework for Providing Tiered Literacy Supports to Adolescents

Researchers at the University of Kansas' Center of Research for Learning (KU-CRL) developed the content literacy continuum (CLC) framework to address the range of literacy needs discussed in this chapter (Lenz, Ehren, & Deshler, 2005; Schumaker & Deshler, 2010). It is one example of how schools can address literacy needs in an inclusive environment. It is described here to provide a conceptual model for how the full range of literacy needs can be addressed in a coordinated and systematic manner. Research on the strategic instruction model covers more than 30 years, with attention to learning strategy instruction, content enhancement, and instructional coaching, among other initiatives. The CLC was conceptualized as a framework to guide implementation of schoolwide literacy instruction and interventions (inclusive of, but not exclusively, CRL intervention programs) in a collaborative and coordinated fashion. The CLC framework focuses on helping secondary schools develop and sustain comprehensive and integrated literacy programs. Table 3.3 provides key implementation objectives of the CLC framework.

The primary goal of the CLC is to establish a coordinated schoolwide approach to improving literacy for all students in secondary schools that will enable all students to meet higher standards. A literacy leadership team (or CLC team) leads this school improvement process and works with administrators, teachers, and staff to develop and implement a standards-based plan to improve literacy and content area learning tied to student performance on state assessments.

The framework consists of a variety of research-based interventions, including the content enhancement routines (Bulgren, Deshler & Lenz, 2007) and learning strategies (Deshler & Schumaker, 1988; Deshler et al., 2001). Some of these interventions focus on helping teachers think about, identify, and present critical content in a learner-friendly fashion. Others focus on helping

Table 3.2. Comprehensive reading instruction in inclusive schools

Reading skills	Level of instruction	What is taught
Word study	Core instruction	Decoding of multisyllabic words
		Morphographs (prefixes, suffixes, roots, word families)
	Additional support	More specific practice with personalized feedback
		Mastery of learning expectations
		Explicit strategy instruction in decoding or word mapping
	Personalized instruction	Intensive, personalized instruction that is appropriately scaffolded and paced
		Linked to instruction in core classes, curriculum, and standards
		Specialized programs
Vocabulary	Core instruction	Explicit vocabulary instruction focused on Tier 2 words (Beck et al., 2004)
		Incidental vocabulary instruction through enriched vocabulary environment
		Systematic and systemic vocabulary instruction (coordinated and intentional)
	Additional support	More specific practice with personalized feedback
		Mastery of learning expectations
		Explicit strategy instruction in vocabulary learning strategies such as LINCS and word maps
		Explicit instruction that promotes generalization of expanded vocabulary use
	Personalized instruction	Intensive, personalized instruction that is appropriately scaffolded and paced
		Linked to instruction in core classes, curriculum, and standards
		Specialized programs
Basic comprehension	Core instruction	Generic strategies of activating and engaging prior knowledge, answering and asking questions, summarizing and paraphrasing, monitoring comprehension, recognizing text structure, and using graphic organizers
	Additional support	More specific practice with personalized feedback
		Mastery of learning expectations
		Explicit strategy instruction
	Personalized instruction	Intensive, personalized instruction that is appropriately scaffolded and paced
		Linked to instruction in core classes, curriculum, and standards
		Specialized programs
Disciplinary literacy	Core instruction	*Vocabulary*
		Discipline-specific vocabulary learning strategies (constrained uses, precise meanings)
		Comprehension
		Selected use of general comprehension strategies adapted to disciplinary text
		Text structure "rules" by discipline
		Development of specific habits of mind used by experts in the discipline
	Additional support	*Vocabulary and comprehension*
		More specific practice with personalized feedback
		Mastery of learning expectations
		Explicit strategy instruction
	Personalized instruction	*Vocabulary and comprehension*
		Intensive, personalized instruction that is appropriately scaffolded and paced
		Linked to instruction in core classes, curriculum, and standards

Table 3.3. Key content literacy continuum (CLC) implementation objectives

Ensure students' mastery of critical core curriculum content to develop the background knowledge required for comprehension, independent learning, and cumulative literacy development.

Integrate key learning strategies into and across core curriculum courses to 1) codevelop literacy skills in conjunction with content mastery, 2) teach students when and how to use strategies, and 3) teach students to value the process of learning how to learn.

Develop support structures to more explicitly and intensively teach the strategies that are required/integrated across core curriculum courses for the students who need more direct instruction than what can be provided by teachers in core curriculum courses.

Identify and support the staff who will lead the CLC effort, including administrators, the literacy leadership team, and site-based professional developers, coaches, and other teacher leaders.

Prepare professionals who support literacy goals, such as speech-language pathologists, to provide clinical support services consistent with schoolwide literacy efforts.

students acquire the skills and strategies they need to learn content. These literacy supports are organized in five levels of increasing intensity that are delivered across general education content classes in all disciplines and in targeted support classes at increasing levels of personalization. The CLC framework mirrors RTI programs in this regard and could be included within a school's RTI model. Figure 3.5 provides a graphic representation of how support is provided—students receive instruction that has scaffolds to improve curriculum access; when needed, teachers explicitly assist students in learning strategic approaches to mastery of increasingly difficult content. Some students might receive supplemental literacy instruction in basic literacy skills (coordinated with what is reinforced and taught in core classes); students who are beginning readers receive instruction at their level and paced for their learning. Finally, personalized support and instruction is provided to students with significant learning or language development challenges or those who are initial ELLs.

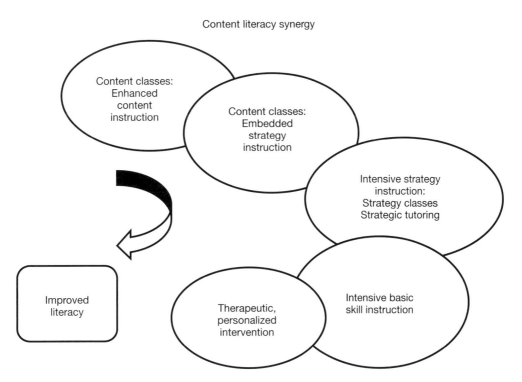

Figure 3.5. Content literacy continuum.

CONCLUSION

To fully participate as an educator in an inclusive school, teachers must embrace their role in advancing the literacy development of their students, regardless of what they teach. They must understand the distinctions among basic literacy skills, intermediate literacy skills, including general comprehension strategies, and advanced disciplinary literacy. This progression in literacy development begins in elementary school and continues through secondary school. There is not a distinct demarcation between these areas of development. Whereas students make a gradual transition to becoming advanced readers with sophisticated literacy skills over their lives, teachers must remain vigilant in their role of providing appropriate literacy instruction across this continuum. Student variability and instructional needs must be taken into account, regardless of what one teaches. Although every teacher must do his or her part to advance disciplinary literacy and literacy development in general, teachers and students will benefit greatly from the support of schoolwide systems that facilitate addressing the range of student needs seen in contemporary schools. The students of 21st-century schools must be equipped to meet 21st-century standards so that they might fully and productively participate in a knowledge-based economy in the United States and in global citizenship.

REFERENCES

"About UDL." (2012). Retrieved April 1, 2102 from http://cast.org.

Almasi, J.F. (2003). *Teaching strategic processes in reading*. New York, NY: Guilford.

Anderson, R.C., & Nagy, W.E. (1992, Winter). The vocabulary conundrum. American Educator, 16(4), 14–18, 44–47.

Anderson, T.H., West, C.K., Beck, D.P., MacDonnell, E.S., & Frisbie, D.S. (1997). Integrating reading and science education: On developing and evaluating WEE science. *Journal of Curriculum Studies,* 29(6), 711–733.

Armbruster, B.B., Lehr, F., & Osborn, J. (2001). *Put reading first: The research building blocks for teaching children to read*. Jessup, MD: National Institute for Literacy.

Barton, M.L. (1997). Addressing the literacy crisis: Teaching reading in the content areas. *NASSP Bulletin,* 81, 22–30.

Baumann, J.F., Edwards, E.C., Font, G., Tereshinski, C.A., Kame'enui, E.J., & Olejnik, S. (2002). Teaching morphemic and contextual analysis to fifth-grade students. Reading Research Quarterly, 37(2), 150–176.

Baumann, J.F., & Kame'enui, E. (2004). *Vocabulary instruction: Research to practice*. New York, NY: Guilford Press.

Beck, I.L., McKeown, M.G. & Kucan L. (2002). *Bringing words to life: Robust vocabulary instruction*. New York, NY: Guilford Press.

Beck, I.L., McKeown, M.G. & Kucan L. (2008). *Creating robust vocabulary: Frequently asked questions & extended examples*. New York, NY: Guilford Press.

Biancarosa, C., & Snow, C.E. (2006). Reading next—A vision for action and research in middle and high school literacy: A report to Carnegie Corporation of New York (2nd ed.). Washington, DC: Alliance for Excellent Education.

Bransford, J.D., Brown, A.L. & Cocking R.C. (Eds.). (1999). *How people learn: Brain, mind, experience, and school*. Washington DC: National Academy Press.

Brown and Palincsar (1984)

Bulgren, J.A. (2006). Integrated content enhancement routines: Responding to the needs of adolescents with disabilities in rigorous inclusive secondary content classes. *Teaching Exceptional Children,* 38(6), 54–58.

Bulgren, J., Deshler, D.D., & Lenz, B.K. (2007). Engaging adolescents with LD in higher order thinking about history concepts using integrated content enhancement routines. *Journal of Learning Disabilities,* 40(2), 121–133.

Bulgren, J. & Lenz, B.K. (2004). *Question Exploration Routine*. Edge Enterprises: Lawrence, KS.

Bulgren, J.A., Marquis, J.G., Lenz, B.K., Schumaker, J.B., & Deshler, D.D. (2009). Effectiveness of question exploration to enhance students' written expression of content knowledge and comprehension. *Reading and Writing Quarterly, 25,* 271–289.

Carnegie Council on Advancing Adolescent Literacy. (2010). Time to act: An agenda for advancing adolescent literacy for college and career success. carnegie.org/fileadmin/Media/Publications/PDF/tta_Main.pdf

Children's Learning Institute. (2009). http://www.childrenslearninginstitute.org/our%2Dprograms/program%2Doverview/tx%2Dreading%2Dfirst/

Conley, M.W. (2012) Cognitive strategy instruction for adolescents: What we know about the promise, what we don't know about the potential. In J. Ippolito, J.L. Steele, and J.F. Samson (Eds.), *Adolescent literacy.* Cambridge, MA: Harvard Educational Review.

Deshler, D.D., & Schumaker, J.B. (1988). An instructional model for teaching students how to learn. In J.L. Graden, J.E. Zins, and M.J. Curtis (Eds.), *Alternative educational delivery systems: Enhancing instructional options for all students* (pp. 391–411). Washington, DC: National Association of School Psychologists.

Deshler, D.D., Schumaker, J.B., Lenz, B.K., Bulgren, J.A., Hock, M.F., Knight, J., & Ehren, B. (2001). Ensuring content-area learning by secondary students with learning disabilities. *Learning Disabilities Research & Practice, 16*(2), 96–108.

Dole, J.A., Valencia, S.W., Greer, E.A., & Wardrop, J.L. (1991). Effects of two types of pre-reading instruction on the comprehension of narrative and expository text. *Reading Research Quarterly, 26*(2), 142–59.

Ellis, E.E. (2000). *The LINCS vocabulary strategy.* Lawrence, KS: Edge Enterprises, Inc.

Faggella-Luby, M.N., & Deshler, D.D. (2008). Reading comprehension in adolescents with LD: What we know; what we need to learn. *Learning Disabilities Research and Practice, 23*(2), 70–78.

Fuson, K.C., Kalchman, M., & Bransford, J.D. (2005). Mathematical Understanding: An Introduction. In M.S. Donovan & J.D. Bransford (Eds.), *How students learn: history, mathemcatics, and science in the classroom.* Washington D.C.: The National Academy Press.

Goldman, S., & Rakestraw, J. (2000). Structural aspects of constructing meaning from text. In R. Barr, M. Kamil, P. Mosenthal, & P.D. Pearson (Eds.), *Handbook of reading research* (Vol. 3, pp. 311–335). New York, NY: Longman.

Graves, M. & Graves, B. (2003). *Scaffolding reading experiences; Designs for student success.* Norwood, MA: Christopher-Gordon Publishers, Inc.

Graves, M.F. (2006). Vocabulary book: Learning and instruction. Urbana, IL: National Council of Teachers.

Harris, M.L., Schumaker, J.B. & Deshler, D.D. (2008). *The word mapping strategy.* Lawrence, KS: Edge Enterprises, Inc.

Hart, B., & Risley, T. (1995). *Meaningful differences in the everyday experience of young American children.* Baltimore, MD: Paul H. Brookes.

Hattie, J. (2009). Visible learning. New York, NY: Routledge.

Honig, B., Diamond, L., & Gutlohn, L. (2008). *Teaching Reading Sourcebook.* Berkeley, CA: Consortium on Reading Excellence (CORE).

IES Best Practice Guide on Adolescent Literacy (2008).

Klingner, J.K., Vaughn, S., & Boardman, A. (2007). *Teaching reading comprehension to students with learning difficulties.* New York, NY: Guilford.

Kosanovich, M.L., Reed, D.K., & Miller, D.H. (2010). *Bringing literacy strategies into content instruction: Professional learning for secondary-level teachers.* Portsmouth, NH: RMC Research Corporation, Center on Instruction.

Lawrence, J., Snow, C. & White, C. (2009). *Results from year 2 of Word Generation.* Paper presented at Society for Scientific Studies of Reading. Boston.

Lee, C.D. & Spratley, A. (2010). *Reading in the disciplines: The challenges of adolescent literacy.* New York, NY: Carnegie Corporation of New York.

Lee, J., Griggs, W., & Donahue, P. (2007). *The nation's report card: Reading 2007 (NCES 2007-496).* Washington, DC: National Center for Education Statistics, Institute of Education Sciences, U. S. Department of Education.

Lenz, B.K., Ehren, B.J., & Deshler, D.D. (2005). The content literacy continuum: A school reform framework for improving adolescent literacy for all students. *Teaching Exceptional Children, 37*(6), 60–63.

Michaels, O'Connor, Hall, & Resnick. (2002). *Accountable talk: classroom conversation that works.* Pittsburgh, PA: University of Pittsburgh.

Moje, E.B., & Lewis, C. (2007). Examining opportunities to learn literacy: The role of critical sociocultural literacy research. In. C.J. Lewis, P. Enciso, & E.B. Moje (Eds.), *Reframing sociocultural research on literacy: Identity, agency, and power.* (pp. 15–48). Mahwah, NJ: Lawrence Erlbaum Associates.

Nagy, W.E. (1988). *Teaching vocabulary to improve reading comprehension.* Newark, DE: International Reading Association.

Nagy, W.E. (2007). Metalinguistic awareness and the vocabulary-comprehension connection. In R.K. Wagner, A.E. Muse, & K.R. Tannenbaum (Eds.), *Vocabulary acquisition: Implications for reading comprehension* (pp. 52–77). New York, NY: Guilford.

Nagy, W.E., Berninger, V.W., & Abbott, R.D. (2006). Contributions of morphology beyond phonology to literacy outcomes of upper elementary and middle-school students. *Journal of Educational Psychology, 98*(1), 134–147.

Nagy, W.E., & Scott, J.A. (2000). Vocabulary process. In M.L. Kamil, P. Mosenthal, P.D. Pearson, & R. Barr (Eds.), *Handbook of reading research* (Vol. 3, pp. 269–284). Mahwah, NJ: Erlbaum.

National Assessment Governing Board (2006). Report of the Ad-hoc Sub-Committee on the future of the NAEP 12th grade Assessments in 2009. http://www.nagb.org/content/nagb/assets/documents/publications/future12.pdf

National Assessment Governing Board (2006). Reading framework for the 2007

National Assessment of Educatonal Progress (NAEP). http://nces.ed.gov/nationsreportcard/

National Institute of Child Health and Human Development. (2000). *Report of the National Reading Panel: Teaching children to read: An evidence-based assessment of the scientific research literature on reading and its implications for reading instruction: Reports of the subgroups.* (NIH Publication No.00–4754). Washington, DC: U.S. Government Printing Office.

Onachukwu, I., Boon, R., Fore, C., & Bender, W. (2007). Use of a story mapping procedure in middle school language arts instruction to improve the comprehension skills for students with learning disabilities. *Insights on Learning Disabilities, 4*(2), 27–47.

Palinscar, A. & Brown, A. (1984). "Reciprocal teaching of comprehension-fostering and comprehension monitoring activities." Cognition and Instruction, I (2), p. 117–175.

Pressley, M., Wood, E., Woloshyn, V.E., Martin, V., Kind, A., & Menke, D. (1992). Encouraging mindful use of prior knowledge: Attempting to construct explanatory answers facilitates learning. *Educational Psychologists, 27*(1), 91–109.

Raphael, T.E. (1986). Teaching question/answer relationships, revisited. *Reading Teacher,* 39, 516–522.

Raphael, T.E., & Au, K.H. (2005). QAR: Enhancing comprehension and test taking across grades and content areas. *Reading Teacher,* 59, 206–221.

Scheiwe, K., Fore, C., Burke, M., & Boon, R. (2007). Teaching a story mapping procedure to high school students with specific learning disabilities to improve reading comprehension skills. *Learning Disabilities: A Multidisciplinary Journal, 14*(4), 233–244.

Schumaker, J.B., & Deshler, D.D. (2010). Using a tiered intervention model in secondary schools to improve academic outcomes in subject-area courses. In *Interventions for achievement and behavior problems in a three-tier model including RTI* (pp. 609–632). Bethesda, MD: National Association of School Psychologists.

Scruggs, T.E., Mastropieri, M.A., Berkeley, S., & Graetz, J. (2011). Do special education interventions improve learning of secondary content? A meta-analysis. *Remedial and Special Education, 36,* 437–449. doi: 10.1177/0741932508327465

Shanahan, T. & Shanahan, C. (2012). Teaching disciplinary literacy to adolescents: Rethinking content-area literacy. In J. Ippolito, J.L. Steele, & J.F. Samson (Eds.), *Adolescent literacy.* Cambridge, MA: Harvard Educational Review.

Snow, C.E. (2002). *Reading for understanding: Toward an R & D program in comprehension.* Santa Monica, CA: RAND Education.

Stagliano, C., & Boon, R. (2009). The effects of a story-mapping procedure to improve the comprehension skills of expository text passages for elementary students with learning disabilities. *Learning Disabilities: A Contemporary Journal, 7*(2), 35–58.

Stone, R., Boon, R., Fore, C., & Bender, W. (2008). Use of text maps to improve reading comprehension skills among students in high school with emotional and behavioral disorders. *Behavioral Disorders, 33*(2), 87–98.

Taboada, A., & Guthrie, J. (2006). Contributions of student questioning and prior knowledge to construction of knowledge from reading information text. *Journal of Literacy Research,* 38(1), 1–35.

The University of Kansas Center for Research on Learning [2002]. Content enhancement presentations [CD-ROM]. Lawrence, KS: The University of Kansas.

Torgesen, J.K., Houston, D.D., Rissman, L.M., Decker, S.M., Roberts, G., Vaughn, S., Wexler, J., Francis, D.J, Rivera, M.O., Lesaux, N. (2007). Academic literacy instruction for adolescents: A guidance document from the Center on Instruction. Portsmouth, NH: RMC Research Corporation, Center on Instruction.

US Department of Education (2008). *Reading First: Student Achievement, Teacher Empowerment, National Success.* http://www2.ed.gov/nclb/methods/reading/readingfirst.html

US Department of Education (2011)

Vaughn Gross Center for Reading and Language Arts at The University of Texas at Austin. (2009). *Texas adolescent literacy academies: Effective instruction for middle school students: Content area instructional routines to support academic literacy* (7th & 8th grades). Austin, TX: Author.

Vaughn, S., Klingner, J.K., & Bryant, D.P. (2001). Collaborative strategic reading as a means to enhance peer-mediated instruction for reading comprehension and content area learning. *Remedial and Special Education,* 22(2), 66–74.

Vygotsky, L.S., (1978). *Mind in society: The development of the higher psychological processes.* Cambridge, MA: The Harvard Press.

4 ||| Using the Embedded Story Structure Routine

Disciplinary Literacy Instruction that Meets the Needs of All Adolescent Learners

Michael N. Faggella-Luby, Sally Valentino Drew, and Yan Wei

Mrs. Jackson is an experienced ninth-grade English teacher who has noticed that large groups of her students struggle to comprehend the textually complex passages recommended in the Common Core State Standards (2010) (e.g., *Romeo and Juliet, The Odyssey, The Tell Tale Heart*). Her students appear to lack the literacy skills to independently read complex texts, causing students to miss critical content and be at-risk for failure.

Mrs. Jackson does not have the background of a reading specialist and is unsure how to adapt instruction within her academically diverse group of students to improve their reading comprehension without boring her high-achieving students. Once she learns the instructional components to boost reading comprehension, Mrs. Jackson cannot imagine how she will embed more content in her already full curriculum with only a short amount of time for instruction each day.

Mrs. Jackson wants to help more of her students but wonders what practices might be feasible to implement in her English class that are also part of the discipline-specific English curriculum. What practices can she embed into what she is already required to teach that will produce better outcomes for all her students?

CONTEXT OF EMBEDDED STRATEGY INSTRUCTION

Mrs. Jackson and countless English teachers like her face the challenge of embedding literacy instruction into their already full curriculum. This challenge is compounded by the lack of teacher preparation in the components of effective literacy instruction for adolescents and the false assumption that English teachers are certified reading specialists. Therefore, English teachers need to be able to teach students who are academically diverse a set of learning strategies that support reading comprehension while simultaneously teaching the discipline-specific content in secondary English curricula. Fortunately, the emerging field of disciplinary literacy (e.g., Shanahan & Shanahan, 2008, 2012) provides a framework for honoring English as a unique content area that requires students to learn to read as literary critics while acknowledging that students need foundational literacy skills. This chapter describes the embedded story structure (ESS) routine (Faggella-Luby, 2006), which is an evidence-based example of a disciplinary literacy intervention that improves reading comprehension for all levels of learners in the English classroom.

English as a Content Area within Disciplinary Literacy Movement

English as a content area or discipline includes a wide array of knowledge and processes (Miller, 2006) and, at times, is misunderstood as a general field for literacy instruction (e.g., Biancarosa & Snow, 2006). The disciplinary nature of English primarily refers to critical analysis of high-quality literary texts (Bialostosky, 2006; Randel, 1958). English teachers will feel increased pressure to teach the specialized strategies students need to understand complex literature and informational texts with the advent of the Common Core State Standards' focus on close reading of increasingly complex text. The disciplinary literacy movement emphasizes that literacy demands become more complex and challenging at the secondary level, and students need to learn how to navigate the unique language structures within a given discipline, such as literature (Fang & Schleppegrell, 2010).

Disciplinary literacy focuses on teaching and learning advanced strategies specific to the content areas (Shanahan & Shanahan, 2008) in order to help students learn to read, write, and think within a discipline. The disciplinary literacy movement assumes students have mastered basic and intermediate literacy skills by the end of middle school and are ready for the advanced study of text particular to the discipline by high school. Many secondary students, however, still lack the foundational reading skills required to gain access to this rich disciplinary content (Faggella-Luby, Graner, Deshler, & Drew, 2012).

One solution is for English (and other content area) teachers to embed interventions that build on general strategy instruction research to develop discipline-specific strategies within their instruction. General strategy instruction is foundational to discipline-specific strategy development and seeks to uncover and teach strategies that can be universally applied to content area learning (e.g., Faggella-Luby & Deshler, 2008). The ESS routine, which is the focus of the remainder of this chapter, is an example of a discipline-specific strategy that builds on students' foundational general strategy knowledge as they are guided through reading a complex narrative.

Challenge of Academic Diversity

English teachers are faced with classrooms of students with increasingly diverse academic needs. These academically diverse classrooms are composed of heterogeneous groups of high-, average-, and low-achieving students (e.g., Schumaker & Deshler, 2006) with varying strengths, background knowledge, academic success, and areas of struggle. For example, National Assessment of Educational Progress data drawing from a national sample of twelfth graders indicated that more than one third of students scored at or above the proficient level on reading measures, whereas approximately two thirds of the remaining students scored at or below the basic level (National Center for Education Statistics [NCES], 2010). *Basic* denotes only partial mastery of the required knowledge and skills fundamental to proficient work. Stated alternatively, almost two out of three students who are about to exit American high schools for the world of college or a career may struggle to proficiently perform when asked to find a main idea or identify a main character in a narrative text (NCES, 2010).

The current climate for educators is one of accountability for the outcomes of all students via federal legislation such as the No Child Left Behind Act (NCLB) of 2001 (PL 107-110) (see also U.S. Department of Education, 2002) and Individuals with Disabilities Education Improvement Act (IDEA) of 2004 (PL 108-446). Related educational initiatives such as response to intervention (RTI) ensure that accountability begins with instruction for all students, including students with disabilities, in the Tier 1 or general education classroom (e.g., Graner, Faggella-Luby, & Fritschmann, 2005).

The general education classroom is the first point of service delivery for all students, including students who struggle with learning. Consequently, English teachers are often expected to be leaders in the RTI efforts to support students who struggle with reading comprehension and writing. Yet, English teachers are often underprepared to meet the needs of struggling readers and writers, resulting in a widening achievement gap between the limited outcomes of these students and their typically developing peers (Faggella-Luby et al., 2012).

Common Core State Standards

The Common Core State Standards movement further heightens the expectations for disciplinary literacy instruction by expecting English teachers to increase the complexity of the literature students are being exposed to—content that many adolescent readers are already struggling to access. Common Core State Standards increases curricular demands by calling for a foundation of college and career readiness that includes: 1) increasing the range and text complexity of independent reading of literary and informational texts; 2) integrating, analyzing, delineating, and evaluating knowledge and ideas; 3) interpreting and analyzing author craft and structure; and 4) close reading to determine key ideas and details. The standards clearly articulate these high-level expectations but do not explicitly suggest access skills—necessary foundational literacy skills, academic language, or prior knowledge—that are essential for meeting each demand. In addition, students in secondary English classes are challenged to think transdisciplinarily, generalizing and solving problems by thinking critically across content and settings (Faggella-Luby et al., in press). Therefore, any move toward disciplinary literacy instruction must consider the breadth of these demands in light of the learner characteristics previously outlined or risk unintentionally widening the achievement gap.

An Instructional Response: Strategy Instruction

Teaching general and discipline-specific comprehension strategies to all students is a research-based approach to improve outcomes in academically diverse English classrooms (Faggella-Luby et al., 2012). Comprehension strategy instruction focuses on teaching students the behaviors of proficient readers in five main categories of reading comprehension: 1) knowledge of text structures (both narrative and expository), 2) vocabulary, 3) prior knowledge, 4) cognitive strategies, and 5) increased motivation/engagement (Faggella-Luby & Deshler, 2008). Cognitive strategy instruction is by far the most well researched with struggling adolescent learners (e.g., Edmonds et al., 2009; Swanson, 1999; Wanzek, Wexler, Vaughn, & Ciullo, 2010).

Considerable research on strategy instruction has been conducted in the area of reading comprehension. Trabasso and Bouchard conducted the review of reading comprehension strategies for the National Reading Panel (National Institute of Child Health and Human Development, 2002) and concluded, "The bottom line is that readers who are given cognitive strategy instruction make significant gains on comprehension compared with students who are trained with conventional instruction procedures" (2002, p. 177). Much of the research includes a combination of individual cognitive reading strategies (e.g., visualizing, self-questioning, comprehension monitoring, summarizing) operationalized in varying ways—reciprocal teaching (Palincsar & Brown, 1984), transactional strategies (Pressley, El-Dinary, Gaskins, & Schuder, 1992), the self-regulated strategy development model (Harris & Graham, 1999), and the strategic instruction model (Schumaker & Deshler, 2006). Each of these teams of investigators has found that struggling learners can learn and effectively apply a range of task-specific strategies resulting in positive effects on reading comprehension and classroom performance (e.g., Swanson, 1999).

Strategies to teach the five areas of reading comprehension previously mentioned require using general strategies as a foundation for discipline-specific strategy development. The ESS routine is an example of an evidence-based, discipline-specific strategy (Faggella-Luby, Schumaker, & Deshler, 2007; Faggella-Luby & Wardwell, 2011). The ESS routine teaches students general (or generalizable) strategies, such as self-questioning and summarizing, and how to use these strategies to deepen comprehension of the structure and overall meaning of complex narrative texts in the English curriculum. In addition, the discipline-specific elements of this routine (narrative elements of text structure) focus on the specialized strategies that do not generalize from English to other contents (Shanahan & Shanahan, 2008). This routine is one example of how English teachers can support the comprehension of increasingly complex literature while addressing the academically diverse needs of all learners in the classroom.

EMBEDDED STORY STRUCTURE ROUTINE

Embedded Story Structure Routine Components

The ESS routine is an evidence-based instructional method that integrates three strategies (self-question, story structure analysis, and summary writing) to improve reading comprehension for

| Name: _Jack Simmons_ | Title: _The Gift of the Magi_ | Date: _11/28_ |

Embedded Story Structure

Who are the main characters?   ❶

	Characters	**Clues/Description**
☺ Protagonist	Della	Mistress of the home; beautiful hair; sparkle; sweetness; one of two foolish children
☹ Antagonist	Money	Pennies saved one and two at a time; former period of prosperity; income shrunk; expenses greater
Other	Jim	Quietness and value; honor; worthy
	Narrator	Storyteller

✍ What is the central conflict?   ❷

Della counts her money and cries. She wants to buy Jim a Christmas present, but she only has $1.87.

Person versus person
Person versus nature
(Person versus ideal)
Person versus self

✎ How does the central conflict begin? (Initiating event)   ❸

It is Christmas Eve. Della counts her money and begins to cry because she doesn't have enough money for a gift worthy of her husband.

🕐 When does the story take place? (Time)   ❹

Christmas Eve

Setting

🏠 Where does the story take place? (Place and background information)   ❺

New York City (implied)

Primarily in a modest flat

↷ Which decision or event is the climax (or turning point)? (Climax)   ❻

The turning point occurs when Della and Jim exchange presents and realize that they have each sold their greatest treasures to buy gifts for the other.

✓ How does the central conflict end/resolve? (Resolution)   ❼

The central conflict ends when Della reassures Jim her hair will grow back, and Jim smiles about the situation and says it is time to eat.

Figure 4.1. Sample embedded story structure.

all learners. The routine is theoretically based on Kintsch (1992, 1998, 2004) and his colleagues' (Van Dijk & Kintsch, 1983) Construction-Integration (CI) model and engages students in a metacognitive reading process to understand text structure in a way that expert readers do. The ESS routine is designed for use in general education classrooms to help heterogeneous groups of students (including struggling adolescent readers and students with learning disabilities) improve their reading comprehension. The ESS routine is designed for use in three phases—before, during, and after reading. In addition to the three strategies, the ESS routine provides students with a graphic organizer to help them visually display pertinent information from the story and to record their notes while integrating the three strategies (see Figures 4.1 and 4.2).

Self-Questioning   Self-questioning is the first strategy in the ESS routine. Students ask themselves questions related to eight story structure elements (main character, initiating event, time, place, central conflict, climax/turning point, resolution, and theme). Seven individual questioning words (*who, what, how, when, where, which,* and *why*) are used to assist students in remembering

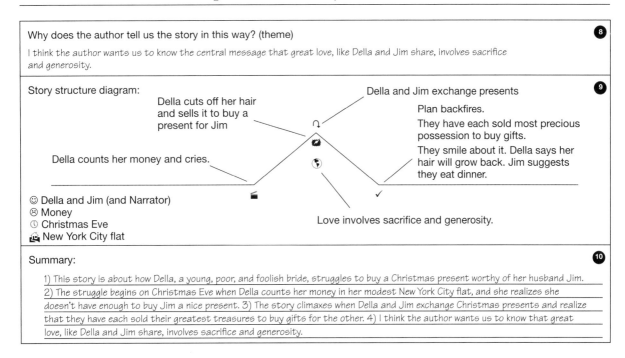

Why does the author tell us the story in this way? (theme)

I think the author wants us to know the central message that great love, like Della and Jim share, involves sacrifice and generosity.

Story structure diagram:

Della cuts off her hair and sells it to buy a present for Jim

Della and Jim exchange presents

Plan backfires.
They have each sold most precious possession to buy gifts.
They smile about it. Della says her hair will grow back. Jim suggests they eat dinner.

Della counts her money and cries.

☺ Della and Jim (and Narrator)
☹ Money
🕑 Christmas Eve
🏘 New York City flat

Love involves sacrifice and generosity.

Summary:

1) This story is about how Della, a young, poor, and foolish bride, struggles to buy a Christmas present worthy of her husband Jim. 2) The struggle begins on Christmas Eve when Della counts her money in her modest New York City flat, and she realizes she doesn't have enough to buy Jim a nice present. 3) The story climaxes when Della and Jim exchange Christmas presents and realize that they have each sold their greatest treasures to buy gifts for the other. 4) I think the author wants us to know that great love, like Della and Jim share, involves sacrifice and generosity.

Figure 4.2. Sample embedded story structure.

each critical story structure component and related questions (see Table 4.1). For example, students can ask the following while reading. Who is the main character? What is the central conflict and how does it begin? How does the central conflict end/resolve? Each question word is used only once to provide a clear mnemonic for students to remember and independently generate each question throughout reading.

The self-questioning strategy is used before and during reading to improve student reading comprehension. Students who ask questions before reading are more likely to activate their prior knowledge of narrative text structure for application when reading new narrative text. Self-questioning during reading requires students to be active in the reading process and provides opportunities for them to reinforce their understanding of the story structure. In addition, the self-questioning strategy becomes a problem-solving activity as students read to identify story structure elements as answers to each question, thus differentiating between main ideas and supporting details and consequently improving comprehension. Moreover, self-questions have the added disciplinary connection because they use literary terms in the English curriculum synonymous with narrative plot structure (e.g., *central conflict, resolution*). Finally, students will be more likely to put

Table 4.1. Embedded story structure routine self-questioning and four-sentence writing formula

Self-questioning	Four-sentence writing formula
Who are the main characters? ☺ ☹ (Main character)	1. This story is about how (main character ☺, supporting detail) struggles with (central conflict 🎬).
What is the central conflict 🎬, and how does it begin 🎬? (Central conflict and initiating event)	2. The struggle begins when (initiating event 🎬) and takes place (time 🕑 and place 🏘).
When 🕑 does the story take place? (Time)	
Where 🏘 does the story take place? (Place)	3. The story climaxes when (climax ⋂), and the conflict is resolved by/when (resolution ✓).
Which decision or event is the turning point ⋂? (Climax)	
How does the central conflict end/resolve ✓? (Resolution)	4. I think the author is trying to tell us that (theme 🌍).
Why did the author tell us the story in this way 🌍? (Theme)	

critical elements of the story structure in sequential order and summarize the story in their own words because self-questioning identifies key elements of narrative text structure.

Story Structure Analysis   Story structure analysis is the second strategy in the ESS routine. Students analyze and label each critical element of the story structure by filling out the story structure diagram on the back of the ESS graphic organizer (see Figure 4.2). Students can use a second mnemonic device in the form of a unique picture cue (e.g., ① = time, 🖤 = central conflict) to identify and label each critical element on the story structure diagram (see Figure 4.2). Students are asked to put each critical element in a chronological (temporal sequence) order to reinforce and review the main ideas of the narrative. Students begin by identifying the protagonist as the main character that the story revolves around and finding the antagonist as the character who creates major obstacles for the protagonist to overcome. Students label the first four story structure components (protagonist, antagonist, time, and place) as exposition at the beginning of the story structure diagram (see Figure 4.2). The initiating event, which signals the start of the central conflict, is placed at the start of the rising action, leading to the climax. Finally, the falling action leads to the resolution, bringing the central conflict to an end.

The story structure analysis is used after reading, when students finish answering self-questions. Analyzing the story structure helps students to immediately review the critical elements of the story structure as well as put these critical elements in chronological order. For example, narrative text may present stories in different ways: some stories are told in a sequential order, beginning with a problem followed by a series of episodes that lead to a resolution, whereas other stories (e.g., *The Odyssey*) begin in the middle (in medias res), introducing a key struggle or point of tension at the beginning before continuing with other critical elements of the plot. Analyzing the structure of these stories helps students put story structure elements in the order of narrative structure and makes these stories more clearly understood. Students can conveniently use this visual map to recall the plot.

Guided Summary   Guided summary is the final strategy in the ESS Routine. Summary writing involves using a four-sentence writing formula (see Table 4.1) in which students generate a complete and well-organized summary based on their responses to the self-questions (see Figure 4.2). For example, the first sentence of the writing formula is derived from the answers of two self-questions: Who is the main character? and What is the central conflict? Answers complete the following guided summary stem: This story is about how (main character ☺, supporting details) struggles with (central conflict 🖤). Table 4.1 provides additional examples to illustrate how each self-question answer is used to direct summary writing.

Summary writing is always used after reading. Generating the summary helps students monitor their understanding of the story. After generating the narrative order of the story structure, summarization requires students to continually keep track of eight critical elements of the story structure as well as provides opportunities for students to transform their perceived understanding of critical elements into a robust synthesis.

Embedded Story Structure Routine Pedagogy

Effective instruction mediates student learning by ensuring the knowledge, skills, and strategies related to an intervention are transferred from teachers to students in an explicit fashion. The ESS routine and its instructional methodology mediate learning through four phases of strategic instruction: 1) teacher demonstration (I Do It), 2) teacher modeling (We Do It), 3) student collaboration and guided practice (Y'all Do It), and 4) independent practice (You Do It; Archer & Hughes, 2011; Faggella-Luby et al., 2007).

Teachers do the following during the I Do It phase: 1) introduce the steps of the three ESS strategies, 2) explain the purpose and how the ESS routine will benefit student learning, 3) specify what students need to do during instruction, 4) model problem solving and use all three ESS strategies through a think aloud, and 5) demonstrate the entire process of the ESS routine that students would carry out. Teachers do the following during the We Do It phase: 1) ask students to perform all ESS strategy steps, 2) ask students to explain what they observed and how they are thinking about the strategy steps, 3) provide corrective feedback through shaping student responses, 4) co-construct meaning from text and fill out the ESS organizer, 5) evaluate student understanding, and 6) reinstruct components or steps of the ESS routine, if necessary.

During the Y'all Do It phase, students: 1) are assigned partners based on student ability level, 2) explain their thinking to one another in small, cooperative learning groups (one to three students), 3) collaboratively problem solve using the ESS routine, 4) engage in a positive and cooperative learning environment, 5) receive corrective feedback as teachers circulate to student groups for additional instruction, and 6) evaluate ESS routine use and understanding. During the You Do It phase, students: 1) independently perform using all ESS strategy steps, 2) receive brief, specific, and constructive feedback from the teacher related to individual ESS routine components the student may be struggling to master, and 3) perform so that instructors are able to identify categories of errors to use in the next session's lesson. This form of mediated instruction is consistent with the principles of explicit instruction (Archer & Hughes, 2011) and research findings indicating that the magnitude of instructional outcomes is related to the level of explicitness during instruction (Swanson, 1999).

An Evidence-Based Intervention

In the age of teacher accountability and evidence-based practice ushered in with NCLB, practitioners require proof of intervention validation prior to implementation. Fortunately, the ESS routine is both a theoretically and empirically validated discipline-specific intervention.

Knowing text structure, or the organizational framework for a piece of prose writing, aids proficient readers by providing a lens through which to view the unique language features and conventions of discipline-specific texts (e.g., science labs, historical documents, novels; Heller & Greenleaf, 2007). Awareness of underlying text structure has been shown to improve basic academic performance and lead to higher-order thinking, including causal reasoning (e.g., Gersten, Fuchs, Williams, & Baker, 2001). Students with reading difficulties, however, typically lack text structure awareness of both expository and narrative text types (Gersten et al., 2001; Stetter & Hughes, 2010). The CI model of reading comprehension (Kintsch, 2004) postulates that to compensate for lack of prior knowledge (e.g., not knowing common story structures), students can and should be taught strategies so that they can not only read to understand, but also read to learn from text. Kintsch described the learnability zone as the gap between what the student already knows (a reader variable) and the information presented in the text (a text variable). Readers with limited understanding of the underlying structure of stories benefit from specific strategy instruction to help improve reading ability to garner information from complex texts. Consequently, the instructional context for the ESS routine includes elements of mediated instruction that allow for the transfer of strategies from teacher to student.

Kintsch (2004) stated that the goal of literacy instruction should be to engage students in processes equivalent to those that expert readers employ. One such process involves categorizing information in light of certain text structures. According to Kintsch, student knowledge and use of text structure favorably affects comprehension, just as world knowledge or vocabulary might. Text structure is believed to be most relevant to the reading process during encoding (as readers construct a text base) and during the reader's organization of the text into higher-order units (integrating knowledge into a situation model). Although syntactic and semantic instruction both foster sentence-level knowledge construction, discourse-level structure construction can be improved by teaching genre-specific text structures. Thus, instruction in the ESS routine explicitly introduces students to the use of narrative text structure to aid in the conceptual understanding of narrative texts.

The ESS routine is also empirically validated. Two research studies have been conducted on the ESS routine with students in high school (Faggella-Luby et al., 2007) and middle school (Faggella-

RESEARCH STUDY 4.1 /// High School
(Faggella-Luby, Schumaker, & Deshler, 2007)

Purpose   The purpose of this experimental study was to investigate the outcome of using the embedded story structure (ESS) routine to improve reading comprehension skills in a general education setting with an academically diverse population of students. Seventy-nine incoming ninth-grade students struggling with reading or mathematics, including 14 students with learning disabilities, were given 9 days of instruction and randomly assigned into two groups: 1) an ESS group and 2) a comprehension skills instruction (CSI) control group.

Procedures   The ESS routine emphasized three strategies: 1) self-questioning, 2) story structure analysis, and 3) written summary. CSI control instruction focused on three research-based strategies for improving reading comprehension: 1) the LINCS vocabulary strategy (Ellis, 2000), which was used for prereading, 2) question-answer relationships (QAR; Raphael, 1982, 1986), which was used during reading, and 3) semantic summary mapping (Englert, Mariage, Garmon, & Tarrant, 1998), which was used after reading. Students in both conditions were taught in groups of 12–14 students over 9 days of block scheduling and with mediated instruction.

Measures   Four dependent measures used in this study included: 1) a strategy-use test, which measured student performance on individual ESS strategies, 2) a knowledge test, which measured student understanding of ESS strategy components, 3) a unit reading comprehension test, which measured student retention of all stories that they read, and 4) two satisfaction surveys, which measured student reading satisfaction with instruction.

Results   The results indicated that ESS students outperformed the CSI control group on all measures, and there were no significant difference in performances between students with or without disabilities in the ESS group. In addition, the ESS students had significant improvements in using strategies compared with the CSI students, and the ESS students at posttests had higher levels of reading satisfaction compared with pretests. Thus, the authors concluded that this study supported the use of the ESS routine as an instructional intervention to improve reading comprehension for all levels of adolescent readers in secondary school classrooms.

Luby & Wardwell, 2011). In the first study, academically diverse high school students who were taught the ESS routine significantly outperformed students receiving another research-based intervention on curriculum and strategy-specific measures. In fact, students both with and without disabilities improved when using the strategy to read literature. In the second study, struggling middle school students receiving Tier 2 RTI instruction in the ESS routine significantly outperformed students engaged in sustained silent reading.

IMPLEMENTING THE EMBEDDED STORY STRUCTURE ROUTINE

The ESS routine is intended as an intervention that can be embedded within a middle or high school English class to improve the strategic abilities of all levels of learners. The intervention, however, is also unique in that it is an example of a discipline-specific package of strategies, which allows teachers to improve student reading comprehension while continuing to teach critical course content. Therefore, the ESS routine can be used with any narrative texts encountered in the curriculum, including those recommended in the new Common Core State Standards (e.g., *The Gift of the Magi, The Odyssey, The Tragedy of Macbeth*).

Teachers should carefully consider the sequence of readings to allow students to develop their own independent mastery of the strategy. For example, the ESS routine might be taught during a set of short story units at the start of the ninth grade. Teachers typically need to cover different short stories related to plot and theme during such units. Therefore, it is helpful during planning to analyze the individual stories for difficulties that students might have, such as a lack

---

RESEARCH STUDY 4.2 /// **Middle School and Response to Intervention**
(Faggella-Luby & Wardwell, 2011)

Purpose   The purpose of this experimental study was to investigate the effects of using three Tier 2 response to interventions (RTIs) (embedded story structure [ESS], typical practice [TP], and sustained silent reading [SSR]) with fifth- and sixth-grade students at-risk in an urban middle school. Eighty-six fifth- and sixth-grade students at-risk were randomly assigned to one of the three treatment conditions.

Procedures   ESS routine instruction used the three strategies from previous research: 1) self-questioning, 2) story structure analysis, and 3) written summary. However, slight modifications were made to ESS instruction to better fit the learning environment: First, the content was changed in two minor ways: 1) the strategy-related mnemonics were posted in the classroom instead of being taught explicitly, and 2) one more sentence was added to the written summary formula (allowing students to include the story's antagonist). Second, the instructional methodology was modified to fit the RTI framework. Specifically, all groups were taught in 30-minute sessions 2–3 days per week over 18 weeks. The TP control instruction was independently designed by teachers, primarily focusing on teaching a package of strategies including previewing, predicting, identifying character, summarizing, visualizing, and questioning. Students in the SSR control instruction were encouraged to bring books to class or borrow from the school library and silently read 30 minutes each day.

Measures   Three key dependent measures used to assess the posttest learning included: 1) a standardized, curriculum-based Cloze measure test—The AIMSweb Maze (Shinn & Shinn, 2003)—which measured student sentence-level reading comprehension, 2) a strategy-use test, which analyzed student understanding of the ESS strategies in the intervention, and 3) the Gates-MacGinitie Reading Comprehension (MacGinitie, MacGinitie, Maria, & Dreyer, 2002), which assessed students' reading comprehension achievements related to text passages.

Results   The results indicated that ESS students reached higher reading achievement than TP and SSR students. And fifth graders and sixth graders benefited equally from using the ESS routine. Thus, the authors concluded that the research on the ESS routine specifically, and the individual components in general, give teachers reason to believe that using the ESS routine as an intervention can effectively improve the reading comprehension of students who are at-risk, including students with disabilities, within an RTI framework.

---

of prior knowledge (including world knowledge, vocabulary, or conceptual understanding) as well as readability level.

Practically, this might mean teaching more straightforward stories such as *The Most Dangerous Game* or *The Necklace* before teaching *The Cask of Amontillado*. Careful sequence of readings allows students to initially focus on developing automaticity with the strategy without struggling with the story content before applying the strategy to more textually complex readings. In addition, sequencing texts with a variety of levels of difficulty may help to increase reader motivation as students' self-efficacy and abilities grow (e.g., McCabe, 2009).

Strategy Teaching Phase 1: I Do It

ESS routine instruction typically begins with teacher explanation of the strategy purpose—helping students improve their understanding of narrative texts by using three strategies that make reading an interactive and engaging process. Teachers then personalize the strategy by discussing the benefits of learning the strategy for individual students (e.g., more enjoyable reading experience, high test and quiz scores, better memory for important story components) as well as types of narrative texts in which the strategy can be used (e.g., short stories, epic poems, graphic novels, plays, realistic fiction). The introduction concludes with teachers and students making a reciprocal commitment: 1) students are asked to commit to being prepared to learn the strategy during the next few weeks and 2) teachers commit to being prepared to teach the strategy each day. It is particularly important that teachers take this opportunity to explicitly state what it means to be prepared (e.g., students bring necessary materials, complete homework, pay attention during instruction).

Strategy Overview   Instruction continues with an overview of the ESS routine components (i.e., self-questioning, story structure analysis, guided summary writing). Each component is presented in sequential order according to the steps of the strategy (e.g., Who is the main character?). Components are written on the board, overhead projector, or presented via PowerPoint and are grouped according to the three strategies (see Figures 4.1 and 4.2). Teachers can provide a brief definition or example of each literary term as each component is presented. For example, after introducing the self-question, "What is the central conflict and how does it begin?" the teacher might define both *central conflict* and *initiating event,* provide examples from previously read stories, and/or show students where these terms appear at the back of their textbook. Finally, the overview concludes by the teacher communicating the expected outcome that students will learn to use the strategy independently when reading narrative texts in their English class, as well as in other classes, or in their own personal reading time.

Strategy Demonstration   The teacher uses a demonstration of the entire strategy to provide students with a "big picture" example of what using the strategy looks like. The demonstration begins with the teacher defining the context of the lesson as an opportunity for students to observe how the strategy will work. It is helpful to choose a short passage (e.g., folktale, fable) with clear conformity to narrative text structure to allow for a complete demonstration of the strategy. The teacher reads the story to the students and asks them to suggest elements of the story that seemed important. The teacher lists these suggestions on the board as they surface. After exhausting the list of student-generated elements, the teacher passes out the ESS organizer and suggests it as one way to organize the material. Students are made aware during the demonstration that eventually they will be expected to independently complete a similar activity. The teacher uses the ESS organizer to demonstrate answering each of the seven self-questions related to critical story components, calling attention to how answering the questions helps to complete the story structure analysis diagram and writes a short paragraph using the four-sentence guided summary formula to the students (see Table 4.1; see Figure 4.2). The demonstration provides a brief visual example of the process for using the strategy and prepares students for the teacher to model the strategy using an oral think aloud to clarify how the strategy works.

Strategy Model   Teacher modeling of the targeted strategies is the most essential feature of introducing the ESS routine in Phase 1. The modeling provides students with a step-by-step example of how an expert learner uses the routine. It is helpful to choose a short narrative passage for the modeling example, although a short story of several pages in length is more helpful than a fable or folktale to illustrate the entire verbal think aloud. The strategy model is often a separate lesson from the introduction, overview, and demonstration and is usually conducted the next time the class meets.

Students are provided with a blank ESS organizer at the beginning of the model while the teacher projects a similar version on an overhead projector. The teacher reads the narrative text and uses predetermined stopping points (approximately every two pages) as opportunities to pause and reflect. These natural breaks in the story allow the teacher to ask self-questions, including vocalizing the desired story structure component, orally paraphrasing the definition, searching the text for the appropriate answer, explaining why the answer is correct, and writing the answer in the appropriate box on the abbreviated ESS organizer. This teacher-centered instruction is followed throughout the first several pause and reflect stops to model how to proceed through the text using the strategy in a sequential manner. In addition, the teacher demonstrates problem solving when obstacles are encountered in the text. For example, the central conflict may appear to be an initial problem for the characters in a story (Rainsford falling overboard at the beginning of *The Most Dangerous Game*, man versus nature). After reading further, however, it may be clear that the central conflict is really a much larger problem, thus requiring revision of earlier self-question answers (e.g., we learn that Rainsford is to be hunted by General Zaroff, man versus man).

Mediation of student learning (from teacher centered to student centered) formally begins with the remaining opportunities to pause and reflect as students are engaged by the teacher to provide answers and explanations for the remaining self-questions. Therefore, student participation is important as learners are engaged by prompting involvement with direct questions (e.g., Where do I record my answer to the self-question about the main character?) or processing questions to check understanding (e.g., What is the next step?). Engagement often is not as in depth as during the following phase of instruction, however.

At the conclusion of the text, the teacher reviews the story by using the answers to the self-questions as content for the story structure analysis diagram and to write the guided summary (see Figure 4.2). Similar to the self-questioning, the teacher uses verbal problem solving to explicitly and successfully engage in both strategies. The teacher should have completed all strategy steps successfully at the conclusion of the model, recording all answers on the ESS organizer as students follow along.

Strategy Teaching Phase 2: We Do It

The second phase of the ESS routine instruction sequence continues to mediate learning through student–teacher collaboration of strategy use and co-construction of knowledge related to the text. Teachers select narrative texts with discernible story structure from the core curriculum (e.g., see the Common Core State Standards documents, for more information) for use during this whole-group instruction. It is helpful if teachers predetermine a reasonable number of pause and reflect stopping points throughout the text. It is ideal if initial stopping points are located just after information relative to the self-questions is presented in the story because this provides a catalyst for students to move forward in the strategy sequence. Instruction begins with a brief review of the previous lesson, including the components of the three strategies that make up the ESS routine. This review might take the form of a game using rapid-fire verbal rehearsal during the course of instruction by having individual students orally share each step of the strategy and then move to another student to provide the next step in the sequence. In addition, teachers might post the strategy components on posters that hang in the room to cue students to use the strategies during reading.

The teacher reads the text to the students; however, when the teacher reaches the first pause and reflect point, he or she now prompts the involvement of the students to get them actively thinking about each strategy step. Prompting can initially be structured by cuing (e.g., "Okay. I have reached a pause and reflect stopping point. What is the first step in the self-questioning strategy?"). Prompting can be more general as students begin to master the strategy steps (e.g., "What questions can we answer here?"). Once a set of strategy steps is exhausted at a given pause and reflect point, reading continues with the teacher prompting readers to search for answers to the self-questions. Reading need not always be done by the teacher. Some classrooms will make use of audio recordings often available for free on the Internet or through the school's textbook publisher as part of ancillary materials.

The teacher continues to prompt student involvement as well as check student understanding during successive stopping points. Frequent monitoring of both student acquisition of strategy-related skills and overall story comprehension is critical. Teachers might ask students to explain what they observe in the story and how they are thinking about the use of the strategy steps. In addition, teachers can correct, expand, or shape student responses as needed. Timely, corrective feedback when errors are encountered will help students to master the strategy more quickly and inform teacher planning if reinstruction or more guided practice is necessary.

Phase 2 concludes after the teacher and students have finished reading the story and completed the ESS organizer. Teachers are able to engineer student success by reinforcing key points and strategy steps throughout the instructional phase. Several opportunities are typically necessary for students to develop the skills necessary to complete the strategy on their own. Therefore, using formal and informal assessment on a daily basis is a critical step in this phase of instruction to inform instruction (and reinstruction) over areas of difficulty in acquiring strategy mastery.

Strategy Teaching Phase 3: Ya'll Do It

The third phase of ESS routine instruction continues to advance student acquisition of strategy mastery through student–peer collaboration (cooperative learning). Although there are many ways to establish partners (e.g., Fuchs, Fuchs, & Kazdan, 1999; Johnson, Johnson, & Holubec, 2008), it is important that teachers have an understanding of the strengths and challenges of each student as they relate to learning the strategy. This will enable teachers to partner students that are not dramatically different in ability, facilitating a relationship of commensalism, or a partnership benefiting both, rather than dependence (see Faggella-Luby et al., 2007).

Students can take turns reading from narrative texts during student–peer collaborations, or the teacher can continue to use an audio recording. However, predetermined pause and reflect breaks should continue to initiate student use of the ESS routine as students take turns using the strategy. In addition to completing the ESS organizer, students are encouraged to take the role of the teacher and ask their partners to explain how they are thinking about using the strategy at each stopping point. Explanation reinforces student knowledge and use of strategy components and provides the opportunity for collaborative problem solving when answers to self-questions are difficult to locate. Students are encouraged to remain engaged and move in a timely fashion; yet, lesson pacing can be flexible based on the class needs. Teachers may want to preteach expectations and procedures for working with partners in order to encourage a positive and cooperative learning environment (e.g., Vernon & Schumaker, 1995).

Student–peer collaborations afford teachers the opportunity to move around the classroom to monitor instruction. Time can be spent providing timely corrective feedback to groups or individual students, evaluating student acquisition of strategy components, reinforcing appropriate cooperative learning behaviors, and using interactive planning to adjust lesson pacing to meet student needs. Moreover, purposeful partnering of students will help the teacher know which groups might need more attention and which groups have sufficient ability to move forward. Given the large numbers of students in secondary English classrooms, partnering can also help reduce the instructional ratio for grading by limiting the necessary feedback to half if teachers choose to have each cooperative group produce a single shared ESS organizer to score. Finally, it is helpful for the teacher to facilitate a class discussion of the essential story elements at the close of the lesson as well as provide feedback on how students feel about progressing in their learning of the strategy.

It is expected that Phase 3 of instruction will require several class meetings to sufficiently build student skill and application of the strategies. However, because the strategy is embedded within the content instruction, the teacher can continue to teach successive narrative texts while reinforcing ESS routine acquisition.

Strategy Teaching Phase 4: You Do It

The final phase of instruction completes mediation of strategy acquisition through independent student practice and performance. Independent practice should appropriately conclude instruction and not be rushed. Therefore, a balance is needed between the cooperative learning previously outlined and independent practice opportunities. Teachers may find it helpful to introduce limited opportunities for independent practice prior to completely releasing students to independent practice to gauge whether students are ready. For example, teachers might identify a particularly clear passage at the start of a narrative text that introduces the main character. It would be appropriate to have students answer the first self-question (e.g., Who is the main character?) on their own and then call the students back together into a larger group to check answers before moving into cooperative learning for the lesson. A similar approach can be used with the resolution of the story, encouraging readers to independently identify how the story ends prior to a large-group discussion. Another option is to use the think-pair-share approach, scaffolding students from independent work to partner work to whole-class sharing.

When teachers have determined students are ready to engage in extended independent practice, the lesson might begin with a brief verbal rehearsal of the strategy steps and overview of the strategy procedures. It is less advantageous to have teachers read out loud at this point and, instead, rely on student reading ability or audio recordings. If students are allowed to read on their own, then it will become necessary to provide them with the predetermined stopping points as well. Students can then progress through the narrative text, completing the ESS organizer to demonstrate knowledge and use of the strategy components. It is recommended that teachers take the opportunity to move around the classroom to monitor instruction. In particular, independent practice allows for individualized and, if necessary, specialized instruction or review with students. In addition, it is helpful during monitoring if the teacher can begin to identify categories of errors for use in the next lesson's review and opportunities for practice.

The teacher can provide targeted feedback when the ESS organizer is complete. Stronger students are more likely to finish early; therefore, the teacher will have an opportunity to correct misconceptions the whole class might struggle with and identify which students are really mastering the strategy steps (see Table 4.2). The teacher should engage students in a discourse grounded in the text when they complete their organizers to process critical content from the passage and tie key ideas back to larger essential questions or unit plan goals.

MRS. JACKSON'S SUCCESS

Mrs. Jackson received professional development in the ESS routine and decided to try it at the start of the school year with her ninth-grade English classes. Students typically read a series of short stories during the first quarter to teach plot structure and theme, giving Mrs. Jackson a chance to embed the ESS routine in her instruction. She was pleased that she could embed the instruction and continue to teach critical course content suggested in the Common Core State Standards.

Although Mrs. Jackson chose to introduce the entire strategy at once, she was able to help students who struggled to learn the strategy during guided practice, cooperative learning, and independent practice so that all of her students were able to master the three strategies. Mrs. Jackson noted that she was able to continue to challenge her high-achieving students because of the mediated instruction and did not have to leave her struggling students behind.

At the end of the quarter, Mrs. Jackson used her unit test scores to confirm that her students had developed the necessary skills to comprehend the complex texts in her core curriculum. Although not all students were receiving *A* grades, it was clear from her assessment data that students had mastered the critical content necessary to move on during the year. Mrs. Jackson committed to cuing the students to use the ESS routine during the second quarter reading of *The Odyssey* in hopes that students would begin to generalize the routine's use to other narrative texts.

CONCLUSION

The ESS routine provides English teachers with an evidence-based intervention to improve literacy instruction in middle and high school classrooms teaching narrative text. The ESS routine fits with the growing literature, suggesting that teachers move beyond general strategy instruction to build disciplinary literacy skills during content area instruction. Because the ESS routine employs three discipline-specific strategies for learning English content, teachers are able to embed strategy instruction in Common Core State Standards curriculum and draw on their own content area expertise during instruction to provide clarity around strategy use, thus helping students read

Table 4.2. Instructional suggestions for academically diverse learners

Student area of difficulty	Instructional suggestion	Examples from *Romeo and Juliet* (or otherwise indicated)
Incomplete background knowledge	Clarify the meaning of key vocabulary from the text prior to reading.	*Pernicious, transgression, sallow, abhor, enjoined, penury*
Limited relevant world knowledge	Facilitate a whole-class discussion prior to reading relative to any concepts, vocabulary, or ideas in the text that may not be part of students' life experience.	*Prejudice, patriarchal compliance, dueling, banishment*
Academic language	Preteach or review any academic language or literary terms the students will need to successfully acquire knowledge from the text.	*Compare, contrast, analyze, synthesize, dramatic irony, tragedy, soliloquy, foil*
Unfamiliar text structure	Begin with narrative texts that have discernible classic text structure that follows a chronological temporal sequence. Then provide students with examples of incomplete or anachronic stories as students become more comfortable.	Classic: *The Most Dangerous Game* Incomplete: *The Lady or the Tiger* Anachronic (e.g., in medias res): *The Odyssey*
Learning the individual strategies	Teach the self-questioning strategy to mastery first. Then introduce the remaining two strategies one at a time until each is mastered. This will avoid overwhelming students.	Use the self-questioning strategy only in Act I and Act II. Introduce the text structure analysis strategy and practice self-questioning in Act III. Introduce summarizing and practice previous strategies in Act IV. Practice all three strategies in the embedded story structure routine in Act V.
Monitoring strategy use	Cue students to use the mnemonic pictures on the graphic organizer to remember the individual steps.	This is particularly helpful when identifying the climax in the middle of the play.
Motivation	If students are having difficulty searching for answers, then it may be helpful to have them make a prediction about the answer to each self-question before reading. This will turn the reading into a problem-solving activity.	Shakespeare's prologue tells the reader the initiating event and resolution to the story, but students can problem solve finding the climax based on the student-identified central conflict.
Text seems overwhelming	Influence the student's first glance by marketing why it is a story they might enjoy.	Share some of the first few pages of Act I with photocopies to get students interested before handing out the play or turning to the entire text.
Text seems too difficult	Provide students with a balance of reading material that is textually complex and at their independent reading level. Use analogies to make knowledge connections to important ideas in the text.	Begin Act I with a discussion of rivalries. Although the Hatfield and McCoy feud may be tempting, more often sports teams (Red Sox versus Yankees), political parties (Democrats versus Republicans), cartoons (Wile E. Coyote versus Road Runner), or Bible stories (David versus Goliath) are more easily accessible.
Difficult syntax	Photocopy short passages for the students to practice.	Practice Shakespearian rhythm (iambic pentameter), word order, and word choice through close reading (and rereading) of short passages to prepare for larger sections. For example, Act I provides action, includes many characters, establishes conflict, is filled with bawdy jokes, and allows for practice of all elements.

closely and understand complex texts. Most important, the ESS routine allows teachers to meet the needs of all students, including academically diverse populations, through mediated instruction.

REFERENCES

Archer, A.L., & Hughes, C.A. (2011). *Explicit instruction: Effective and efficient teaching.* New York, NY: Guilford Press.

Bialostosky, D. (2006). Should college English be close reading? *College English, 69*(2), 111–116.

Biancarosa, C., & Snow, C.E. (2006). *Reading next—A vision for action and research in middle and high school literacy: A report to Carnegie Corporation of New York* (2nd ed.). Washington, DC: Alliance for Excellent Education.

Common Core State Standards Initiative. (2010). *Common Core State Standards for English language arts and literacy in history/social studies, science, and technical subjects. Appendix B: Text exemplars and sample performance tasks.* Retrieved from http://www.corestandards.org/assets/Appendix_B.pdf

Edmonds, M.S., Vaughn, S., Wexler, J., Reutebuch, C., Cable, A., Klingler Tackett, K., & Wick Schnakenberg, J. (2009). A synthesis of reading interventions and effects on reading comprehension outcomes for older struggling readers. *Review of Educational Research, 79*(1), 262–300.

Ellis, E.S. (2000). *The LINCS vocabulary strategy* (2nd ed.). Lawrence, KS: Edge Enterprises.

Englert, C.S., Mariage, T.V., Garmon, M.A., & Tarrant, K.L. (1998). Accelerating reading progress in early literacy project classrooms: Three exploratory studies. *Remedial and Special Education, 19*(3), 142–159.

Faggella-Luby, M. (2006). *Embedded learning strategy instruction: Story-structure pedagogy in secondary classes for diverse learners.* (Doctoral dissertation, University of Kansas). *ProQuest Dissertations and Theses,* , 170 p. Retrieved from http://ezproxy.lib.uconn.edu/login?url=http://search.proquest.com/docview/305319438?accountid=14518.

Faggella-Luby, M., & Deshler, D. (2008). Reading comprehension in adolescents with LD: What we know; what we need to learn. *Learning Disabilities Research and Practice, 23*(2), 70–78.

Faggella-Luby, M., Graner, P., Deshler, D., & Drew, S. (2012). Building a house on sand: Why disciplinary literacy is not sufficient to replace general strategies for adolescent learners who struggle. *Topics in Language Disorders, (32)*1, 69–84.

Faggella-Luby, M., Schumaker, J.S., & Deshler, D.D. (2007). Embedded learning strategy instruction: Story-structure pedagogy in heterogeneous secondary literature classes. *Learning Disability Quarterly, 30*(2), 131–147.

Faggella-Luby, M., & Wardwell, M. (2011). RTI in middle school: Findings and practical implications of a tier-2 reading comprehension study. *Learning Disability Quarterly, 34,* 35–49.

Fang, Z., & Schleppegrell, M.J. (2010). Disciplinary literacies across content areas: Supporting secondary reading through functional language analysis. *Journal of Adolescent and Adult Literacy, 53*(7), 587–597.

Fuchs, L.S., Fuchs, D., & Kazdan, S. (1999). Effects of peer-assisted learning strategies on high school students with serious reading problems. *Remedial and Special Education, 20,* 309–318.

Gersten, R., Fuchs, L.S., Williams, J.P., & Baker, S. (2001). Teaching reading comprehension strategies to students with learning disabilities: A review of research. *Review of Educational Research, 71*(2), 279–320.

Graner, P.S., Faggella-Luby, M., & Fritschmann, N. (2005). An overview of responsiveness to intervention: What practitioners ought to know. *Topics in Language Disorders, 25*(2), 93–105.

Harris, K.R., & Graham, S. (1999). Programmatic intervention research: Illustrations from the evolution of self-regulated strategy development. *Learning Disability Quarterly, 22*(4), 251–262.

Heller, R., & Greenleaf, C. (2007). *Literacy instruction in the content areas: Getting to the core of middle and high school improvement.* Washington, DC: Alliance for Excellent Education.

Individuals with Disabilities Education Improvement Act (IDEA) of 2004, PL 108-446, 20 U.S.C. §§ 1400 *et seq.*

Johnson, D.W., Johnson, R., & Holubec, E. (2008). *Cooperation in the classroom* (8th ed.). Edina, MN: Interaction Book Company.

Kintsch, W. (1992). A cognitive architecture for comprehension. In H.L. Pick, P. van den Broek, & D.C. Knill (Eds.), *The study of cognition: Conceptual and methodological issues* (pp. 1143–1164). Washington, DC: American Psychological Association.

Kintsch, W. (1998). *Comprehension: A paradigm for cognition.* New York, NY: Cambridge University Press.

Kintsch, W. (2004).The construction-integration model of text comprehension and its implications for instruction. In R.B. Rudell & N.J. Unrau (Eds.), *Theoretical models and processes of reading* (5th ed., pp. 1270–1324). Newark, DE: International Reading Association.

MacGinitie, W.H., MacGinitie, R.K., Maria, K., & Dreyer, L.G. (2002). *Gates-MacGinitie Reading Tests* (4th ed.). Itasca, IL: Riverside Publishing.

McCabe, P. (2009). Enhancing adolescent self-efficacy for literacy. In D. Wood & W.E. Blanton (Eds.), *Literacy instruction for adolescents: Research-based practice* (pp. 54–76). New York, NY: Guilford Press.

Miller, T. (2006). What should college English be doing? *College English, 69*(2), 150–155.

National Center for Education Statistics. (2010). *The nation's report card: Grade 12 reading and mathematics 2009* (NCES 2011-455). Washington, DC: U.S. Department of Education.

National Institute of Child Health and Human Development. (2000). *Report of the National Reading Panel. Teaching children to read: An evidence-based assessment of the scientific research literature on reading and its implications for reading instruction* (NIH Publication No. 00-4769). Washington, DC: U.S. Government Printing Office.

No Child Left Behind Act of 2001, PL 107-110, 115 Stat. 1425, 20 U.S.C. §§ 6301 *et seq.*

Palincsar, A.S., & Brown, A.L. (1984). Reciprocal teaching of comprehension-fostering and comprehension-monitoring activities. *Cognition and Instruction, 1*(2), 117–175.

Pressley, M., El-Dinary, P.B., Gaskins, I.W., & Schuder, T. (1992). Beyond direct explanation: Transactional instruction of reading comprehension strategies. *Elementary School Journal, 92*(5), 513–555.

Randel, W. (1958). English as a discipline. *College English, 19*(8), 359–361.

Raphael, T. (1982). Question-answering strategies for children. *The Reading Teacher, 36*(2), 186–190.

Raphael, T.E. (1986). Teaching question-answer relationships, revisited. *The Reading Teacher, 39*(6), 516–522.

Schumaker, J.B., & Deshler, D.D. (2006). Teaching adolescents to be strategic learners. In J.B. Schumaker & D.D. Deshler (Eds.), *Teaching adolescents with disabilities: Accessing the general education curriculum* (pp. 121–156). Thousand Oaks, CA: Corwin.

Shanahan, T., & Shanahan, C. (2008). Teaching disciplinary literacy to adolescents: Rethinking content-area literacy. *Harvard Educational Review, 78*(1), 40–59.

Shanahan, T., & Shanahan, C.R. (2012). What is disciplinary literacy and why does it matter? *Topics in Language Disorders, 32*(1), 7–18.

Shinn, M.R., & Shinn, M.M. (2003). AIMSweb *training workbook: Administration and scoring of reading maze for use in general outcome measurement.* Eden Prairie, MN: Edformation.

Stetter, M., & Hughes, M. (2010). Using story grammar to assist students with learning disabilities and reading difficulties improve their comprehension. *Education and Treatment of Children, 33*(1), 115–151.

Swanson, H.L. (1999). Instructional components that predict treatment outcomes for students with learning disabilities: Support for a combined strategy and direct instructional method. *Learning Disabilities Research and Practice, 14*(3), 129–140.

Trabasso, T., & Bouchard, E. (2002). Teaching readers how to comprehend text strategically. In C. Collins Block & M. Pressley (Eds.), *Comprehension instruction: Research-based best practices* (pp. 176–200). New York, NY: Guilford Press.

U.S. Department of Education. (2002). *The Elementary and Secondary Education Act (The No Child Left Behind Act of 2001).* Retrieved from http://www2.ed.gov/policy/elsec/leg/esea02/index.html

Van Dijk, T.A., & Kintsch, W. (1983). *Strategies of discourse comprehension.* San Diego, CA: Academic Press.

Vernon, D., & Schumaker, J.B. (1995). Programs to teach cooperation and teamwork. *Intervention in School and Clinic, 31*(2), 121–125.

Wanzek, J., Wexler, J., Vaughn, S., & Ciullo, S. (2010). Reading interventions for struggling readers in the upper elementary grades: A synthesis of 20 years of research. *Reading and Writing: An Interdisciplinary Journal, 23*(8), 889–912.

5 ||| Using Graphic Organizers in Secondary, Inclusive Content Classes

Colleen Klein Reutebuch, Stephen Ciullo, and Sharon Vaughn

Educators teaching secondary learners in inclusive content area classrooms have considerable challenges, including 1) teaching students with a wide array of academic needs and reading abilities, 2) equipping students with strategies to enable the acquisition of content and the ability to read for understanding, and 3) preparing students to graduate from high school and pursue postsecondary aspirations. Heightened academic standards have led educators to seek instructional practices that are based on research and are associated with improving academic outcomes in content area classrooms (Bulgren, Deshler, & Lenz, 2007). Content area teachers in secondary school must teach a required curriculum while also fostering an environment in which students are actively engaged in higher-order thinking and applying learning strategies.

This chapter highlights the use of the graphic organizer as an instructional tool that is associated with improving content area learning and reading comprehension for students with varying academic skills. Graphic organizers are visual and spatial displays of information that are used to highlight important information and help make abstract concepts more comprehensible (Ausubel, 1968). They aid in organizing information or depicting relationships within a learning task. Graphic organizers can be used to teach vocabulary, summarize content, and display relationships or connections between different ideas or concepts. Common examples of graphic organizers include visual displays such as time lines or flowcharts, Venn diagrams, story maps, cognitive maps, semantic maps, matrices, or a sequence chart (Dexter & Hughes, 2011; Kim, Vaughn, Wanzek, & Wei, 2004). Graphic organizers can be independently or collaboratively generated and completed by students or teachers and can even incorporate technology.

This chapter provides educators with information regarding the use of graphic organizers for secondary learners in inclusive content area classrooms. This chapter is organized to provide 1) a rationale for why graphic organizers work and reasons for using them, 2) a brief review of research that summarizes the evidence supporting this teaching practice, 3) tips for designing graphic organizers to use for English language arts, math, social studies, and science, 4) a framework for teaching students how to generate their own graphic organizers to become learners who can collaboratively and independently use graphic organizers to enhance academic potential, and 5) a chapter wrap-up including future directions for this instructional practice and considerations for using graphic organizers.

WHY USE GRAPHIC ORGANIZERS?
THE RATIONALE AND EVIDENCE FOR THE TEACHING PRACTICE

Decades of cognitive psychology research suggested that graphic organizers benefit learning (Dexter, 2010). Graphic organizers can help students understand and remember information because they make abstract concepts more concrete and offer an organizational structure to learn new content. The dual coding theory (Clark & Paivio, 1991; Paivio, 1986) attempts to explain why graphic organizers work. The theory suggests that people contain two cognitive systems for remembering and processing information. The visual system helps process images, such as a flow-charts, diagrams, or pictures. The verbal system processes language when it is used as input, such as listening to a lecture. The visual and verbal systems are separate, but they work together to help us learn. When verbal (e.g., lecture, speech) and visual information (e.g., a graphic organizer or Venn diagram that compares and contrasts the geography of the United States and China) are presented together, students can process the information and remember it more effectively than if information was only presented verbally (Clark & Paivio, 1991; Dexter, 2010). Although the dual coding theory is only one of the various learning theories supporting the use of graphic organizers, it is an example of the contribution of cognitive research to education.

There are practical reasons that make graphic organizers appealing tools for enhancing content. First, learning from informational text can be challenging. Informational text often contains unfamiliar vocabulary, is organized in a manner that may be confusing, and often requires the integration of prior knowledge regarding specific subject matter (Gajria, Jitendra, Sood, & Sacks, 2007; Twyman, McCleery, & Tindal, 2006). Although any student could potentially have academic difficulty, students with reading difficulties and students with learning disabilities in inclusive classrooms often have additional needs to consider. Issues that impede learning for students with reading difficulties and students with learning disabilities include decoding ability that is below grade level, delayed reading comprehension skills, and an absence of strategic reading strategies that good readers possess (Gersten, Fuchs, Williams, & Baker, 2001; Griffin, Simmons, & Kame'enui, 1991). Given the heterogeneity in student performance in most classrooms, students benefit when teachers incorporate instructional practices that reflect the learning needs of all students.

Although several instructional options for teaching material in content area classrooms exist, such as the integration of technology- or web-based learning, purposeful discussion, and lecture and notetaking, textbooks also play a prominent role. Reading informational text for understanding is important beginning in upper elementary school (Wanzek, Wexler, Vaughn, & Ciullo, 2010), and this continues to be an important skill during secondary school and college. The Common Core State Standards, which many states have adopted, are indicative of how crucial informational text learning has become. They indicate that reading to ascertain content and applying knowledge to academic tasks involving evaluation, inference, and synthesis are ways in which students must demonstrate content mastery and comprehension. The graphic organizer is a tool that can support students as they read text and strive to organize, remember, and apply information in content areas.

Graphic organizers are particularly useful in inclusive classes because they are associated with improved outcomes for students with disabilities and students who have reading difficulties as well as students who are typical learners. Although there are several syntheses that describe the impact of graphic organizers on students' reading and learning (Dexter & Hughes, 2011; Kim et al., 2004; Moore & Readence, 1984), a few studies are summarized to illustrate this impact. For example, above-average middle school students in science classes randomly assigned to a group that received graphic organizers at the outset of each of seven chapters significantly outperformed the comparison group that read and studied the chapters without graphic organizers on posttest measures (Hawk, 1986).

Another investigation addressing science content demonstrated that seventh graders in an inner-city general education setting benefited from a graphic organizer known as a concept map (Guastello, Beasley, & Sinatra, 2000). Students were randomly assigned to two groups. The treatment group learned about the circulatory system via a pre-reading prediction activity, a detailed overview, text reading, discussion, and completion of a concept map with the teacher. The only difference with the comparison group is that they did not use a concept map. Students receiving the treatment scored much higher than students in the comparison group, confirming that student and teacher collaboration to construct concept maps in science contributed to attainment of science knowledge (Guastello et al., 2000).

In a systematic review of the literature on graphic organizers, students with learning disabilities outperformed students in typical practice conditions in content area tests of social studies, science, English language arts, and math across 29 studies (Dexter & Hughes, 2011). The majority of the studies in the review relied on content area and researcher-developed measures to capture the impact of graphic organizers on learning. The following depicts examples of research studies for students with learning disabilities.

A study involving middle school students with learning disabilities demonstrated that students who received scripted and explicit instruction and graphic organizers following social studies reading significantly outperformed students in a typical practice comparison group on written essays (DiCecco & Gleason, 2002). The graphic organizer condition consisted of reading with corrective feedback on word reading errors. The teacher went through the graphic organizer step by step, explaining the relationships between concepts and asking students to chorally state the information that was written on the graphic organizer. Students occasionally filled in partially completed graphic organizers independently to maintain active participation.

Another example measured the acquisition of science vocabulary and reading comprehension with multiple-choice items and written recalls of an accompanying passage immediately following intervention and four weeks later (Bos & Anders, 1990). Students engaged in a semantic mapping condition in which the students and teacher created a graphic organizer that demonstrated the relationships among the science concepts significantly outperformed students in the comparison condition. The comparison group learned the science vocabulary via traditional word definition instruction. Students engaged in producing the science vocabulary semantic maps significantly outperformed the control condition on a researcher-generated short- and long-term assessment that evaluated students' knowledge of content-related meanings of vocabulary and reading comprehension of a science passage with multiple-choice responses (Bos & Anders, 1990). In summary, research studies suggested that students engaged in various graphic organizer interventions improved content area learning across all subject areas (Dexter & Hughes, 2011; Kim et al., 2004; Moore & Readence, 1984).

Finally, technologically based graphic organizers have a developing body of research. Boon, Burke, Fore, and Spencer (2006a) compared the relative effects of traditional textbook instruction to graphic organizers generated using a software program. Students in the computer-based condition completed and reviewed the graphic organizer collectively with the teacher before inserting the graphic organizer's content into a software program. The software created a graphic organizer of the content. Students reviewed the content in a whole-group setting and also studied independently. The results indicated that students in an inclusive ninth-grade social studies classroom (including 20 students with mild disabilities) significantly outperformed students in the textbook-based condition on a social studies test covering the Cold War (Boon et al., 2006a). Other studies suggested that concept mapping via computers is related to improved performance on content learning (Boon, Burke, Fore, Hagan-Burke, 2006b) and expository writing (Sturm & Rankin-Erickson, 2002) for students with learning difficulties and learning disabilities in secondary school.

DESIGNING AND USING GRAPHIC ORGANIZERS ACROSS THE CONTENT AREAS

This section describes teaching practices for incorporating graphic organizers into inclusive content area classes. Examples of graphic organizers for English language arts, math, social studies, and science are presented. The chapter concludes with a brief section highlighting the use of student-generated graphic organizers.

Ideas for Designing Graphic Organizers

The design of the graphic organizer you choose to incorporate into your instructional activities will depend on the learner outcomes you want to achieve and the type of text that students will be working with (narrative or expository). A variety of formats can be used to organize a particular type of information. Basic shapes such as boxes or ovals can be used to arrange ideas, facts, or concepts with lines or arrows to demonstrate connections, sequence, or stages (see Figure 5.1).

Examples of graphic organizers that display order, sequence, or stages

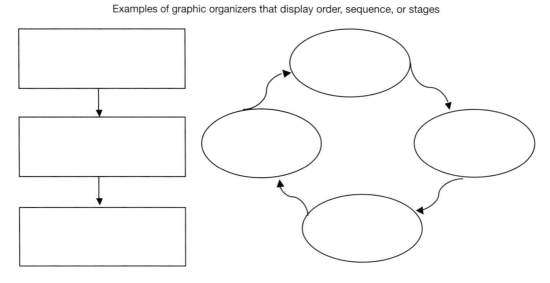

Examples of graphic organizers that display connections

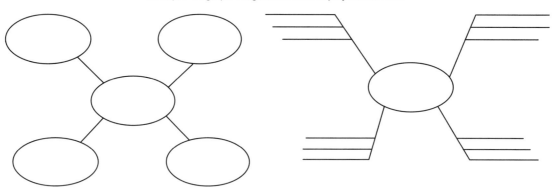

Figure 5.1.   Examples of graphic organizers that display order, sequence, stages or connections.

The following steps should serve as a guide to the graphic organizer's design, regardless of whether it is constructed by the teacher or students (Merkley & Jefferies, 2000; Vacca & Vacca, 2008).

1.   Analyze the learning activity for words, concepts, ideas, categories, or events important to understanding the topic.

2.   Position terms to illustrate the connections and patterns of organization (consider whether your aim is to show a relationship, a pattern, or stages or to sequence information, identify main ideas and supporting details, or compare and contrast).

3.   Evaluate the clarity of relationships (Does your arrangement make sense? Are relationships clear and accurate?).

The following steps are for teachers constructing a graphic organizer with sections that need to be completed.

1.   Leave the graphic organizer only partially completed when providing it to students. Substitute empty slots for certain words, concepts, ideas, categories, and events to promote active reading, listening, thinking, and interacting with the text and others.

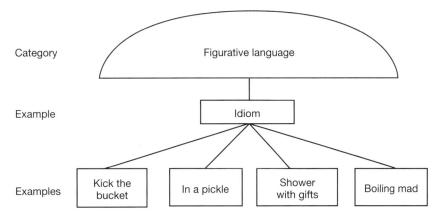

Figure 5.2. Example of a concept map.

2. Promote discussion to draw on students' understanding of and experience with the concepts being used to complete the graphic organizer.

The following directions and guidance are for constructing graphic organizers for specific content areas.

English Language Arts   English language arts involves active processes to include reading, writing, speaking, and listening that are used to construct meaning. The processes have been further expanded to also include 21st-century activities related to visually representing and creating multimedia and viewing and reading multimedia. These English language arts processes are an essential part of the English language arts content area, involve specific strategies for learning in a wide range of content areas, and comprise the means by which learning is constructed in nearly all the content areas (Hall & Strangman, 2002).

A major responsibility of English language arts teachers is to develop students' ability to read for knowledge; to think critically about print, which includes the skills to approach printed material with critical analysis, inference, and synthesis; to write with accuracy and coherence; and to use information and insights from text as the basis for informed decisions and creative thought. Acquiring vocabulary and concept knowledge is key to reading and content comprehension and learned best through direct, concrete, purposeful learning encounters (Nagy, 1988). Graphic organizers can be used to: 1) activate students' prior knowledge about vocabulary and concepts to be covered in an assignment or unit and 2) clarify their understanding of the words and concepts as they study. Educators across content areas can help students build vocabulary and conceptual knowledge by teaching and reinforcing preidentified targeted terms in relation to other key words and concepts prior to reading, listening to lectures, or hearing or viewing an audio or video clip (see Figure 5.2).

The following are steps to teach and/or reinforce word and concept learning.

1. Preselect terms that students will encounter while listening, reading, or viewing material that is essential to understanding the big idea or develops academic vocabulary. For instance, idioms are sometimes applied in literature to describe something. An idiom is an expression whose meanings cannot be inferred from the meanings of the words that make it up (e.g., it's raining cats and dogs). Idioms are difficult for English language learners (ELLs) and those with language learning difficulties. Idioms are part of a larger category called figurative language, which includes metaphors and similes.

2. Display a concept map with the targeted term. If *idiom* is the target word, then it would be inserted in the map as the targeted concept.

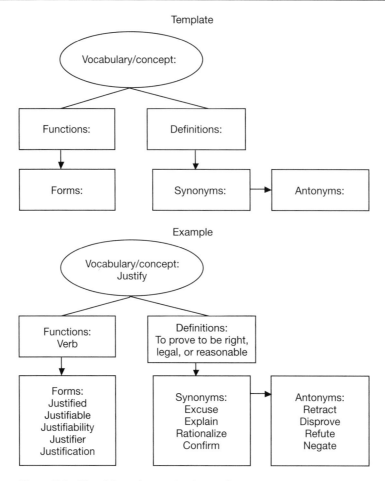

Figure 5.3.   Template and example of a word map.

3.   Provide guidance and promote discussion to help students determine the larger classifica-
     tion of the word. For instance, an idiom is classified under the larger category of figurative
     language.

4.   Write in the classification or category. Figurative language would be written in the box above
     the concept of idiom.

5.   Provide several examples to guide students before asking them to come up with their own idi-
     oms to place in the example boxes. Some common idioms that students may be familiar with
     include frog in my throat, fork in the road, and put your foot in your mouth.

6.   Ask students for examples that they have encountered and write them in if they are accurate
     representations of the concept. Some acceptable examples of idioms include in a pickle, kick
     the bucket, shower with gifts, boiling mad, up a tree, and crocodile tears. If students provide
     nonexamples, such as metaphors or similes, then explain why these are not idioms.

Further word and concept study can be targeted using a word map to build a frame of reference
for unknown words or concepts and to extend word generation to other forms (see Figure 5.3).
     The following are steps for using a word map:

1.   Preselect terms that are important to the meaning of the lesson.

2.   Display a word map (you may provide copies to individual students or small groups).

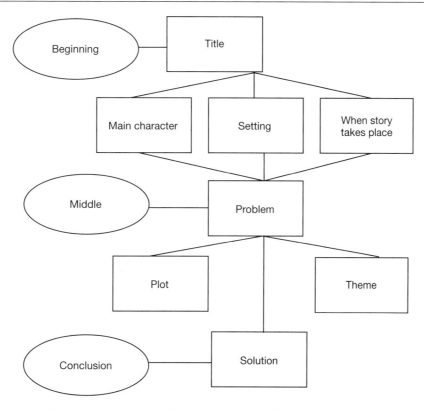

Figure 5.4. Narrative text story elements graphic organizer.

3. Write the word in the oval with the caption vocabulary/concept.

4. Indicate the function of the word in the form box (e.g., noun, verb, adjective, adverb) as it will be used in the lesson.

5. Help students generate other forms of the word by adding affixes.

6. Include a definition, or have students help write one.

7. Generate a list of synonyms and antonyms for the targeted word (students can be asked to independently perform this task after sufficient modeling, teacher guidance, and student practice).

Graphic organizers can also play a critical role in helping students frame information revealed in text patterns in a meaningful way. The traditional outline format often assigned for completion during and after a reading assignment or in preparation for a writing assignment, which is typically organized with headings and subheadings, uses a linear form that requires the learner to have familiarity with the topic to complete it. Students who lack the background knowledge needed to make sense of a topic or to associate it with previously learned material may require a more visual display to connect main and supporting ideas, connect new knowledge with prior learning, or draw inferences that can assist in interpreting and comprehending text.

Story maps are often used in English language arts classrooms to help students record the major parts of narrative text. Think about the story elements you want students to identify, including major characters, plot, setting, and/or sequence of events (see Figure 5.4). Hand draw or make a story elements organizer using presentation software or other commercially available products that are used to design graphic organizers and visual displays.

The following are steps for using a story map organizer:

1. Discuss the main components of a story (e.g., characters, setting, plot, and theme, as well as beginning, middle, and conclusion).

2. Provide each student with a blank story map organizer and model its completion.

3. Have students complete the story map as they read. They should fill in any missing parts after they are done reading. This can be done independently or with a partner.

Readers typically have an easier time understanding narrative text because it is more relatable to everyday experiences (i.e., pursuing dreams, facing barriers, and reacting to circumstances) (Graesser, Singer, & Trabasso, 1994). Reviewing a completed story map in order to create an organized composition that recounts the story structure or conveys sequence can enrich writing to retell or summarize information from narrative text. Reading and writing about expository text differs because it is primarily constructed to communicate information and ideas using text structures that express cause and effect, compare and contrast, problem and solution, and sequence classification. According to Sturm and Rankin-Erickson (2002), "Expository writing in the secondary classroom is more cognitively demanding because the writer is expected to compose longer documents, to use complete text and sentence structures, and to integrate and manipulate information from a wide variety of sources" (p. 124).

The English language arts processes discussed here are essential in teaching and learning mathematics, social studies, science, and more. In particular, reading and writing across curricular areas can be enhanced by using graphic organizers to guide students in communicating their ideas and what they know. The following sections provide graphic organizer tips and examples for content areas other than English language arts.

Mathematics   Math courses make use of common graphic organizers such as hierarchical diagrams, sequence charts, and compare and contrast charts (Baxendell, 2003). Hierarchical organizers provide a systematic arrangement of objects, usually in rows and columns, that help students understand relationships among related terms or ideas. Hierarchical maps are often arranged in a top-down manner in which the main category is placed at the top of the page and the subcategories are placed below (see Figure 5.5). Sequencing organizers denote a series of events, order of steps, operations, or procedures that flow in a linear pattern. Comparing and contrasting differences and similarities across two or more ideas or groups of information and clarifying relationships lend themselves to graphic organizers that use columns, matrices, or Venn diagrams. The Venn diagram shows what characteristics the items being compared have in common within the intersection of two circles. Characteristics that vary are written within the parts of the circle that do not overlap (see Figure 5.6).

The following are steps to promote conceptual understanding and problem solving with graphic organizers:

1. Select mathematical vocabulary and concepts to be pretaught.

2. Identify comprehension skills that students will need to acquire in order to successfully read and interpret problems.

3. Select the appropriate graphic organizer to use with the math lesson and concepts to be taught.

4. Incorporate Steps 1 and 2 into your lesson planning and model how to use the graphic organizer.

Vocabulary knowledge is vital to mathematical learning. Therefore, vocabulary activities similar to those used in English language arts classrooms should be integrated to safeguard that students are assimilating and using vocabulary and concepts essential to learning math. Concept and word map activities can be applied to teach discipline-specific words in mathematics (e.g., quotient,

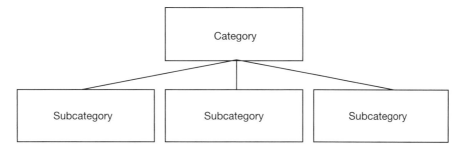

Example: Measures of central tendency hierarchical graphic organizer

Measures of central tendencies		
Sample data: 5, 5, 10, 10, 10, 15, 15, 15, 20, 25		
Mean	Medium	Mode
Average	Middle value	Number(s) occurring most frequently
Sum of data Total number of data $130 \div 10 = 13$	5 5 10 10 **(10)** **(15)** 15 15 20 25 $10 + 15 \div 2 = 12.5$	10 and 15

Figure 5.5. Template and example of a hierarchical diagram for mathematics.

factorization, binomial) as well as academic vocabulary that has potential for generalization across content areas (e.g., analyze, inference, elaborate, justify).

The following are steps to promote vocabulary development using graphic organizers in math:

1. Preteach math vocabulary prior to a lesson.

2. Model vocabulary when teaching new concepts.

3. Require students to practice using the targeted math words and concepts in reading, writing, speaking, and generating visual representations to demonstrate what they know.

Social Studies and Science Instruction in social studies and science relies on reading and learning from informational text. Comparison and contrast organizers (e.g., Venn diagram, matrix) work well for showing similarities and differences between people, places, or concepts. Events are typically presented in sequential order, so a time line (see Figure 5.7) or visual representation depicting a chain of events (e.g., first, next, last) can be utilized in these content areas.

Students who struggle tend to have problems with content area material because learning key concepts relies heavily on technical and abstract text with complex vocabulary (Bulgren et al., 2007), so using the word and concept maps previously discussed is applicable. Table 5.1 shows an example of a vocabulary and concept map designed for teaching social studies and science. Unlike previous examples, this graphic organizer contains built-in supports that provide many opportunities for students to use the target word or concept, as well as to visually organize attributes of the word (definition, form, synonyms), which may contribute to a student deeply understanding the meaning of the word as well as its use.

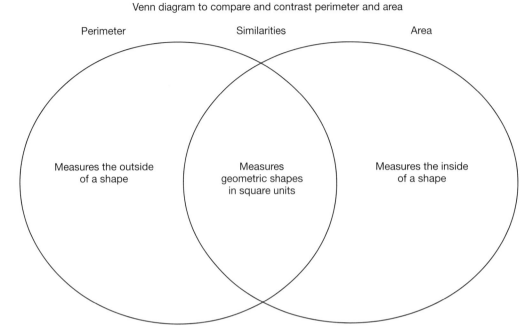

Figure 5.6.   Example of a compare and contrast chart using a Venn diagram in mathematics.

The following are steps for explicitly teaching vocabulary and concepts in social studies and science.

1.   Select appropriate words for preteaching.

2.   Display concept and vocabulary graphic organizer, and have students follow along with their own copy as you introduce the target term.

3.   Pronounce the word and/or concept.

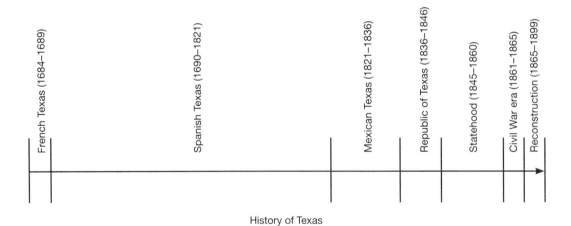

Figure 5.7.   Example time line for social studies.

Table 5.1. Example word and concept map for social studies and science

Vocabulary/concept: Rotation

Student-friendly definition: The spinning of the Earth on its axis

Visual/graphic representation (draw it or paste a picture)	Word forms: Verb	Synonyms
	Rotate Rotating Rotates Rotated	Spin

Read it	The *rotation* of Earth causes day and night. It takes Earth 24 hours to complete a *rotation* on its axis.
Write it (fill in the blanks)	My dad took the car to have its tires _____. My class schedule _____ so that I have gym class every Monday, Wednesday, and Friday.
Use it	Rotation is different from revolution because . . .
Speak it	Describe something that you can rotate.
Think it	Think about why planets rotate.

4. Define the word with a student-friendly definition.

5. Illustrate the word and/or concept with something visual (use hand-drawn art, a picture from the Internet, or a picture taken with a smartphone camera).

6. Ask or tell students how the illustration or visual is representative of the word.

7. Provide an example of the word in two sentences (one in a historical context or that describes a scientific method, process, or event and a second one that is more pertinent to the students' experiences).

8. Use prompts to help students make connections between the unit of study and what they know.

9. Give students opportunities to repeatedly encounter and use the word throughout instruction.

Graphic organizers can be designed to support initial content area instruction, develop vocabulary or reading comprehension of text throughout the reading process (before, during, and/or after the reading), and respond to reading through writing, and can, as well, be used for review and retention of information as in a study guide. Next is a discussion about how graphic organizers can be applied in situations that are student led rather than teacher led.

STUDENT-GENERATED GRAPHIC ORGANIZERS

The preceding part of this chapter primarily describes teacher-led, whole-class application of graphic organizers. The steps and ideas for each content area were influenced by research studies using graphic organizers to help students improve content learning. This section briefly highlights ways in which students can generate their own graphic organizers to help organize abstract concepts, use as a study guide, or use as a springboard for writing. These student-led activities can be done independently or in small, collaborative groups, which have been acknowledged for their ability to promote academic discussion and deeper understanding (Griffin, Malone, & Kame'enui, 1995; Maheady, Harper, & Mallette, 2001).

Independent Creation

One way to encourage students to independently use graphic organizers is to demonstrate how they can be used during tests or when reading for homework. For example, research suggested that story maps can be used to improve reading comprehension when used to organize setting, plot, and theme (Gardill & Jitendra, 1999). Graphic organizers can also be used to develop a time line or sequence chart that may be helpful during an examination regarding major events or in constructing an essay to explain the causes of some phenomenon and its impact.

Fostering Independence Through Collaboration

Teachers can promote student collaboration in pairs or small groups to encourage effective collaboration, productivity, and discourse aided by implementation of graphic organizers. Matching students with varying levels of skills (i.e., heterogeneous grouping) may improve learning of complex concepts for all students because of the more interactive and motivating structure for promoting academic and language acquisition in which all students are responsible for contributing to the group's learning (Maheady et al., 2001). Teachers should facilitate to make sure that all students in the groups are contributing to the completion of the graphic organizer.

The following are steps to promote successful peer-mediated learning with graphic organizers.

1. Pair or group students using assessment and other data sources to reflect a moderate range of abilities (not too high or too low) so that each group has students with the abilities to support each other, especially with literacy and language development.

2. Teach prerequisite skills for collaborating (e.g., using an appropriate voice level and proximity for working in groups, taking turns, listening, speaking, coming to consensus, disagreeing respectfully, self-monitoring, making contributions to the learning task).

3. Ensure students understand the task and how to contribute to developing the graphic organizer to match the learning objective and the steps necessary for successfully completing the task as well as the expected individual and collective outcomes.

CONCLUSION

This chapter described using graphic organizers to improve the academic outcomes of adolescents in inclusive content area classrooms. We reviewed the conceptual framework for graphic organizers, summarized relevant research for students in general education and students with mild disabilities, explained how to design and incorporate graphic organizers into content area instruction, and provided a guided framework for implementation based on research and our instructional experience.

Although there is evidence to suggest that the application of graphic organizers for students with various learning needs is a promising instructional practice or academic intervention (Dexter & Hughes, 2011), researchers and practitioners should continue to investigate the broad efficacy of these practices. Areas for future experimentation include using graphic organizers for ELLs or students with emotional and/or behavioral disorders and continuing to investigate the impact of computer software and technology-based practices on content area learning.

REFERENCES

Ausubel, D.P. (1968). *Educational psychology: A cognitive view.* Austin, TX: Holt, Rinehart & Winston.
Baxendell, B.W. (2003). Consistent, coherent, creative: The 3c's of graphic organizers. *Teaching Exceptional Children, 35*(3), 46–53.
Boon, R.T., Burke, M.D., Fore, C., & Spencer, V.G. (2006). The impact of cognitive organizers and technology-based practices on student success in secondary social studies classrooms. *Journal of Special Education Technology, 21*(1), 5–15.

Boon, R.T., Burke, M.D., Fore, C., & Hagan-Burke, S. (2006). Improving student content knowledge in inclusive social studies classrooms using technology-based cognitive organizers: A systematic replication. *Learning Disabilities: A Contemporary Journal, 4*(1), 1–17.

Bos, C.S., & Anders, P.L. (1990). Effects of interactive vocabulary instruction on the vocabulary learning and reading comprehension of junior-high learning disabled students. *Learning Disability Quarterly, 13,* 31–42.

Bulgren, J., Deshler, D., & Lenz, K. (2007). Engaging adolescents with LD in higher order thinking about history concepts using integrated content enhancement routines. *Journal of Learning Disabilities, 40,* 121–133.

Clark, J.M., & Paivio, A. (1991). Dual coding theory and education. *Educational Psychology Review, 3,* 149–210. doi: 10.1007/BF01320076

Dexter, D.D. (2010). Graphic organizers and their effectiveness for students with learning disabilities. *Thalamus, 26*(1), 51–67.

Dexter, D.D., & Hughes, C.A. (2011). Graphic organizers and students with learning disabilities: A meta-analysis. *Learning Disability Quarterly, 34,* 1–15.

DiCecco, V., & Gleason, M.M. (2002). Using graphic organizers to attain relational knowledge from expository text. *Journal of Learning Disabilities, 35,* 306–320.

Gajria, M., Jitendra, A.K., Sood, S., & Sacks, G. (2007). Improving comprehension of expository text in students with LD: A research synthesis. *Journal of Learning Disabilities, 40,* 210–225.

Gardill, M.C., & Jitendra, A.K. (1999). Advanced story map instruction: Effects on the reading comprehension of students with learning disabilities. *Journal of Special Education, 33,* 2–17.

Gersten, R., Fuchs, L.S., Williams, J.P., & Baker, S. (2001). Teaching reading comprehension strategies to students with learning disabilities: A review of research. *Review of Educational Research, 71,* 279–320.

Graesser, A.C., Singer, M., & Trabasso, T. (1994). Constructing inferences during narrative text comprehension. *Pyschological Review, 10*(3), 371–395.

Griffin, C.C., Malone, L.D., & Kame'enui, E.J. (1995). Effects of graphic organizer instruction on fifth-grade students. *Journal of Educational Research, 89*(2), 98–107.

Griffin, C.C., Simmons, D.C., & Kame'enui, E.J. (1991). Investigating the effectiveness of graphic organizer instruction on the comprehension and recall of science content by students with learning disabilities. *Journal of Reading, Writing, and Learning Disabilities International, 7,* 355–376.

Guastello, E.F., Beasley, T.M., & Sinatra, R.C. (2000). Concept mapping effects on science content comprehension of low-achieving inner city seventh graders. *Remedial and Special Education, 20*(6), 356–364.

Hall, T., & Strangman, N. (2002). *Graphic organizers.* Retrieved from http://aim.cast.org/learn/historyarchive/backgroundpapers/graphic_organizers

Hawk, P. (1986). Using graphic organizers to increase achievement in middle school life science. *Science Education, 70*(1), 81–87.

Kim, A., Vaughn, S., Wanzek, J., & Wei, S. (2004). Graphic organizers and their effects on the reading comprehension of students with LD: A synthesis of research. *Journal of Learning Disabilities, 37,* 105–118.

Maheady, L., Harper, G.F., & Mallette, B. (2001). Peer-mediated instruction and interventions and students with mild disabilities. *Remedial and Special Education, 22*(1), 4–14.

Merkley, D.M., & Jefferies, D. (2000). Guidelines for implementing a graphic organizer. *The Reading Teacher, 54*(4), 350–357.

Moore, W.D., & Readence, J.E. (1984). A quantitative and qualitative review of graphic organizers. *Journal of Educational Research, 78*(1), 11–17.

Nagy, W.E. (1988). *Teaching vocabulary to improve reading comprehension.* Newark, DE: International Reading Association.

Paivio, A. (1986). *Mental representations: A dual coding approach.* New York, NY: Oxford University Press.

Sturm, J.M., & Rankin-Erickson, J.L. (2002). Effects of hand-drawn and computer-generated concept mapping on the expository writing of middle school students with learning disabilities. *Learning Disabilities Research and Practice, 17*(2), 124–139.

Twyman, T., McCleery, J., & Tindal, G. (2006). Using concepts to frame history content. *Journal of Experimental Education, 74,* 331–349.

Vacca, R.T., & Vacca, J.A.L. (2008). *Content area reading: Literacy and learning across the curriculum* (9th ed.). Boston, MA: Pearson Education.

Wanzek, J., Wexler, J., Vaughn, S., & Ciullo, S. (2010). Reading interventions for struggling readers in the upper elementary grades: A synthesis of 20 years of research. *Reading and Writing: An Interdisciplinary Journal, 23,* 889–912.

6 | Supporting Struggling Readers in High School

A Peer-Mediated Approach

Jessica R. Toste, Douglas Fuchs, and Lynn S. Fuchs

One can expect to find considerable academic diversity in a typical high school classroom—students with varying skills, abilities, and interests. In the upper-elementary grades, the number of words read correctly in 1 minute ranges from 0 to 183 in an average class of 22 students (L.S. Fuchs & Fuchs, 2003). This range in reading skill increases as students move up in grade level and presents a challenge for most teachers in addressing students' learning needs. As such, there is often a disconnect between student diversity and classroom instruction; with teachers implementing lessons that are directed toward the average student in the class and failing to meet the needs of those who perform below or above average (e.g., Baker & Zigmond, 1990; D. Fuchs, Fuchs, Mathes, & Simmons, 1997; McIntosh, Vaughn, Schumm, Haager, & Lee, 1993). It is easy to understand why many high school students struggle with content area instruction that does not account for widely varying reading skills in the classroom.

READING IN THE CONTENT AREAS

Only 35% of eighth graders in the United States read at or above proficiency levels (National Assessment of Educational Progress [NAEP], 2009). Thus, it is not surprising that many students struggle to engage with and learn from texts at their grade level in content areas. Science and social studies classes can be particularly difficult for students with reading disabilities (e.g., Scruggs, Mastropieri, & Boon, 1998; Scruggs, Mastropieri, & Okolo, 2008). Textbooks are written at levels that generally exceed the reading levels of these students (Mastropieri, Scruggs, & Graetz, 2003). Instruction is often based on textbook reading and teacher lecture—with content being covered at a rapid pace to ensure that students have adequate knowledge for state tests that they will be required to take at the end of the year. Students with disabilities may be overwhelmed with the demands of such learning environments (Mastropieri & Scruggs, 2000).

Previous studies have found that the classroom's instructional environment can have a positive effect on the process of learning for students (Rohrbeck, Ginsburg-Block, Fantuzzo, & Miller, 2003; Ryan & Deci, 2000; Swanson & Hoskyn, 1998). Students with reading disabilities require instruction that is more explicit, intensive, and supportive than what is provided in the general classroom (Foorman & Torgesen, 2001; Torgesen, 2004). General education teachers, however, often find it difficult to extend the time and effort required to adapt their content curriculum to meet individual students' learning needs (Vaughn & Schumm, 1995).

Nonetheless, in a report from the U.S. Department of Education's Institute of Education Sciences (IES), there is resounding agreement that literacy must be a primary goal for adolescent learners. The authors of the IES document stated that

> The time has come to consider seriously the support that needs to be given to struggling readers and the role that every teacher needs to play in working toward higher levels of literacy among all adolescents, regardless of their reading abilities. (Kamil et al., 2008, p. 4)

Kamil et al. (2008) outlined recommendations for improving adolescent literacy, including the need to enhance pedagogical practices that increase reading engagement and conceptual learning by providing opportunities for self-directed and collaborative learning. These classroom activities not only augment the learning and motivation of struggling readers, but also support general social and cognitive needs during the developmental period of adolescence. Nevertheless, the IES report begs the question of how students with disabilities receive this type of instruction in general education classrooms without the necessity of awaiting referral for special education services.

HIGH-QUALITY CLASSROOM INSTRUCTION

Response to intervention (RTI) is a policy and instructional initiative that has attempted to reconceptualize service delivery into a multitiered system oriented toward prevention and early intervention (Fletcher & Vaughn, 2009; L.S. Fuchs & Fuchs, 2007, 2008). In RTI models, schools organize their efforts into three levels that represent a continuum of increasing intensity of support (D. Fuchs, Compton, Fuchs, Bryant, & Davis, 2008; O'Connor, Bocian, Beebe-Frankenberger, & Linklater, 2010; Simmons et al., 2011; Vaughn et al., 2010). These levels can be framed as primary prevention, secondary prevention, and tertiary prevention.

Primary prevention refers to high-quality classroom instruction that takes place within the general education classroom. This includes the core instructional program and practices that provide opportunity for instructional differentiation, as well as accommodations that permit all students to gain access to instruction. Secondary prevention provides more targeted intervention for struggling readers. This intervention often takes the form of small-group instruction that relies on a scientifically validated program; the teacher implementing this program will meet with students several times each week (e.g., 3 or 4 days per week). Tertiary prevention efforts involve the most intensive support services and intervention for students who have not responded adequately to previous instruction. This generally involves one-to-one intervention with increased frequency (e.g., 5 days per week).

Through the lens of RTI, it may be assumed that high school students would receive remedial support for reading difficulties outside of the classroom. It would be an inadequate application of this multitiered model, however, if these same students were not also receiving high-quality instruction in their general education classroom. We then return to the concern that teachers often do not adapt instruction to meet the diverse learning needs presented in each classroom. A possible remedy is using differentiated instruction, which has been discussed as an essential approach for supporting the needs of diverse learners (Carolan & Guinn, 2007). Teachers who differentiate instruction have been described by some as using knowledge about their students' varying experiences, interests, learning styles, and readiness levels; tapping multiple sensory modalities in their instruction; grouping students flexibly; varying the pace of instruction; and assessing student learning with varied and balanced procedures (Kapusnick & Hauslein, 2001; Tomlinson, 1999).

Various approaches have been characterized as supporting differentiation. All aim to supplement core instruction and, thereby, make general education more accommodating to a greater diversity of students. Regardless of its effectiveness, however, differentiated instruction does not and will not replace secondary and tertiary prevention, which are needed by some students to master basic reading skills. This chapter discusses peer-mediated approaches to learning to address academic diversity within the context of the general education classroom.

PEER-MEDIATED APPROACHES TO LEARNING

A peer-mediated approach to instruction has been shown to create increased opportunities for direct instruction and the repeated practice often required by struggling students at the high school level (L.S. Fuchs, Fuchs, & Kazdan, 1999; D. Fuchs et al., 2010; Marshak, Mastropieri, & Scruggs, 2011; Mastropieri, Spencer, Scruggs, & Talbott, 2000). Several approaches to peer-mediated learning are described next, and Peer-Assisted Learning Strategies (PALS) for reading, which requires the classroom teacher to reorganize all students in dyads, are emphasized.

Peer tutoring is inherently a social process that simultaneously engages students in the experience of teaching and learning. Although academic gain for the tutee by exposure and rehearsal of learned material is the most common goal of peer tutoring (Fulk & King, 2001; Osguthorpe & Scruggs, 1986), peer tutoring may also provide support for students to learn how to become better learners. That is, peer tutoring presents a learning structure for the tutor and tutee that provides individualization, modeling, and motivation (Johnson-Pynn & Nisbet, 2002; Topping & Ehly, 1998). Individualization through the one-to-one attention given to each student in some peer tutoring arrangements maximizes the active participation of tutor and tutee because it involves focused attention, explanation, demonstration, direct feedback, and reinforcement of the tutee's responses. Tutors test their knowledge and receive feedback through the questioning and understanding of the tutee. Teachers are also able to adjust the level of the materials and pace of the activities within each dyad. Second, using peers as models maximizes the possibility that students will benefit from their demonstration. Students often look to peers as models because they may be similar in age, knowledge, and experience. In addition, the motivational system often used in peer tutoring consists of systematic reinforcement. Tangible rewards can be effective motivators, but the most frequent reward tends to be social in nature, such as attention and verbal feedback (Chun & Winter, 1999; Cohen, 1986; Medcalf, Glynn, & Moore, 2004).

Reciprocal Teaching

Palincsar and Brown's (1984) reciprocal teaching method focuses on improving reading comprehension. Reciprocal teaching addresses the lack of comprehension instruction in classrooms (Durkin, 1979; Rosenshine & Meister, 1994) by providing a framework to teach students four cognitive strategies (i.e., questioning, summarizing, clarifying, predicting). Students work in small groups and read expository text together, paragraph by paragraph. They learn and practice how to generate questions, summarize text, clarify meanings (at word and sentence levels), and predict subsequent paragraphs. These strategies form the basis of reciprocal teaching, which has been found to be an effective approach with older students.

The nature of reciprocal teaching is grounded in Vygotsky's (1978) theoretical work on the role of cognition in mediated learning. Specifically, he posited that optimal learning takes place when instruction is targeted between the actual skill level of the student and his or her level of potential development. Palincsar and Brown's (1984) work attempted to present a practical application of this theory through apprenticeship modeling. Scaffolding instruction is the process underlying reciprocal teaching. The teacher provides direct instruction and models the four strategies during the early stages of reciprocal teaching; then students practice them as the teachers provide feedback by modeling, coaching, and explaining. The teacher gradually transfers responsibility for the program's implementation to the students, while observing and supporting the students as needed. The reciprocal teaching sessions eventually become a dialogue among the students as they work with and support one another. They prompt each other to use strategies, explain their strategy use, and comment on the application.

Rosenshine and Meister (1994) conducted a meta-analytic review of 16 studies that investigated the efficacy of reciprocal teaching for improving students' reading comprehension skills. Their analysis concluded that there was a median effect size of 0.32 for studies that utilized standardized measures of reading comprehension compared with a median effect size of 0.88 for studies that used comprehension tests that were designed by the experimenter. Overall, results did not vary significantly if students were taught the four cognitive strategies or a variable number of strategies (two, three, or ten). Rosenshine and Meister did find that the instructional timing of the cognitive strategies made a difference when measuring performance on tests designed by the experimenter; specifically, they found that when strategies were explicitly taught before engaging in the reciprocal teaching procedure (e.g., Palincsar, David, & Brown, 1989; Pearson & Dole, 1987), students' comprehension skills increased more than when the strategies were taught during the process of reciprocal teaching. Although this review suggested that question generation and summarization may be the strategies that result in greatest gains for students, analysis of the results from these empirical investigations did not provide a clear answer regarding the most effective cognitive strategies for improving comprehension.

There has been ample support for using reciprocal teaching approaches and the notion that reading comprehension should be explicitly taught. Pressley (1997), however, wrote that reciprocal teaching may be difficult for teachers and students to use because of their relative unfamiliarity with the use of explicit strategies to strengthen reading comprehension. Another concern has been that students who are low achievers may inadvertently become marginalized through the peer-mediation process (cf. Hacker & Tenant, 2002).

Classwide Peer Tutoring

Organizing students into same-age dyads is the instructional format adopted by most peer tutoring activities. Delquadri and colleagues have done much to explore this in the context of classwide peer tutoring (CWPT; Delquadri, Greenwood, Whorton, Carta, & Hall, 1986). CWPT has been shown to be an effective academic intervention for basic skill acquisition and content area learning (Greenwood, Delquadri, & Hall, 1989; Hughes & Fredrick, 2006; Maheady & Harper, 1987; Mastropieri, Scruggs, Spencer, & Fontana, 2003; Utley et al., 2001).

CWPT requires that students are randomly paired with a peer each week and given lists of spelling words, simple mathematical problems, or reading assignments from a shared text. Following a structured teacher-developed lesson, the students tutor one another on the same material. The tutor presents an instructional item and provides feedback following the tutee's response. The pair takes turns as tutor and tutee each day and earns points for providing correct answers, reading without errors, and correcting mistakes. Each pair is assigned to one of two classroom teams and the points accumulated by each pair go to their team, with a winner being declared each week.

There is evidence to suggest that participation in CWPT results in improvement of basic skills mastery (Greenwood, Terry, Arreaga-Mayer, & Finney, 1992). Greenwood et al. (1989) examined the efficacy of CWPT when students participated in the program from first through fourth grade. Classrooms were randomly assigned to either an experimental or control condition. CWPT students demonstrated superior reading, language, and mathematics scores at the end of fourth grade. Furthermore, students in CWPT classes were less likely to have been identified with a learning disability or emotional and/or behavioral disorder. CWPT has also been shown to be beneficial for students with disabilities in general education classrooms (e.g., Sideridis et al., 1997).

Although the efficacy of CWPT has been demonstrated, there is concern that it focuses only on basic skills. Although repeated practice and corrective feedback is essential for struggling readers (e.g., Torgesen et al., 1999), CWPT does not promote the use of higher-order skills that may be necessary for success in the curriculum.

Peer-Assisted Learning Strategies

PALS was developed with the goal of combining the supportive, engaging, and effective dyadic format of CWPT with some of the more challenging, higher-order tasks of reciprocal teaching (McMaster, Fuchs, & Fuchs, 2006). PALS provides teachers with the opportunity to modify instructional materials, activities, rewards, and expectations for performance. Because students are divided into dyads, teachers have the opportunity to assign different tasks to different dyads and the flexibility to include virtually all students in the activities.

PALS programs in reading have been developed and field tested for preschool (D. Fuchs et al., 2004), kindergarten (D. Fuchs, Fuchs, Thompson, Al Otaiba et al., 2001; D. Fuchs, Fuchs, Thompson, Svenson et al., 2001; D. Fuchs, Fuchs, Thompson et al., 2002), first grade (D. Fuchs, Fuchs, Svenson et al., 2001; D. Fuchs, Fuchs, Yen et al., 2001), second through sixth grade (D. Fuchs, Fuchs, Mathes, & Martinez, 2002; D. Fuchs et al., 2008; D. Fuchs et al., 1997), and high school (L.S. Fuchs et al., 1999).

Partner Reading

The first reader reads aloud for 5 minutes.
The second reader reads aloud for 5 minutes.
1. For 2 minutes, the FIRST READER and SECOND READER alternate retelling the main ideas that happened in the story.

Figure 6.1.   Posted guidelines for Peer-Assisted Learning Strategies (PALS) partner reading activity. (Reprinted with permission from manual, *Peer-Assisted Learning Strategies [PALS] for High School Students.* [http://kc.vanderbilt.edu/pals/])

IMPLEMENTING PEER-ASSISTED LEARNING STRATEGIES

The PALS program was originally developed by researchers at Vanderbilt University for students in second through sixth grade (see D. Fuchs et al., 1997) to promote reading fluency and comprehension. There are several important features of PALS. First, all students in a class are paired to form tutoring dyads. Second, students are trained to use specific prompts, corrections, and feedback. Third, PALS incorporates frequent verbal interactions between tutors and tutees, increasing students' opportunities to respond (Delquadri et al., 1986; Greenwood et al., 1989). Fourth, roles are reciprocal so that both students in a pair serve as tutor and tutee during each session. Fifth, PALS consists of a set of structured activities, and students are trained to implement them independently. These activities include partner reading with retell, paragraph shrinking, and prediction relay.

Structure of Peer-Assisted Learning Strategies Activities

Training   Teachers use a set of brief, scripted lessons to train all students. The training lessons for each activity last 30–60 minutes per session and take 2–3 sessions to implement. These lessons include scripted teacher presentations, student practice, and teacher feedback. Following training, students participate in 35-minute PALS sessions, 3 times per week.

Pairs and Teams   The teacher determines the pairs for each dyad by first rank-ordering all the students from the strongest to the weakest reader. The teacher then divides the rank-ordered list in half, pairs the strongest reader from the top half with the strongest reader from the bottom half and so forth until all students are paired. Although the tutoring roles are reciprocal during each tutoring session, the strongest reader always reads aloud first to serve as a model for the weaker reader. Each pair is assigned to one of two teams for which they earn points during PALS. These points are awarded for correct responses during the activities. Each pair marks their points by slashing through numbers on a scorecard. Teachers also circulate among the pairs during PALS to monitor performance and award bonus points for cooperative behavior and following the PALS procedures. The pairs report the number of points they earned for their teams at the end of each week, and the teacher adds them up to determine the winning team. The teacher creates new pairs and teams every 4 weeks.

Partner Reading   Partner reading with retell is the first activity during each PALS session (see Figure 6.1). Each student reads aloud from connected text for 5 minutes. This text comes from the literature selected by the teacher and should be at an appropriate level for the weaker reader in each pair. The stronger reader goes first, then the weaker reader recites the same text. Whenever the reader makes an error, the tutor says, "Stop, you missed that word. Can you figure it out?" If the reader does not figure out the word in 4 seconds, then the tutor says, "That word is ____. What word?" The reader says the word and continues reading. After both students have read, the weaker reader retells the sequence of events just read for 2 minutes. Students earn 1 point for each sentence read correctly and 10 points for the retell.

Paragraph Shrinking   Paragraph shrinking is designed to develop comprehension through summarization and main idea identification (see Figure 6.2). Students use a questioning strategy to direct their attention to the important ideas or events in the text (e.g., Jenkins, Heliotis, Stein,

Paragraph Shrinking

Main idea statement:

Name who or what. (The main person, animal, place, or thing).
Tell the most important thing about the who or what.
Tell the main idea in 10 words or less.

Figure 6.2.   Posted guidelines for Peer-Assisted Learning Strategies (PALS) paragraph shrinking activity. (Reprinted with permission from manual, *Peer-Assisted Learning Strategies [PALS] for High School Students.* [http://kc.vanderbilt.edu/pals/])

& Haynes, 1987). Students continue reading orally during this activity, but they stop at the end of each paragraph to identify the main idea. The tutor asks the reader to identify who or what the paragraph is mainly about and the most important detail about the who or what. The reader must condense (or shrink) this information into 10 words or fewer. If the tutor determines that the reader's answer is incorrect, then he or she says, "That's not quite right. Skim the paragraph and try again." After the reader provides a new answer, the tutor decides whether the answer is correct. If so, then he or she gives 1 point each for correctly identifying the who or what, stating the most important detail, and using 10 words or fewer to state the main idea. If the tutor determines that the answer is incorrect, then he or she provides a correct answer and the pair continues reading. The partners switch roles after 5 minutes.

Prediction Relay   Prediction relay requires students to make predictions and then confirm or disconfirm them. This activity is included in PALS because making predictions is a strategy associated with improvements in reading comprehension (Palincsar & Brown, 1984). It consists of four steps: the reader makes a prediction about what will happen on the next half page to be read, reads the half page aloud, confirms or disconfirms the prediction, and summarizes the main idea (see Figure 6.3). If the tutor disagrees with the prediction, then he or she says, "I don't agree. Think of a better prediction." Students earn points for each reasonable prediction, for reading each half page, for accurately confirming or disconfirming the prediction, and for identifying the main idea in 10 words or fewer. Again, the students switch roles after 5 minutes.

Prediction Relay

Predict
What do you predict will happen next?

⬇

Read
Read the next half page

⬇

Check
Did the prediction come true?

⬇

Shrink
Name who or what the page was about.
Tell the most important things discussed.

Figure 6.3.   Student procedure for Peer-Assisted Learning Strategies (PALS) prediction relay activity. (Reprinted with permission from manual, *Peer-Assisted Learning Strategies [PALS] for High School Students.* [http://kc.vanderbilt.edu/pals/])

High School Modifications High School PALS is similar to PALS for second through sixth grades in that students work reciprocally in pairs, earn points for their teams, and work on the same three activities. High school PALS has three unique elements, however. First, students switch partners every day instead of every 4 weeks. This accommodates the more frequent absences of high school students, which makes partner consistency difficult. High school students also seem to prefer interacting with different classmates. Second, the motivational system is based on a "work" theme. Pairs earn PALS dollars, which they deposit into checking accounts. They maintain these accounts and write checks to order items from a PALS catalog (e.g., music, fast-food restaurant gift cards, donated sports apparel). Finally, students typically read from expository text, rather than narrative, during PALS. The text is targeted to address issues pertinent to their lives, such as work and social relationships.

EVIDENCE TO SUPPORT PEER-ASSISTED LEARNING STRATEGIES

PALS programs in reading have been applied to students in preschool through high school classrooms. Multiple investigations of PALS implementation have demonstrated that this approach improves the reading achievement of students who are low, average, and high achievers (e.g., D. Fuchs et al., 1997; D. Fuchs, Fuchs, Thompson, Svenson et al., 2001; McMaster et al., 2006; Simmons, Fuchs, Fuchs, Hodge, & Mathes, 1994). Ample evidence also supports the effectiveness of PALS in supporting the academic performance of English language learners (e.g., Saenz, Fuchs, & Fuchs, 2005) and students with emotional and/or behavioral disorders (e.g., Spencer, 2006; Spencer, Scruggs, & Mastropieri, 2003; Spencer, Simpson, & Oatis, 2009).

Researchers documented positive outcomes from PALS implementation in academic and social domains. In a large-scale experimental field trial (D. Fuchs et al., 1997), 12 schools in three districts (one urban and two suburban) were stratified by student achievement and socioeconomic status and randomly assigned to PALS or non–PALS conditions. PALS was implemented for 15 weeks in 20 classrooms as a supplement to the reading curriculum. Twenty additional non–PALS classrooms continued with their regular reading programs. After the 15 weeks, students in PALS classrooms significantly outperformed their control counterparts in terms of growth on the Comprehensive Reading Assessment Battery (L.S. Fuchs, Fuchs, & Hamlett, 1989), a measure of reading fluency and comprehension. These effects held for average and low achievers, including students with learning disabilities who had been mainstreamed in general education classrooms. Results in another study (D. Fuchs, Fuchs, Mathes et al., 2002) indicated that students with learning disabilities in PALS classes enjoyed greater social acceptance than those with learning disabilities in non–PALS classes. These findings suggest that PALS has social and academic benefits—an important consideration in planning instructional practices that address the developmental needs of adolescents.

Peer-Assisted Learning Strategies in High School Classrooms

PALS has been demonstrated to be a promising instructional strategy for adolescents struggling with reading (L.S. Fuchs et al., 1999). The following section describes several studies at Vanderbilt University and elsewhere that have examined the effectiveness of high school PALS.

L.S. Fuchs et al. (1999) investigated the impact of PALS on struggling readers' fluency, reading comprehension, and attitudes toward reading. Eighteen special education and remedial reading teachers in 10 high schools were assigned to PALS or contrast treatments. PALS was implemented 5 times every 2 weeks (e.g., 2.5 times per week) over a 16-week period. The PALS lessons included partner reading, paragraph shrinking, and prediction relay. Contrast teachers taught reading in accordance with their usual approaches, which did not include peer-mediated methods. After 16 weeks of intervention, students in the PALS condition demonstrated significantly greater growth in reading comprehension than students in non–PALS classrooms. There were no differences between conditions in terms of reading fluency or general attitudes toward reading.

Mastropieri et al. (2001) randomly assigned struggling readers to either traditional teacher-led instruction or a comprehension strategy-based peer tutoring condition during seventh-grade

English classes. This study replicated the PALS procedures described in L.S. Fuchs et al. (1999), and students in the peer tutoring condition were explicitly trained to use the three-step paragraph shrinking strategy. Activities in the traditional instruction condition were teacher led and comprised round-robin oral reading, silent reading, accompanying worksheets, and teacher questioning for comprehension. After 5 weeks, students in the tutoring condition significantly outperformed their peers in the control condition on reading comprehension measures. When interviewed about their experiences, students in the PALS group reported that they liked spending more time reading during tutoring than in their English classes, reading to a single partner than to an entire class of students, and working with peer tutors. Students also expressed concerns, however, about their partners and the decoding and comprehension activities. Some disliked their teachers assigning partners, favoring an opportunity to select their own partners. Many students expressed the fact that they had difficulty decoding texts. Some said that they could not read as fast as their partners and they felt bad about it. Teachers also reported benefits and challenges with implementing PALS with their struggling readers. Reported benefits included enjoying the tutoring, acknowledging the value-added component of reading comprehension strategy instruction, and reporting that more instructional time was devoted to reading during tutoring activities. Challenges included handling absences, monitoring dyads, and making appropriate dyad matches. Finally, teachers found that mixed-gender dyads were almost completely unworkable in these seventh-grade classes.

Armani, Mastropieri, and Scruggs (2001) replicated these procedures in inclusive ninth-grade classes of students with reading difficulties. Again, students were randomly assigned to tutoring and traditional instruction during their English classes. Tutoring took place during reading of an assigned novel study. The intervention occurred throughout the length of time necessary to cover the novel and was cotaught by the special education and general education teachers. Partner groups included one strong reader and one weak reader for the peer tutoring activities. The partners engaged in oral reading and text summarization (paragraph shrinking) during the peer tutoring. Differing from previous results, no significant differences were obtained between treatment conditions on oral reading fluency, comprehension, or recall from the novel. In follow-up interviews, the special education teacher reported that she liked the tutoring, but the general education teacher did not appear to be receptive to the intervention and was somewhat reluctant to give up instructional time. These suggest that the values of the teacher, as well as the fidelity of PALS implementation, may be very much related to the success of this instructional approach for students.

Mastropieri, Scruggs, Spencer, and Fontana (2003) investigated the use of peer tutoring versus teacher-directed guided notes in world history for secondary-level students with mild disabilities. Sixteen students participated in 9 weeks of one of the two instructional conditions. The same special education teachers taught students during world history classes. Findings indicated that students who participated in peer tutoring significantly outperformed those who participated in the guided notes condition on content area tests. No significant differences were obtained on oral reading fluency measures, but students in the tutoring condition performed significantly better at using a reading comprehension summarization strategy independently and at remembering the strategy steps.

The studies that investigated PALS at the high school level found that this is a promising approach for adolescents who struggle with reading. High school students who participated in PALS significantly improved their reading comprehension scores in comparison to similar students in non–PALS programs. In addition, PALS students reported working harder with their peers and working harder to improve their reading. Nevertheless, taken together, the findings from these studies require a closer examination of the implementation of PALS. In the one study that did not show significant gains among the PALS versus non–PALS programs (Armani et al., 2001), there are questions regarding fidelity of implementation if teachers are not receptive to using evidence-based practices in their classes. Many researchers observed that fidelity of treatment implementation and teacher attitude toward interventions profoundly influence the impact of any intervention

(Scruggs & Mastropieri, 1996). Introducing a variable that may dramatically change the administration of an otherwise efficacious intervention is something else to consider; in the case of Armani and colleagues' study (2001), PALS was delivered using a coteaching format that differed from other PALS studies and may have influenced the teachers' commitment to implementation.

IMPLICATIONS FOR PRACTICE

The close involvement of classroom teachers in developing and implementing PALS has been particularly important to its research (e.g., D. Fuchs & Fuchs, 1998; D. Fuchs, Fuchs, & Burish, 2000; D. Fuchs, Fuchs, Thompson, Al Otaiba, et al., 2001). Teachers' collaboration with PALS researchers has led to a set of programs that are not only effective for many students, but are also efficient and feasible for classroom use. Many schools and districts have adopted PALS as part of their reading curricula. Of course, important considerations exist regarding the implementation of PALS.

Fidelity of Implementation

Results of the large-scale studies reviewed in this chapter demonstrate that teachers can implement PALS with success. Consistently implementing the program with fidelity is a key to this success; that is, the activities follow the procedures that have been established during PALS development. Several efforts are made to ensure the fidelity of PALS implementation when conducting research studies—professional development, technical support, and scheduling of instructional time (D. Fuchs & Fuchs, 2005).

Teachers participate in a full-day training session prior to beginning PALS. This training provides teachers with the opportunity to see demonstrations of PALS, practice the activities with guidance and support, and ask questions before implementing the program in their classrooms. The program can be implemented using the comprehensive PALS manuals, but it is recommended that teachers participate in a training workshop. In studies of PALS development, teachers were provided with on-site technical support from research staff who made regular classroom visits to observe, answer questions, and troubleshoot problems that arose. Although this support is not generally available to classroom teachers, it can be helpful for a teacher to videotape the activities or have a colleague (also trained in PALS) to observe his or her implementation. Finally, PALS must be implemented at least 3 times per week for 15–20 weeks. This may seem like a significant time commitment, but teachers have found it to be feasible. Many have implemented PALS during their scheduled independent reading time, finding the program to be practical and efficient (D. Fuchs et al., 1997, 2000).

Nonresponders

Although PALS appears to benefit many students, including students with disabilities, some children do not make adequate achievement gains despite participating in the program. An estimated 20% of students without disabilities who are low achievers (Mathes, Howard, Allen, & Fuchs, 1998) and more than 50% of students with disabilities (D. Fuchs, Fuchs, Thompson, Al Obtaiba et al., 2002) have not responded to PALS, as measured by growth on tests of phonological awareness, decoding, and word recognition. Al Otaiba and Fuchs (2002) attempted to identify characteristics of children predictive of their responsiveness to PALS. They found nonresponders to have relatively weak phonological awareness, attention and behavior control, and cognitive development or to attend high-poverty Title I schools.

Given this knowledge, we know that even generally effective treatment programs will never fully address the learning needs for all students—even best practice programs will not be universally effective (Al Otaiba & Fuchs, 2002; Fuchs & Young, 2006). Hence, beyond primary prevention efforts, including supplemental programs such as PALS, there is the need to design instruction specifically for students who remain unresponsive to these programs. We would expect that high-quality classroom instruction and differentiated instructional practices within an RTI framework will meet the needs of a wider range of students than are currently being addressed in many general education classrooms. But it is necessary to recognize that there will be a considerable minority of students that do not show improvement and, thus, will require access to more intensive and individualized services (secondary and tertiary prevention).

CONCLUSION

Adolescent literacy has often gone overlooked in content area learning, assuming that students' reading abilities are not the responsibility of the general education teacher at this level. As it becomes clear that a large number of high school students continue to read below proficiency level (NAEP, 2009), it has been noted that practices that address struggling readers at the secondary level must be improved (Kamil et al., 2008). Peer tutoring is one approach that enhances classroom instruction at the high school level by providing students with opportunities to engage in self-directed and collaborative learning.

PALS is one particular approach that transforms knowledge about reading instruction into routines and programs that real teachers can implement. The materials developed for PALS are concrete, specific, and user friendly—they can complement most instructional approaches and content areas as it supplements, rather than replaces, teachers' ongoing classroom practices. PALS researchers are identifying the kinds of students for whom PALS is not beneficial and finding ways to increase its effectiveness for them (McMaster, Fuchs, Fuchs, & Compton, 2005). In addition, researchers are examining how to maximize the accessibility of PALS to teachers who struggle to find ways to implement evidence-based instruction amid all of the other challenges they face.

REFERENCES

Al Otaiba, S., & Fuchs, D. (2002). Characteristics of children who are unresponsive to early literacy intervention: A review of the literature. *Remedial and Special Education, 23,* 300–315.

Armani, L., Mastropieri, M.A., & Scruggs, T.E. (2001). *Peer tutoring as an inclusion strategy in secondary English classes.* Fairfax, VA: George Mason University, Graduate School of Education.

Baker, J.M., & Zigmond, N. (1990). Are regular education classes equipped to accommodate students with learning disabilities? *Exceptional Children, 56,* 515–526.

Carolan, J., & Guinn, A. (2007). Differentiation: Examining how master teachers weave differentiation into their daily practice can help reluctant teachers take the plunge. *Educational Leadership, 64*(5), 44–47.

Chun, C.C., & Winter, S. (1999). Classwide peer tutoring with and without reinforcement: Effects on academic responding, content coverage, achievement, intrinsic interest, and reported project experience. *Educational Psychology, 19,* 191–205.

Cohen, J. (1986). Theoretical considerations of peer tutoring. *Psychology in the Schools, 23,* 175–193.

Delquadri, J., Greenwood, C.R., Whorton, D., Carta, J.J., & Hall, R.V. (1986). Classwide peer tutoring. *Exceptional Children, 52,* 535–542.

Durkin, D. (1979). What classroom observations reveal about reading comprehension. *Reading Research Quarterly, 14,* 518–544.

Fletcher, J.M., & Vaughn, S. (2009). Response to intervention: Preventing and remediating academic difficulties. *Child Development Perspectives, 3,* 30–37.

Foorman, B.R., & Torgesen, J. (2001). Critical elements of classroom and small-group instruction promote reading success in all students. *Learning Disabilities Research and Practice, 16*(4), 203–212.

Fuchs, D., Compton, D.C., Fuchs, L.S., Bryant, J., & Davis, G.N. (2008). Making "secondary intervention" work in a three-tier responsiveness-to-intervention model: Findings from the first-grade longitudinal reading study at the National Research Center on Learning Disabilities. *Reading and Writing: An Interdisciplinary Journal, 21*(4), 413–436.

Fuchs, D., & Fuchs, L.S. (1998). Researchers and teachers working closely together to adapt instruction for diverse learners. *Learning Disabilities Research and Practice, 13,* 126–137.

Fuchs, D., & Fuchs, L.S. (2005). Peer-Assisted Learning Strategies: Promoting word recognition, fluency, and reading comprehension in young children. *Journal of Special Education, 39*(1), 34–44.

Fuchs, D., Fuchs, L.S., & Burish, P. (2000). Peer-Assisted Learning Strategies: An empirically-supported practice to promote reading achievement. *Learning Disabilities Research and Practice, 15,* 85–91.

Fuchs, D., Fuchs, L.S., Eaton, S., Young, T., Mock, D., & Dion, E. (2004). *Hearing sounds in words: Preschoolers helping preschoolers in a downward extension of peer-assisted learning strategies.* Paper presented at the National Learning Disabilities Association Annual Conference, Atlanta, GA.

Fuchs, D., Fuchs, L.S., Mathes, P.G., & Martinez, E.A. (2002). Preliminary evidence on the social standing of students with learning disabilities in PALS and no-PALS classrooms. *Learning Disabilities Research and Practice, 17,* 205–215.

Fuchs, D., Fuchs, L.S., Mathes, P.G., & Simmons, D.C. (1997). Peer-assisted learning strategies: Making classrooms more responsive to diversity. *American Educational Research Journal, 34,* 174–206.

Fuchs, D., Fuchs, L.S., Mathes, P.G., & Simmons, D.C. (2008). *Peer-assisted learning strategies in reading: Second through sixth grade reading manual (Revised).* Nashville, TN: Vanderbilt University.

Fuchs, D., Fuchs, L.S., Shamir, A., Dion, E., Saenz, L., & McMaster, K. (2010). Peer mediation: A means of differentiating classroom instruction. In R. Allington & A. McGill-Franzen (Eds.), *Handbook of reading disabilities* (pp. 362–373). Mahwah, NJ: Lawrence Erlbaum Associates.

Fuchs, D., Fuchs, L.S., Svenson, E., Yen, L., Thompson, A., McMaster, K.L., . . . Kearns, D. (2001). *Peer-assisted learning strategies: First grade reading manual.* Nashville, TN: Vanderbilt University.

Fuchs, D., Fuchs, L.S., Thompson, A., Al Otaiba, S., Yen, L., Yang, N.J., . . . O'Connor, R.E. (2001). Is reading important in reading-readiness programs? A randomized field trial with teachers as program implementers. *Journal of Educational Psychology, 93,* 251–267.

Fuchs, D., Fuchs, L.S., Thompson, A., Al Otaiba, S., Yen, L., Yang, N.J., . . . O'Connor, R.E. (2002). Exploring the importance of reading programs for kindergartners with disabilities in mainstream classrooms. *Exceptional Children, 68,* 295–311.

Fuchs, D., Fuchs, L.S., Thompson, A., Svenson, E., Yen, L., Al Otaiba, S., . . . Saenz, L. (2001). Peer-Assisted Learning Strategies in reading: Extensions for kindergarten, first grade, and high school. *Remedial and Special Education, 22,* 15–21.

Fuchs, D., Fuchs, L.S., Yen, L., McMaster, K.L., Svenson, E., Yang, N.J., . . . King, S. (2001). Developing first-grade reading fluency through peer mediation. *Teaching Exceptional Children, 34,* 90–93.

Fuchs, L.S., & Fuchs, D. (2003). Can diagnostic reading assessment enhance general educators' instructional differentiation and student learning? In B. Foorman (Ed.), *Preventing and remediating reading difficulties: Bringing science to scale* (pp. 325–351). Timonium, MD: York Press.

Fuchs, L.S., & Fuchs, D. (2007). Progress monitoring within a multi-tiered prevention system. *Perspectives on Language and Literacy, 33*(2), 43–47.

Fuchs, L.S., & Fuchs, D. (2008). The role of assessment within the RTI framework. In D. Fuchs, L.S. Fuchs, & S. Vaughn (Eds.), *Response to intervention: A framework for reading educators* (pp. 27–39). Newark, DE: International Reading Association.

Fuchs, L.S., Fuchs, D., & Hamlett, C.L. (1989). Monitoring reading growth using student recalls: Effects of two teacher feedback systems. *Journal of Educational Research, 83,* 103–111.

Fuchs, L.S., Fuchs, D., & Kazdan, S. (1999). Effects of peer-assisted learning strategies on high school students with serious reading problems. *Remedial and Special Education, 20,* 309–318.

Fuchs, D., & Young, C.L. (2006). On the irrelevance of intelligence in predicting responsiveness to reading instruction. *Exceptional Children, 73,* 8–30.

Fulk, B., & King, K. (2001). Classwide peer tutoring at work. *Teaching Exceptional Children, 34*(2), 49–53.

Greenwood, C.R., Delquadri, J.C., & Hall, R.V. (1989). Longitudinal effects of classwide peer tutoring. *Journal of Educational Psychology, 81,* 371–383.

Greenwood, C.R., Terry, B., Arreaga-Mayer, C., & Finney, D. (1992). The ClassWide Peer Tutoring Program: Implementation factors that moderate students' achievement. *Journal of Applied Behavior Analysis, 25,* 101–116.

Greenwood, C.R., Terry, B., Utley, C.A., Montagna, D., & Walker, D. (1993). Achievement, placement, and services: Middle school benefits of classwide peer tutoring used at the elementary school. *School Psychology Review, 22,* 497–516.

Hacker, D.J., & Tenant, A. (2002). Implementing reciprocal teaching in the classroom: Overcoming obstacles and making modifications. *Journal of Educational Psychology, 94*(4), 699–718.

Hughes, T.A., & Fredrick, L.D. (2006). Teaching vocabulary with students with learning disabilities using Classwide Peer Tutoring and constant time delay. *Journal of Behavioral Education, 15,* 1–23.

Jenkins, J.R., Heliotis, J.D., Stein, M.L., & Haynes, M.C. (1987). Improving reading comprehension by using paragraph restatements. *Exceptional Children, 54,* 54–59.

Johnson-Pynn, J.S., & Nisbet, V.S. (2002). Preschoolers effectively tutor novice classmates in a block construction task. *Child Study Journal, 32,* 241–255.

Kamil, M.L., Borman, G.D., Dole, J., Kral, C.C., Salinger, T., & Torgesen, J. (2008). *Improving adolescent literacy: Effective classroom and intervention practices.* Washington, DC: U.S. Department of Education.

Kapusnick, R.A., & Hauslein, C.M. (2001). The 'silver cup' of differentiation. *Kappa Delta Pi Record, 37,* 156–159.

Maheady, L., & Harper, G. (1987). A classwide peer tutoring program to improve the spelling test performance of low-income, third- and fourth-grade students. *Education and Treatment of Children, 10,* 120–133.

Marshak, L., Mastropieri, M.A., & Scruggs, T.E. (2011). Curriculum enhancements for inclusive secondary
social studies classes. *Exceptionality, 19,* 61–74.

Mastropieri, M.A., & Scruggs, T.E. (2000). *The inclusive classroom: Strategies for effective teaching.* Upper Saddle
River, NJ: Prentice Hall.

Mastropieri, M.A., Scruggs, T.E., & Graetz, J. (2003). Reading comprehension for secondary students. *Learning Disability Quarterly, 26,* 103–116.

Mastropieri, M.A., Scruggs, T.E., Mohler, L., Beranek, M ., Boon, R., Spencer, V., & Talbott, E. (2001). Can
middle school students with serious reading difficulties help each other and learn anything? *Learning Disabilities Research and Practice, 16,* 18–27.

Mastropieri, M.A., Scruggs, T.E., Spencer, V, & Fontana, J. (2003). Promoting success in high school world
history: Peer tutoring versus guided notes. *Learning Disabilities Research and Practice, 18,* 52–65.

Mastropieri, M.A., Spencer, V., Scruggs, T.E., & Talbott, E. (2000). Students with disabilities as tutors: An
updated research synthesis. In T.E. Scruggs & M.A. Mastropieri (Eds.), *Advances in learning and behavioral
disabilities* (pp. 247–279). Oxford, UK: Elsevier Science/JAI Press.

Mathes, P.M., Howard, J.K., Allen, S.H., & Fuchs, D. (1998). Peer-assisted learning strategies for first-grade
readers: Responding to the needs of diversity. *Reading Research Quarterly, 31,* 268–289.

McIntosh, R., Vaughn, S., Schumm, J.S., Haager, D., & Lee, O. (1993). Observations of students with learning
disabilities in general education classrooms. *Exceptional Children, 60*(3), 249–261.

McMaster, K.L., Fuchs, D., & Fuchs, L.S. (2006). Research on peer-assisted learning strategies: The promise
and limitations of peer-mediated instruction. *Reading and Writing Quarterly, 22,* 5–25.

McMaster, K.L., Fuchs, D., Fuchs, L.S., & Compton, D.L. (2005). Responding to nonresponders: An experimental field trial of identification and intervention methods. *Exceptional Children, 71*(14), 445–463.

Medcalf, J., Glynn, T., & Moore, D. (2004). Peer tutoring in writing: A school systems approach. *Educational
Psychology in Practice, 20,* 157–178.

National Assessment of Educational Progress. (2009). *The nation's report card: Reading 2009.* Washington, DC:
National Center for Education Statistics.

O'Connor, R.E., Bocian, K., Beebe-Frankenberger, M., & Linklater, D.L. (2010). Responsiveness of students
with language difficulties to early intervention in reading. *Journal of Special Education, 43,* 220–235.

Osguthorpe, R.T., & Scruggs, T.E. (1986). Special education students as tutors: A review and analysis. *Remedial and Special Education, 7,* 15–25.

Palincsar, A.M., & Brown, A.L. (1984). Reciprocal teaching of comprehension-fostering and comprehension-
monitoring activities. *Cognition and Instruction, 2,* 117–175.

Palincsar, A.S., David, Y.M., & Brown, A.L. (1989). *Using reciprocal teaching in the classroom: a guide for teachers.*
Unpublished manuscript.

Pearson, P.D., & Dole, J.A. (1987). Explicit comprehension instruction: A review of research and a new conceptualization of instruction. *Elementary School Journal, 88,* 151–165.

Pressley, M. (1997). *Remarks on reading comprehension.* Notes prepared for the Chesapeake Institute, Washington, DC.

Rohrbeck, C.A., Ginsburg-Block, M.D., Fantuzzo, J.W., & Miller, T.R. (2003). Peer-assisted learning interventions with elementary school students: A meta-analytic review. *Journal of Educational Psychology, 95*(2),
240–257.

Rosenshine, B., & Meister, C. (1994). Reciprocal teaching: A review of research. *Review of Educational Research,
64,* 479–530.

Ryan, R.M., & Deci, E.L. (2000). Self-determination theory and the facilitation of intrinsic motivation, social
development, and well-being. *American Psychologist, 55,* 68–78.

Saenz, L.M., Fuchs, L.S, & Fuchs, D. (2005). Peer-Assisted Learning Strategies for English language learners
with learning disabilities. *Exceptional Children, 71,* 231–247.

Scruggs, T.E., & Mastropieri, M.A. (1996). Teacher perceptions of mainstreaming and inclusion, 1958–1995:
A research synthesis. *Exceptional Children, 63,* 59–74.

Scruggs, T.E., & Mastropieri, M.A. (2003). Science and social studies. In H.L. Swanson, K. Harris, & S. Graham (Eds.), *Handbook of learning disabilities* (pp. 364–379). New York, NY: Guilford Press.

Scruggs, T.E., Mastropieri, M.A., & Boon, R. (1998). Science for students with disabilities: A review of recent
research. *Studies in Science Education, 32,* 21–44.

Scruggs, T.E., Mastropieri, M.A., & Okolo, C. (2008). Science and social studies for students with disabilities.
Focus on Exceptional Children, 41(2), 1–24.

Sideridis, G.D., Utley, C., Greenwood, C.R., Delquadri, J., Dawson, H., Palmer, P., & Reddy, S. (1997). Classwide peer tutoring: Effects on the spelling performance and social interactions of students with mild
disabilities and their typical peers in an integrated instructional setting. *Journal of Behavioral Education, 7,*
435–462.

Simmons, D.C., Coyne, M.D., Hagan-Burke, S., Kwok, O., Johnson, C., Zuo, Y., . . . Crevecoeur, Y.C. (2011). Effects of supplemental reading interventions in authentic contexts: A comparison of kindergarteners' response. *Exceptional Children, 77,* 207–228.

Simmons, D.C., Fuchs, D., Fuchs, L.S., Hodge, J.P., & Mathes, P.G. (1994). Importance of instructional complexity and role reciprocity to classwide peer tutoring. *Learning Disabilities Research and Practice, 9,* 203–212.

Spencer, V.G. (2006). Peer tutoring and students with emotional or behavioral disorders: A review of the literature. *Behavioral Disorders, 31*(2), 204–222.

Spencer, V., Scruggs, T.E., & Mastropieri, M.A. (2003). Content area learning in middle school social studies classrooms and students with emotional or behavioral disorders: A comparison of strategies. *Behavioral Disorders, 28,* 77–93.

Spencer, V.G., Simpson, C.G., & Oatis, T.L. (2009). An update on the use of peer tutoring and students with emotional and behavioural disorders. *Exceptionality Education International, 19*(1), 2–13.

Swanson, H.L., & Hoskyn, M. (1998). Experimental intervention research on students with learning disabilities: A meta-analysis of treatment outcomes. *Review of Educational Research, 68,* 277–321.

Tomlinson, C.A. (1999). *The differentiated classroom: Responding to the needs of all learners.* Alexandria, VA: Association for Supervision and Curriculum Development.

Topping, K., & Ehly, S. (Eds.). (1998). *Peer-assisted learning.* Mahwah, NJ: Lawrence Erlbaum Associates.

Torgesen, J.K. (2004). Preventing early reading failure and its devastating downward spiral. *American Educator, 28,* 32–39.

Torgesen, J.K., Wagner, R.K., Rashotte, C.A., Lindamood, P., Rose, E., Conway, T., & Garvan, C. (1999). Preventing reading failure in young children with phonological processing disabilities: Group and individual responses to instruction. *Journal of Educational Psychology, 91,* 579–593.

Utley, C.A., Reddy, S.S., Delquadri, J.C., Greenwood, C.R., Mortweet, S.L., & Bowman, V. (2001). Classwide peer tutoring: An effective teaching procedure for facilitating the acquisition of health education and safety facts with students with developmental disabilities. *Education and Treatment of Children, 24,* 1–27.

Vaughn, S., Cirino, P.T., Wanzek, J., Wexler, J., Fletcher, J.M., Denton, C.A., & Francis, D.J. (2010). Response to intervention for middle school students with reading difficulties: Effects of a primary and secondary intervention. *School Psychology Review, 39,* 3–21.

Vaughn, S., & Schumm, J.S. (1995). Responsible inclusion for students with learning disabilities. *Journal of Learning Disabilities, 28,* 264–270, 290.

Vygotsky, L. (1978). *Mind in society: The development of higher psychological process.* Cambridge, MA: Harvard University Press.

7 Using Mnemonics in Content Areas

Margaret E. King-Sears and Nancy Johnson Emanuel

Recalling and retrieving information learned in academic content areas can be particularly difficult for students with mild learning disabilities, emotional and/or behavioral disorders, and intellectual disabilities (Scruggs, Mastropieri, Berkeley, & Graetz, 2010). Mnemonics are ways to help students or individuals remember unfamiliar information, such as terms' definitions, steps in a process, and a list of what to purchase at a store. Teaching students how to use mnemonics has been shown to increase their memory of academic content, and students with disabilities often remember more than their peers without disabilities who do not use mnemonics (Wolgemuth, Cobb, & Alwell, 2008).

The premise behind using mnemonics is that this technique provides the opportunity for the brain to encode complex information in a way that is much easier to remember (Fritz, Morris, Acton, Voelkel, & Etkind, 2007; Scruggs, Mastropieri, Berkeley, & Marshak, 2010). Levin (1983) referred to the three *R*s as the process students use when associating new information with mnemonics.

- Recode: Find some part of the new term that sounds familiar or rhymes (i.e., the acoustic link). The new term is recoded for a keyword rhyme, which makes the connection between the term and the keyword.

- Relate: Connect the keyword mnemonic in some way with the new term and the new term's definition (i.e., interactive illustration). Students may imagine the relating visual imagery, draw a picture of the relating image, or someone else may draw the relating image for them.

- Retrieve: The keyword mnemonic and interactive illustration must be studied enough so students can retrieve the accurate and complete definition of the new term.

Memory is defined in the study of cognitive psychology as the ability to store and recall information and experiences. This may sound fairly simple and is sometimes taken for granted, but the process of remembering a fact or experience is actually very complex and requires a series of learned associations (Gray, 2010). Storing and then retrieving information can be difficult for almost everyone, depending on what they are learning and their background for that content. Think about studying for the Scholastic Aptitude Test (SAT), Graduate Record Exam (GRE), or any other standardized test that incorporates infrequently used words or unfamiliar concepts. In order to remember words, concepts, or information, you first have to find them somewhere in your memory. The task of getting information into your memory, however, may require some effort and, in many cases, a great deal of work (Gray, 2010). This is where mnemonics can be very helpful. Learning something new becomes a process of weaving and blending something known with something unknown. Mnemonics help train the brain to put information into memory and retrieve information when it is needed.

Secondary students are also learning more vocabulary. In one study, high school students with learning disabilities were taught 30 SAT vocabulary words (Terrill, Scruggs, & Mastropieri,

2004). Their teacher alternated instruction on the targeted terms by using direct instruction one week on one set of terms, then keyword mnemonic instruction on a new set of terms the following week. Results indicated out of 30 terms in which students received direct instruction with mnemonics, they averaged almost 93% for recall of definitions. Conversely, when students received direct instruction only on another set of 30 terms, they averaged about 49% accuracy. The power of mnemonics is evident by the students' scores, which were immensely different when mnemonics were used.

Mnemonic instruction links new information to prior knowledge by using visual or acoustic cues. Several comprehensive reviews about various methods of improving memory for secondary students have been published, some going back to the 1980s and Mastropieri and Scruggs. Their research began with identifying the impact of memory on learning as well as what the impact of weak memory skills would be for students with learning disabilities and students at-risk for educational failure (Mastropieri & Scruggs, 1998; Mastropieri, Scruggs, & Levin, 1983, 1987). Mnemonic strategies for enhancing memory involve several techniques, including keywords, pegwords, and letter strategies (Mastropieri, Emerick, & Scruggs, 1988; Mastropieri, Scruggs, Bakken, & Brigham, 1992).

KEYWORD MNEMONICS

A keyword is a known word, easily recognized, and similar in sound to the new word or concept being studied, which is connected to the unknown, unfamiliar, and not easily recognized information. For example, a student may need to learn two different parts of the brain for a science class. The cerebrum is the largest part of the brain, and the cerebellum is a smaller part of the brain. The keyword for cerebrum could be *drum,* which is larger than the keyword for cerebellum, which is *bell.* The following shows how Levin's (1983) three *R*s are applied to cerebrum.

- Recode: Cerebrum's keyword is *drum.*

- Relate: The cerebrum is the largest and most highly developed part of the brain, so think of a drum as being the largest sound of some bands. The cerebrum's functions include thinking, talking, and touching. Think of a drum in the brain, and the drum is taking up a large amount of space. The person touching the drum is using highly developed beats (ba boom ta ta ta). Draw a picture of that large drum in the brain (use clip art if you need to) where the cerebrum is located. Make some tallies together to show that the person's thinking and touching of the drum results in highly developed beats (//_///_//_///).

- Retrieve: When you hear the term *cerebrum,* think of the keyword *drum.* When you think of drum, remember the picture of that large drum with highly developed beats. Remembering that picture of the drum in the brain where the cerebrum is should take you to cerebrum's definition—the largest and most highly developed part of the brain. If you need to remember the cerebrum's functions, then think of touching the drum and how the person had to think to make those beats.

The keyword method of linking a known word with something new strengthens the brain's connections to put the new word or knowledge into memory. Creating a connection and an image in the "mind's eye" makes the new information easier to store in memory and, more important, easier to retrieve when needed. A visual link strengthens the connection between old and new ideas. By imagining that interactive illustration (or picture), keywords can be helpful for students studying vocabulary words that may not have any particular meaning to them unless they can somehow be connected to a concrete fact or familiar object they already know.

The keyword technique can be useful for a variety of learning experiences, including remembering words from foreign languages, long lists of information, and words that are not typically encountered every day. For example, the French word *chapeau* means hat. A keyword or familiar

Chapeau, the French word for hat; think of a "chap" wearing a hat

Assail: to attack someone with words or actions; think of a sailboat crashing into someone as the interactive illustration—to assail (sailboat) is to attack someone (to crash) with words or actions

Expunge: to destroy or get rid of something; think of a large *X* and a plunger getting rid of something unpleasant—to expunge (*X*) is to get rid of something, such as destroying it

Figure 7.1. Keyword mnemonics for terms with explanations of how to retrieve the recoded term that has been related to a more familiar term.

word can be connected to the new word along with a visual cue to improve student recall. In this case, a "chap" wearing a hat can be easily imagined and the connection can be made (see Figure 7.1). The student is guided through the process in the following manner.

The French word for hat is chapeau. *The keyword for chapeau is* chap, *which means a man or gentleman (show a picture of man wearing a hat). Look at what this chap is wearing. It is a hat. When I ask you what chapeau means, picture the chap, or the man, wearing a chapeau, which is a hat. Remember that the hat is on the chap's head. Now think back to the picture and think about the chap wearing a hat, a chapeau. The hat is connected to chap, and the chap is connected to chapeau. Chapeau is the French word for hat.*

A foreign word is connected to its English translation by a chain of two links when this method is used. The first link is the similarity in sound (acoustic link), and the second link is the mental (or pictorial) image of the interaction between the two words (imagery link). Numerous studies involving students with and without mild disabilities have produced results clearly indicating that mnemonic strategies are effective for improving memory in the content areas for students at the secondary level (King-Sears, Mercer, & Sindelar, 1992; Mastropieri, Scruggs, Levin, Gaffney, & McLoone, 1985).

The following is another example of how a student might remember the definition of an unfamiliar word using a keyword mnemonic. The word *assail* means to attack someone with words or actions. A keyword for assail can be *sailboat*. After identifying the term and the term's definition and finding a keyword that sounds similar to the term, the next step is to imagine the term's definition doing something with the keyword. Simply showing a sailboat does not yet work with the definition of *assail,* which is to attack someone with words or actions, so students need to work on finding a way that would connect sail and assail to remember the new definition. Here is one way.

Imagine a sailboat in rough water. The water seems to be attacking the sailboat. What if someone forgot to pack all the life jackets for people to wear? Imagine the captain of the sailboat using harsh words to scold someone about the missing life jackets.

Now students are getting closer to using the keyword mnemonic technique in a way that helps them connect the term to the keyword and the interactive illustration to the term's definition.

- Recode: *Assail* means to attack someone with words or actions. The mnemonic keyword for assail is *sailboat.*

- Relate: Imagine a sailboat in rough waters, and someone on the boat has forgotten to pack enough life jackets. The water is attacking the sailboat with its violent waves, and the person who forgot to bring all the life jackets is hearing some harsh words for not doing his or her job.

- Retrieve: When you hear *assail,* think of a sailboat in rough water with not enough life jackets on board. *Assail* means to attack someone with words or actions.

The students should recognize the familiar word *sail* after using the keyword mnemonic technique and envision a sailboat crashing through rough water and attacking the waves. This connection will help recall the meaning of the new vocabulary word *assail* (see Figure 7.1).

Here is a final example of keyword mnemonics. *Expunge* means to destroy or get rid of something. Visualize a giant letter *X* and a plumber using a plunger to get rid of something nasty (see Figure 7.1). Students recode expunge as *X,* relate the *X* to a plumber using a plunger to get rid of something, and retrieve the definition of *expunge*—to destroy or get rid of something.

PEGWORD MNEMONICS

The pegword mnemonics technique is used for memorizing lists of items. The student learns a list of words or rhymes that can be connected with the numbers that they will represent. By teaching students the "pegs" connected to numbers, the information has to be memorized just once and the connection can be used every time a list of items needs to be memorized. See Table 7.1 for a list of pegwords and how to remember Newton's three laws of motion.

These associations create the pegs of this technique. To memorize a list of objects, each object is associated with the appropriate peg. Once students know pegwords well, they can associate them using rhymes and visual imagery or illustrations. For example, spiders and their close relatives have eight legs, so the pegword is *eight.* Visualize a spider with eight legs sitting on a gate (Mastropieri & Scruggs, 1998).

Using pegwords is another way of linking new information with familiar or previously known information. Quite literally, pegwords are words onto which new information can "hang." Several variations exist for pegword rhyming and it can be adapted to suit the requirements of linking this type of rhyme to new information (Higbee, 1996). Students who struggle to learn their multiplication facts would first be taught to connect the appropriate pegword to the number being multiplied followed by making the pegword connection to the answer or product. For example, to teach the math fact 6×6, the students would first be taught the pegword *sticks* to associate with six. "Sticks times sticks" would remind the students to think of six sticks bundled together six times. Creating additional pegwords such as "30 is dirty" will help students remember larger numbers and the answer to this multiplication fact. Because the answer is 36, combining 30 with 6 can now

Table 7.1. Pegword mnemonics

1	2	3	4	5	6	7	8	9	10
One ate a bun	Two in a shoe	Three for free	Four on the floor	Five is alive	Six on sticks	Seven in heaven	Eight on a gate	Nine down a mine	10 in a pen
Make up your own pegword rhymes (once one set is memorized, there is no need to memorize more than one set)									
Sun	Blue	Tree	Door	Hive	Mix	Leaven	Late	Whine	Alien
Run	Flew	Glee	Pour	Dive	Fix	Kevin	Crate	Sign	Children
				Drive		Devon	Date		Den
				Survive					Garden
Content in a sequence or order retains numbers Mix up numbers for other items									

Identify and describe Newton's three laws of motion.
- One is bun; the bun does not move until someone or something touches it (also think of inertia).
- Two is flew; the airplane flew at the same speed until the wind became stronger (an object maintains velocity unless something acts on it to increase the speed).
- Three is glee; the child was full of glee one moment and then began to cry (for every action there is an opposite and equal reaction).

be associated with "dirty sticks." The student can then combine the pegwords to remember: 6×6 (sticks $\times$ sticks) = 36 (dirty sticks).

ACRONYM MNEMONICS

Acronym mnemonics use letter associations to create a memorable phrase using only the first letters of the information being learned. For example, students learn about the five Great Lakes during a geography lesson focused on bodies of water in North America and are expected to remember their names. Teachers can share an acronym mnemonic (HOMES) with the students to help them remember the names of the Great Lakes: *H*uron, *O*ntario, *M*ichigan, *E*rie, *S*uperior. Teachers should remind students to create a link between the mnemonic and the new information.

If you get rid of all the letters of the lakes except the first letter in each name, you get HOMES. Think of all the homes that people live in right next to the Great Lakes. Because it is probably very cold in the north, you would need to live in a home in order to stay warm and cozy. When you think of all the HOMES near the Great Lakes, you will remember their names.

ACROSTIC LETTER SENTENCE MNEMONICS

Acrostic letter mnemonics can be used to remember information that may not actually have a relationship to the memory statement. Educators can teach students to remember a simple silly sentence that will trigger their memory for factual information. For example, here is an acrostic letter mnemonic to remember the names of the Great Lakes in order of size: *S*ara's *H*ippo *M*ust *E*at *O*ranges—*S*uperior, *H*uron, *M*ichigan, *E*rie, *O*ntario. Now envision that Sara lives near one of these lakes and think about how silly it is that a hippo is there and that the hippo eats oranges. It is this visual image (or illustration) that is essential to help students retrieve which acrostic mnemonic goes with what piece of information. What if students remembered HOMES for the size of the Great Lakes? Their response would be wrong. It is critical for students to connect the correct mnemonic with the corresponding accurate information. Here's another basic, yet memorable, acrostic letter sentence. *N*ever *E*at *S*our *W*atermelon is a great way to remember the directions on a compass rose—*N*orth, *E*ast, *S*outh, *W*est. Starting at the top of a compass rose, teach students to say the silly sentence and label the directional points in a clockwise fashion.

COMBINING MNEMONIC METHODS

Mnemonic methods can also be combined. For example, using keywords and acronyms to form acoustic reconstructions can be used effectively when the terminology or information is unfamiliar (Mastropieri & Scruggs, 2010). Spending a short amount of time teaching the mnemonic along with the connected content can make a huge difference to students.

Scientific terminology such as *lithosphere, atmosphere,* and *pedosphere* are very appropriate for acoustic reconstructions and could be more readily learned when transformed into familiar-sounding keywords and into an acoustically connected phrase. The prefix *lith* means "related to rock or stone," and the lithosphere layer contains the crust and uppermost layer of the Earth. The keyword *list* can remind students to start at the top of the list of Earth layers and remember "lithosphere is on top of the list." *Atmosphere* refers to the layer of air and gasses surrounding a planet. *At most* could be the keyword. "At most, you will want to breathe on a planet." Pedosphere is the layer of the Earth that forms soil and on which we walk. *Pedestrian* could be the keyword here. "Pedestrians walk on the pedosphere." Your students will thank you for not only teaching the content, but also for teaching them how to remember the important facts.

Pictorial or mimetic reconstruction is another way of combining mnemonic methods. This method uses recognizable pictures or mental representations to recall information. When information is relatively familiar, being reminded to think of something specific will help trigger the connection to the required terminology or facts. This makes new information more concrete and more readily recalled. For example, display a picture depicting frogs in the water and toads on dry land and then envision that frogs are amphibians and prefer water, whereas toads are also amphibians but live on land. Use the picture to recall the information—frogs are swimming in the water doing a "frog kick" swimming stroke, whereas the toads are hopping on the land on their toes. There are a lot of connections here, and learning mnemonics is all about making connections to create a memory.

WHEN SHOULD MNEMONICS BE INTRODUCED?

The best time to teach students about how to develop and use mnemonics is at the beginning of the quarter or semester. Take the time for all students to learn the mnemonic techniques well. The investment of time pays off later when students will spend less time throughout the school year having problems remembering new terms and definitions; students can more efficiently focus on higher level skills using the new terms when their focus can shift from "What does that word mean?" to "How do these terms apply to characters' traits in this novel?" Keep in mind, too, that teaching students how to use mnemonics as a remembering technique is not the same as teaching students the content. That is, students need to first learn what the content is (e.g., What is the term? What is the term's definition?) before they can apply mnemonics to remember the content. Graves and Levin (1989) found students who monitored their thinking using self-questioning and rereading passages to identify main ideas were more accurate in identifying main ideas. Students who used mnemonics to remember the main ideas, however, performed significantly better on assessments given immediately and one week later.

Ways to Incorporate Mnemonics in English, Science, and Social Studies Classrooms

Mnemonic strategies can be useful across all content areas. The following are a few examples of how specific strategies can be used in the English, science, and social studies classroom. Any of the examples could be adjusted to reflect the topic of that day's lesson. Expect to demonstrate for students how to develop and remember the mnemonics, such as the following.

- Present each term and definition.

- Focus on one term at a time, telling the students the keyword mnemonic and explaining how the keyword and term's definition interact together.

Strategies for Keyword Mnemonics

English teachers can help students define unfamiliar words by teaching them how to use a keyword mnemonic technique or showing students how to use morphemic cues (e.g., prefix, root words, suffix meanings.) IT FITS (King-Sears et al., 1992) and LINCS (Ellis, 1992) are two popular strategies used for teaching students how to develop their own mnemonics.

The IT FITS strategy was used to teach science vocabulary and definitions to middle school students with learning disabilities (King-Sears et al., 1992). Initially, the teacher provided students with the keywords and interactive illustrations. After receiving a week of instruction using teacher-developed keywords and interactive illustrations, then students learned the IT FITS strategy so they could develop their own keywords and interactions. Students used individual index cards to write the terms, keywords, and definitions.

- *I*dentify the term (including the pronunciation).

- *T*ell the definition of the term.

- *F*ind a keyword that sounds like the term.

- *I*magine the keyword doing something with the term (interactive illustration).

- *T*hink about this interaction.

- *S*tudy this until you know it.

The last step in IT FITS seems simplistic. Some students with disabilities, however, may think that they are done once they have developed the keywords and interactive illustrations. But they are not done until they know the terms' definitions. Students can study frontward (given the term, tell the definition) and backward (given the definition, tell the term) using their index cards. See Figure 7.2 for how IT FITS is used to teach students a keyword and interactive illustration for *alveoli* (a science term).

Students who learn to develop their own keywords and interactive illustrations can be more independent in all classes when they need to learn new vocabulary and remember definitions. When students can be taught strategies that promote their independence, teachers can consider the time investment in initially teaching the strategy to the time saved when students can use the strategy on their own. The LINCS keyword mnemonic technique (Ellis, 1992) is similar to IT FITS because LINCS also has students develop their own keyword and imagine an interactive illustration for unfamiliar terms. The LINCS steps are as follows.

- *L*ist the term and the essential definition.

- *I*ndicate a familiar rhyming word.

- *N*ote the auditory LINCS device (through a LINCing story).

- *C*onstruct the visual LINCS device (LINCing picture).

- *S*elf-test.

   The new term is *palisades,* which are steep cliffs alongside the ocean or river.

   - The keyword mnemonic for palisades is *pal.*

   - The LINCing story, drawn by students, shows "My pal, Joe, dove from the cliff into the . . ." (Harris, Schumaker, & Deshler, 2011, p. 25).

Keyword Mnemonics

Some mnemonics can seem easier than others, so teachers should incorporate more difficult keywords and picture interactions during instruction. For example, remembering that Annapolis is

Identify the term.
    Alveoli

Tell the definition of the term.
    Alveoli are tiny air sacs within the lungs where the exchange of oxygen and carbon dioxide takes place.

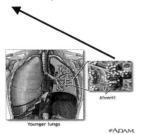

Find a keyword.
    Eye

Imagine the definition doing something with the keyword.
    The eye can look like each tiny air sac in the lungs.

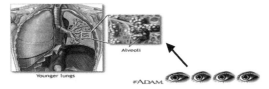

Think about the definition doing something with the keyword.
    I think of eyes, or alveoli, which are the tiny air sacs in the lungs where the exchange of oxygen and carbon dioxide takes place.

Study what you imagined until you know the definition.

Term: alveoli	Definition: Alveoli (eye) are the tiny air sacs in the
Keyword: eye	lungs where the exchange of oxygen and carbon dioxide takes place.

Figure 7.2. IT FITS strategy for students developing keyword mnemonics. (From King-Sears, M.E., Mercer, C.D., & Sindelar, P.T., *Remedial and Special Education* [Vol. 13, No. 5], pp. 22–33, copyright © 1992 by SAGE Publications. Reprinted by Permission of SAGE Publications.)

the capital of Maryland can seem difficult initially. Yet, Scruggs, Mastropieri, Berkeley, and Marshak (2010) reported that one teacher of students with intellectual disabilities creatively connected Annapolis with "two apples" and then had students imagine two apples getting married, with *married* as the keyword for Maryland. So students hearing Annapolis think of "two apples getting married; Annapolis is the capital of Maryland." Scruggs et al. noted the students with intellectual disabilities averaged 94% accuracy for states and capitals taught using mnemonics over a 4-week period. This score is quite impressive for students who typically experience memory issues.

Keyword mnemonics are not limited to terms and definitions. Educators are encouraged to consider curriculum content that lends itself to using some type of mnemonics. For example, students with learning disabilities learned states and their capitals using keyword mnemonics (Mastropieri et al., 1992). For example, to teach students that Olympia is the capital of Washington, the keyword phrase for Washington was "wash-a-ton," and the keyword for Olympia was the *Olympics*. The interactive illustration showed people at an Olympic event washing a ton of their laundry (wash-a-ton). Interestingly, students learned a forward and backward way of remembering the states' keywords and capitals' keywords. That is, when students heard Olympia, they needed to

Table 7.2. Sample material instructors may teach at each stage of HOMER

Step	Material
Hypothesize	Characteristics of the scientific method, development of research ideas, differences between theories and hypotheses, induction, deduction, literature searches
Operationalize	Translation of conceptual variables into operational definitions, scales of measurement, types of data (e.g., self-report, observation), reliability, validity
Measure	The three basic types of research (descriptive, correlational, experimental) and the characteristics of each, variations on the three basic research designs (e.g., quasi-experiments, factorial designs)
Evaluate	Appropriate statistical analyses for each type of research design, internal and external validity, statistical validity and Type I and II errors, power
Replicate/revise/report	Types of replications, importance of revisions, oral presentations, conference-style poster presentations, APA-style written reports

J.L. Lakin, R.B. Giesler, K.A. Morris, & J.R. Vosmik, *Teaching of Psychology* (34, 2) p. 95, copyright 2007 by SAGE Publications, Reprinted by Permission of SAGE Publications Inc.

think of the Olympics and the ton of laundry washed there to remember Washington. Conversely, when asked to identify the capital of Washington, they needed to think of washing a ton of laundry at the Olympics to remember Olympia.

Acronym Mnemonics

The terms that appear in key science texts are often complex. Using an acronym mnemonic can help students recall certain formulas and procedures. For example, students can use the acronym mnemonic HOMER (from the animated television show *The Simpsons*) to remember the different steps of the scientific method: *h*ypothesize, *o*perationalize, *m*easure, *e*valuate, and *r*eplicate (Lakin, Giesler, Morris, & Vosmik, 2007; see Table 7.2). Students can recall these complicated steps by combining keywords, a simple visual, and the acronym mnemonic.

Pegword Mnemonics

Using a pegword in the social studies classroom can help students with mild disabilities remember the content of narrative texts and expository texts. For example, using rhymes for words is a variation of using pegword mnemonics (e.g., one is fun, two is blue). Sometimes using a rhyming pattern of words can make recalling important dates and facts easier and fun. The following sentence can help students remember when the final two states were admitted into the Union: '59 was the date when Alaska and Hawaii became new states.

Acrostic Letter Mnemonics

A simple sentence can help students in a social studies classroom recall information in the correct order. For example, using an acrostic to visualize the order of the first five American presidents can be helpful. Imagine that *W*ashington's *A*rmy *J*ogged *M*any *M*iles. The first five presidents of the United States were Washington, Adams, Jefferson, Madison, and Monroe.

Brigham, Scruggs, and Mastropieri (1995) combined acrostic and other mnemonics and taught middle school students with high-incidence disabilities how to develop symbols to recall American Revolution battle names, depictions of soldiers and buildings, and other information by using map-like displays. Map symbols included 1) reconstructive elaborations of battle names and associated event information, 2) mnemonic keywords of battle names, and 3) realistic drawings of soldiers, buildings, and so forth. Students taught with mnemonics remembered much more than their peers who were not taught using mnemonics.

CONCLUSION

Mnemonics is a memory-enhancing instructional strategy that involves teaching students how to link new information to information they already know. Mnemonics provide a visual or verbal

Table 7.3.   Web sites with mnemonic information

Teaching academic skills: http://www.nsttac.org/content/using-mnemonics-teach-academic-skills
Studying homework: http://homeworktips.about.com/od/homeworkhelp/tp/mnemonics.htm
Learning the 50 states and capitals: http://mrsjonesroom.com/themes/usa.html
Spelling mnemonics: http://www.audiblox2000.com/spelling-mnemonics.htm
Selecting mnemonic sentence generator: http://spacefem.com/mnemonics

prompt for students who have difficulty receiving and retaining information, particularly content information that is unfamiliar and contains vocabulary that is infrequently used. Mnemonics can be a valuable tool that students of all ages can utilize to improve factual recall and memory skills. Several web sites are available that students and teachers can access to help them develop mnemonics (see Table 7.3).

Mnemonics words, phrases, and pictures can be developed by teachers or students. Teachers should provide clear instruction for students as they are learning about keywords, pegwords, acrostic sentences, and other types of mnemonics. After teacher-led instruction and students' use of teacher-developed mnemonics, teachers should consider instructing students on how to develop their own mnemonics. Students who develop their own mnemonics acquire more instructional independence and learn techniques they can use across content areas. Mnemonics can be valuable tools that enable students to remember vocabulary definitions, lists of information, and items that go together. When students remember foundational content, they are better able to learn, remember, and apply concepts and procedures related to higher level content. Students can create meaningful connections to information taught through the general curriculum with some simple reminders and inexpensive materials and discover a way to take charge of their own learning.

REFERENCES

Brigham, F.J., Scruggs, T.E., & Mastropieri, M.A. (1995). Elaborative maps for enhanced learning of historical information: Using spatial, verbal and imaginal information. *Journal of Special Education, 28,* 440–460.

Ellis, E.S. (1992). *The vocabulary (LINCS) strategy.* Lawrence, KS: Edge Enterprises.

Fritz, C.O., Morris, P.E., Acton, M., Voelkel, A.R., & Etkind, R. (2007). Comparing and combining retrieval practice and the keyword mnemonic for foreign vocabulary learning. *Applied Cognitive Psychology, 21,* 499–526.

Graves, A.W., & Levin, J.R. (1989). Comparison of monitoring and mnemonic text-processing strategies in learning disabled students. *Learning Disability Quarterly, 12,* 232–236. doi:10.2307/1510693

Gray, P.O. (2010). *Psychology* (6th ed.). New York, NY: Worth Publishers.

Harris, M.L., Schumaker, J.B., & Deshler, D.D. (2011). The effects of strategic morphological analysis instruction on the vocabulary performance of secondary students with and without disabilities. *Learning Disability Quarterly, 34,* 17–33.

Higbee, K.L. (1996). *Your memory.* New York, NY: Marlowe & Company.

King-Sears, M.E., Mercer, C.D., & Sindelar, P.T. (1992). Toward independence with keyword mnemonics: A strategy for science vocabulary instruction. *Remedial and Special Education, 13*(5), 22–33. doi:10.1177/074193259201300505

Lakin, J.L., Giesler, R.B., Morris, K.A., & Vosmik, J.R. (2007). HOMER as an acronym for the scientific method. *Teaching of Psychology, 34*(2), 94–96.

Levin, J.R. (1983). Pictorial strategies for school learning: Practical illustrations. In M. Pressley & J.R. Levin (Eds.), *Cognitive strategy research: Educational applications* (pp. 63–87). New York, NY: Springer-Verlag.

Mastropieri, M.A., & Scruggs, T. (1998). Enhancing school success with mnemonic strategies. *Intervention in School and Clinic, 33,* 201–208. doi:10.1177/105345129803300402

Mastropieri, M.A., & Scruggs, T.E. (2010). *The inclusive classroom: Strategies for effective instruction* (4th ed.). Upper Saddle River, NJ: Prentice Hall.

Mastropieri, M.A., Emerick, K., & Scruggs, T.E. (1988). Mnemonic instruction of science concepts. *Behavioral Disorders, 14,* 48–56.

Mastropieri, M.A., Scruggs, T.E., Bakken, J.P., & Brigham, F.J. (1992). A complex mnemonic strategy for teaching states and their capitals: Comparing forward and backward associations. *Learning Disabilities Research and Practice, 7,* 96–103.

Mastropieri, M.A., Scruggs, T.E., & Levin, J.R. (1983). Pictorial mnemonic strategies for special education. *Journal of Special Education Technology, 6,* 24–33.

Mastropieri, M.A., Scruggs, T.E., & Levin, J.R. (1987). Learning-disabled students' memory for expository prose: Mnemonic versus nonmnemonic pictures. *American Educational Research Journal, 24,* 505–519.

Mastropieri, M.A., Scruggs, T.E., Levin, J.R., Gaffney, J., & McLoone, B. (1985) Mnemonic vocabulary instruction for learning disabled students. *Learning Disability Quarterly, 8,* 57–63.

Scruggs, T.E., Mastropieri, M.A., Berkeley, S., & Graetz, J.E. (2010). Do special education interventions improve learning of secondary content? A meta-analysis. *Remedial and Special Education, 31,* 437–449. doi: 10.1177/0741932508327465

Scruggs, T.E., Mastropieri, M.A., Berkeley, S., & Marshak, L. (2010). Mnemonic strategies: Evidence-based practice and practice-based evidence. *Intervention in School and Clinic, 46,* 79–86. doi:10.1177/1053451210374985

Terrill, M., Scruggs, T.E., & Mastropieri, M.A. (2004). SAT vocabulary instruction for high school students with learning disabilities. *Intervention in School and Clinic, 39,* 288–294.

Wolgemuth, J.R., Cobb, R.B., & Alwell, M. (2008). The effects of mnemonic interventions on academic outcomes for youth with disabilities: A systematic review. *Learning Disabilities Research and Practice, 23,* 1–10. doi:10.1111/j.1540-5826.2007.00258.x

8 ||| Using Collaborative Strategic Reading to Improve Comprehension

Alison G. Boardman, Karla Scornavacco, and Janette K. Klingner

In the following excerpt from a middle school language arts classroom, students are in mixed-ability cooperative learning groups. They are engaged in the final step of the Collaborative Srategic Reading (CSR) process, Wrap Up. Students are sharing their review statements and providing textual evidence to support their ideas about what they have learned from a text on global warming.

Laura: I wrote "The temperatures are increasing so the perennial ice is melting." And the perennial ice is thick, thick ice. Didn't it say that? It's really thick.

Ms. Thompson was standing near this group of middle school students, listening before entering the conversation to give support.

Katy: I said the same thing as Laura [pointing to her learning log], that "The perennial ice is melting and that's worrying because the ice has been frozen for many, many years."

Laura: And it's like really thick ice. Like it shouldn't be melting.

Cinthia: I wrote that "Temperatures are not the usual, which has brought lots of damage like the annual ice," which is like vulnerable because that's the ice that's been there too.

Katy: Are you finished, David?

David: Yeah, I wrote that "The temperatures are increasing and causing the thick ice to melt."

Katy: That's mostly what I put.

Cinthia: Yeah. (Klingner, Vaughn, Boardman, & Swanson, 2012, p. 13)

Ms. Thompson continued to observe, noticing how students were interacting with one another and how well they had understood the text. Ms. Thompson and her students look forward to "Nonfiction Friday," a time to use CSR to lead students through nonfiction texts connected to the unit's goals. It was mid-February and by this time of the year Ms. Thompson and her students were familiar with the CSR routines that structure discussions and activities. Although topics and content vary according to the curriculum, students, as well as Ms. Thompson, are busy, active, and engaged in each CSR lesson (Klingner et al., 2012).[1]

HOW DO STUDENTS BENEFIT FROM COLLABORATIVE STRATEGIC READING?

CSR (Klingner, Vaughn, & Schumm, 1998) is a multicomponent reading comprehension instructional model that engages students in text by teaching them to use a set of reading strategies in student-led cooperative learning groups. This chapter describes the CSR strategies and sugges-

The Collaborative Strategic Reading research described in this chapter is supported in part by grant R305A080608 from the Institute of Education Sciences, U.S. Department of Education. The content is solely the responsibility of the authors and does not necessarily represent the official views of the Institute of Education Sciences or the U.S. Department of Education.
    [1]Ms. Thompson is one of several teachers we have worked with over the years in studies about the effectiveness of collaborative strategic reading (e.g., Klingner & Vaughn, 2000; Vaughn et al., 2011). Teaching in an urban public school district in the western United States, Ms. Thompson taught diverse seventh-grade language arts classes that included students with disabilities, a large proportion of English language learners, and several students identified as gifted.

tions for introducing them to students for maximum effect. The teacher's role in guiding students to be collaborative, strategic readers is highlighted, and real-life examples from classrooms such as Ms. Thompson's are provided.

Consider for a moment a well-documented instructional task common to classrooms across grade levels and subject areas. First, the class reads a selection of text. Next, a question and answer session is offered in which the teacher guides students to extract the meaning of the text through a series of questions and answers that are marked by extensions and explanations by the teacher. Although the students who are engaged in this discussion may indeed leave the classroom with an understanding of the content at hand, they are not provided with skills to approach a text in subsequent encounters. Thus, the teacher has become an essential purveyor of reading comprehension. How do these same students handle difficult content they must read in situations when a teacher is not present? What about navigating homework, a reading assessment, a novel, or an instruction manual?

CSR has increased reading comprehension outcomes for students with a range of abilities, including students with learning disabilities, students at risk for reading difficulties, students who are average and high achievers (e.g., Bryant et al., 2000; Klingner, Vaughn, & Schumm, 1998; Vaughn et al.; 2000; 2011), and English language learners (ELLs; Klingner & Vaughn, 1996). CSR includes explicit teaching of before, during, and after reading strategies that are used to facilitate discussions about text. Students apply reading strategies and conduct text-based discussions in student-led cooperative learning groups during CSR (Johnson & Johnson, 1989). Figure 8.1 presents the four CSR components—Preview, Click and Clunk, Get the Gist, and Review. CSR was initially designed to be used with expository, content-specific texts. Over the years, teachers have also successfully used CSR with a range of texts, including primary source documents, novels, and poetry.

CSR, and reading comprehension strategy instruction in general, is founded on the principle that struggling readers can improve their ability to comprehend text when they learn to apply reading behaviors that are used by good readers (Kamil et al., 2008; Klingner et al., 2012; Paris, Wasik, & Turner, 1991; Pressley & Afflerbach, 1995). Because struggling readers may not naturally employ effective tactics to unpack understanding, students are taught specific strategies in CSR to use before, during, and after reading in a routine that is easy to learn and apply. Yet, CSR is not just for students who are below grade level. Research demonstrates that CSR is effective for all readers and is especially important for those who struggle with reading comprehension.

TEACHING COLLABORATIVE STRATEGIC READING

CSR strategies are introduced one at a time using reading materials that are a part of the curriculum. Teachers provide explicit instruction to introduce each strategy while allowing students to contextualize its practical application and usefulness in the reading process. Introducing each strategy addresses the following questions (Klingner, Vaughn, Dimino, Schumm, & Bryant, 2001).

- What is the strategy?

- Why is the strategy important?

- How is the strategy used?

- When is the strategy used?

As students learn the CSR strategies through teacher modeling and guided practice, they begin to apply them in student-led cooperative learning groups. Many teachers choose to teach individual CSR strategies several times each week so that students are able to move into using the full CSR process within about a month's time.

Cooperative grouping offers multiple opportunities for students in mixed-ability classrooms to discuss what they are reading and thinking and to help one another gain access to high-level content in text. Cooperative grouping also creates a scaffold that allows the teacher to facilitate learning without being the sole translator of understanding from text to student. The combination of reading comprehension strategies and cooperative learning addresses several essential reading goals.

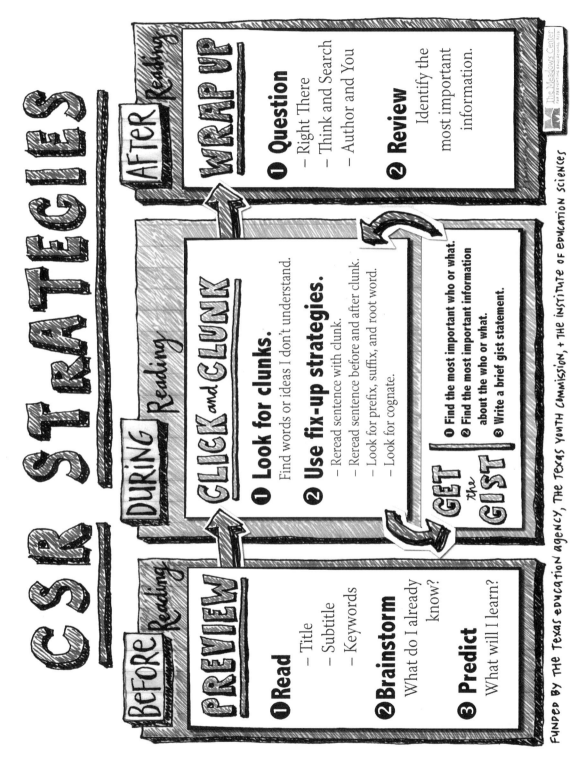

CSR STRATEGIES

BEFORE Reading

PREVIEW

❶ Read
– Title
– Subtitle
– Keywords

❷ Brainstorm
What do I already know?

❸ Predict
What will I learn?

DURING Reading

CLICK and CLUNK

❶ Look for clunks.
Find words or ideas I don't understand.

❷ Use fix-up strategies.
– Reread sentence with clunk.
– Reread sentence before and after clunk.
– Look for prefix, suffix, and root word.
– Look for cognate.

GET the GIST
① Find the most important who or what.
② Find the most important information about the who or what.
③ Write a brief gist statement.

AFTER Reading

WRAP UP

❶ Question
– Right There
– Think and Search
– Author and You

❷ Review
Identify the most important information.

The Meadows Center

FUNDED BY THE TEXAS EDUCATION AGENCY, THE TEXAS YOUTH COMMISSION, + THE INSTITUTE OF EDUCATION SCIENCES

Figure 8.1. Collaborative strategic reading (CSR) strategies. (Reprinted with permission from the Meadows Center for Preventing Educational Risk at The University of Texas at Austin [2009]. *CSR strategies.* Austin, TX: Author.)

- Increase reading comprehension, especially in content area expository text.

- Address reading and language needs of all students in mixed-ability classrooms where ELLs, students with learning disabilities, and struggling readers are included with peers who are average and high-achieving readers.

- Promote active engagement in high-level discussions with peers.

- Increase opportunities for students to develop academic language.

Collaborative Strategic Reading Resources and Planning

Many teachers ask which texts to use during CSR. Perhaps the most important aspect of text selection is utilizing text that supports curriculum and content learning goals. Teachers often use textbooks or other support materials provided in their curriculum. If students need additional information on a topic, then teachers can find materials that supplement what students are learning or provide alternative perspectives, such as those provided in primary source documents in social studies, literary analyses in language arts, or research articles in science.

Teachers choose a portion of text that can be read in about one class session and divide it into about three sections. The class will begin by previewing the entire text. Next, students will cycle through Click and Clunk and Get the Gist for each section of text. After reading the entire passage. the class will apply the strategies in the CSR Wrap Up. Several materials support the implementation of CSR, including the CSR learning log and CSR cooperative learning roles.

Collaborative Strategic Reading Learning Log   Students record their work in a student learning log throughout the reading process (Klingner et al., 2012; see Figure 8.2). A key aspect of CSR is that it not only involves reading but also listening, writing, and speaking. For each strategy, students first write individual responses in their learning logs and then share and discuss with their group members. The process of using the learning log allows for built-in wait time because students have a minute or longer to write down their thoughts (e.g., ideas, predictions) before they provide a verbal response. The learning log also serves as a reminder of the CSR routine; students are more prepared for what to do next, and they can go back to their work at any time to review or improve it. After the lesson, students can use learning logs to study for quizzes or as prompts for discussions. In addition, the learning log becomes a record of student thinking and learning. Teachers refer to the learning log when targeting their feedback to students and determining the focus and content of subsequent instruction.

Cooperative Learning Group Roles   CSR uses cooperative group roles to facilitate peer-mediated discussion and learning. Students use CSR cue cards to guide them through their roles (Klingner et al., 2012; Figure 8.3). All students engage in every component of CSR, which is different from other group role formats. In this way, students are individually accountable for completing their own work. At the same time, they are relied on by group members to fulfill their expert roles and engage in sharing and discussing. The teacher forms mixed-ability groups of about four students who utilize the following group roles.

- Leader: Guides the group in implementing CSR by keeping track of time, prompting students to read, and saying which strategy to do next.

- Clunk expert: Leads the group in trying to figure out difficult words or concepts.

- Gist expert: Guides the group to write individual gists and to discuss their quality to determine which gists contain the most important ideas from a section of text.

- Question expert: Prompts students to generate and answer questions and to share these questions in the group.

As teachers introduce the CSR strategies they can begin to integrate the use of cooperative learning and group roles. For example, after students learn Preview and Click and Clunk, the teacher

CSR Learning Log

Name _____ Date _____ Period _____

Today's Topic _____

BEFORE READING: Preview

Brainstorm: Connections to prior knowledge

Key Vocabulary:

_____ = _____

_____ = _____

_____ = _____

Predict: What I might learn about the topic

DURING READING: Section 1

Clunks   **Fix-up Strategies**

_____ = _____   1   2   3   4

_____ = _____   1   2   3   4

_____ = _____   1   2   3   4

Gist:

Figure 8.2. Collaborative Strategic Reading (CSR) learning log. (From Klingner, J.K., Vaughn, S., Boardman, A.G., & Swanson, E. [2012]. *Now we get it! Boosting comprehension with collaborative strategic reading.* Copyright 2012 Jossey-Bass. This material is reproduced with permission of John Wiley & Sons, Inc.; adapted by permission.)

(continued)

Figure 8.2.   (*continued*)

DURING READING: Section 2

Clunks   **Fix-up Strategies**

_____ = _____   1   2   3   4

_____ = _____   1   2   3   4

_____ = _____   1   2   3   4

Gist:

DURING READING: Section 3

Clunks   **Fix-up Strategies**

_____ = _____   1   2   3   4

_____ = _____   1   2   3   4

_____ = _____   1   2   3   4

Gist:

AFTER READING: Wrap Up

Questions: (write questions and answers)

Q:
A:

Q:
A:

Q:
A:

Review:

CSR CUE CARD
CSR Leader

Job Description

The leader's job is to guide the group through all the steps of CSR. The leader keeps track of time, keeps the group working together and leads the review.

DURING READING

Read

- Who would like to read the next section?

Click and Clunk

- Write your clunks in your learning log.
- Clunk expert, please help us.

Get the Gist

- It's time to get the gist. Gist expert, please help us.

[Repeat all of the steps in this section.]

AFTER READING

Questions
- It's time to ask questions. Question expert, please help us.

Review
- Now it's time to write the most important ideas in your log.
  [When everyone is done.]
- Who would like to share?
- Remember to say why your ideas are the most important.

Compliments and Suggestions
- Something that went well today was _____.
- Next time we need to work on _____.
- Is there anything else that would help us do better next time?

CSR CUE CARD
Clunk Expert

Job Description

The clunk expert makes sure that students write their clunks in their learning logs. The clunk expert also helps students use fix-up strategies to figure out the meaning of unknown words or ideas.

DURING READING

Click and Clunk

- Who has a clunk?
- Does anyone know the meaning of the clunk?

If YES

- Please explain what the clunk means and why you think so.
- Let's reread the sentence and make sure that definition makes sense.

[Check for understanding.]

If NO, Use Fix-Up Strategies

[After you come up with a definition.]

- Write the definition in your learning log.
- Let's reread the sentence and make sure that definition makes sense.

CSR CUE CARD
Gist Expert

Job Description

The gist expert makes sure that all students in the group write their own gists. The gist expert also leads the group in sharing their gists and discussing the quality of the gists. High-quality gists contain the topic (the most important "who" or "what") and the most important information about the topic. Gists should be about 10 words.

DURING READING

Get the Gist

- What is the most important "who" or "what" in this section?

[Ask students to share.]

- Everyone, think of your own gist and write it in your learning log.

[When everyone is done.]

- Who would like to share their gist?

[Help your group come up with a gist that includes the most important information, leaves out the details, and contains about 10 words.]

CSR CUE CARD
Question Expert

Job Description

The question expert guides the group in coming up with questions that address important information from the reading. The question expert makes sure that students ask different levels of questions. The question expert checks to see that all students write questions and answers.

AFTER READING

Wrap Up

- Let's think of some questions to check whether we really understood what we read. Write your questions and the answers in your learning log.

  Remember to write different types of questions:

  a. "Right there"
  b. "Think and search"
  c. "Author and you"

  [After everyone is finished writing questions, ask:]

- Who would like to share his or her best question?

  [Check that the question begins with "who," "what," "when," "where," "why," or "how."]

- Who would like to answer that question?
- Where did you find the information to answer that question?

Figure 8.3. Collaborative Strategic Reading (CSR) cue cards. (From Klingner, J.K., Vaughn, S., Boardman, A.G., & Swanson, E. [2012]. *Now we get it! Boosting comprehension with collaborative strategic reading.* Copyright 2012 Jossey-Bass. This material is reproduced with permission of John Wiley & Sons, Inc.; reprinted by permission.)

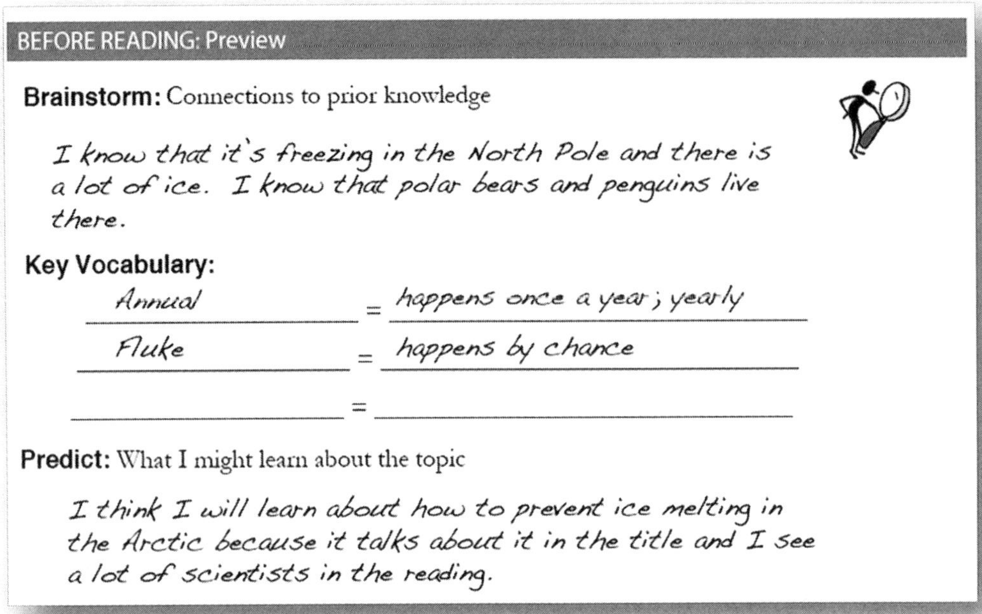

BEFORE READING: Preview

Brainstorm: Connections to prior knowledge

I know that it's freezing in the North Pole and there is a lot of ice. I know that polar bears and penguins live there.

Key Vocabulary:

Annual	=	*happens once a year; yearly*
Fluke	=	*happens by chance*
	=	

Predict: What I might learn about the topic

I think I will learn about how to prevent ice melting in the Arctic because it talks about it in the title and I see a lot of scientists in the reading.

Figure 8.4. The Preview component of Collaborative Strategic Reading (CSR). (From Klingner, J.K., Vaughn, S., Boardman, A.G., & Swanson, E. [2012]. *Now we get it! Boosting comprehension with collaborative strategic reading.* Copyright 2012 Jossey-Bass. This material is reproduced with permission of John Wiley & Sons, Inc.; adapted by permission.)

may then introduce cooperative learning groups and the first two roles, Leader and Clunk Expert. Students begin to use their roles as they practice the strategies.

Preview

Before Ms. Thompson asked her class to read the text, they previewed the passage together. The Preview component is guided by the teacher and includes four activities to build and activate prior knowledge and to motivate students' interest about the content of the passage (see Figure 8.4).

1. The teacher introduces the topic and purpose of the reading and preteaches key words or concepts that are important to text comprehension and content learning.

2. Students brainstorm what they already know about the topic. They write down their ideas and share them with each other. Teachers also provide additional background as needed.

3. Students preview the passage, looking specifically at text features such as headings and graphics.

4. Students predict what they think they will learn from the passage. Students record their predictions in their learning log and share them with each other.

Preview is a great opportunity for students to become comfortable with sharing ideas, which is something they will do throughout CSR. Whereas during and after the reading, CSR strategies require students to discuss, provide feedback, and evaluate each other's responses. In Preview, students can simply share what they already know about the topic (brainstorm) and what they think they will learn (predict).

Introducing Collaborative Strategic Reading and Preview to Students Teachers first introduce students to the CSR process during Preview. Teachers often choose to discuss why reading is

---

BOX 8.1 /// **Collaborative Strategic Reading**

C: Collaborative Strategic Reading (CSR) is collaborative. Students learn to work together to discuss what they are reading. The process helps students develop academic language and discussion skills. It is also fun to work in small, student-led groups.

S: Students use strategies before, during, and after reading to become strategic readers. (Discuss strategies students already use and show plan for strategic reading.)

R: CSR is a process used during reading. Students become better readers when they use strategies as they read.

---

important and how the students might benefit from the CSR strategies. Teachers introduce the CSR acronym with discussion about each word in CSR.

Teachers tell students that the first strategy they will learn is Preview. They might relate a reading preview to a movie preview, noting how the preview provides images and information that gives the viewer a quick overview (Klingner et al., 2001). Next, teachers walk students through the Preview strategy with a short section of text. They make sure students are not just told about the strategy, but learn the "what," "why," "when," and "how" with many opportunities to see it (modeling and think aloud) and to practice. Students learn that preteaching vocabulary calls attention to important terms, increases the number and types of exposures, and provides visuals and other tools to help them understand and remember. They learn that brainstorming activates prior knowledge, helps students make connections, and reveals misconceptions that may require further clarification by the teacher. They also learn that previewing and predicting what you will learn draws attention to important text features and piques student interest.

In this first opportunity to convey the importance of peer-mediated discussion, teachers allow students to write responses on their own and then share with a partner or small group (see Klingner et al., 2012).

BOX 8.2 /// **Preview**

What: Preview

Why: Preteaching key vocabulary calls attention to important terms, increases the number and types of exposures, and provides visuals and other tools to help students understand and remember. Brainstorming activates prior knowledge, helps students make connections, and reveals misconceptions that may require further clarification by the teacher. Previewing text and predicting what you will learn draws attention to important text features and piques student interest.

When: Students preview prior to reading.

How:

- The teacher introduces the topic and purpose of the reading and preteaches key words or concepts.
- Students brainstorm what they already know about the topic and share with their group members.
- Students preview the passage.
- Students predict what they think they will learn from the passage and share the predictions with their group members.

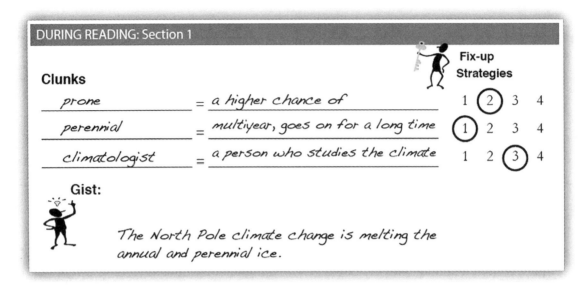

Figure 8.5. Example of clunks that a student has written in his or her learning log. (From Klingner, J.K., Vaughn, S., Boardman, A.G., & Swanson, E. [2012]. *Now we get it! Boosting comprehension with collaborative strategic reading.* Copyright 2012 Jossey-Bass. This material is reproduced with permission of John Wiley & Sons, Inc.; adapted by permission.)

Click and Clunk

Students using CSR monitor and deepen their understanding of the text in strategic ways. Click and Clunk is the first "during reading" strategy, with *click* referring to times when students are understanding what they are reading and *clunk* signaling when students have hit a breakdown in understanding. This metacognitive strategy teaches students to recognize when they need to take action to repair comprehension.

Students identify words or concepts they do not understand and then apply fix-up strategies to figure out the meaning of these clunks. After reading a short section of text (usually a few paragraphs), students identify clunks and write them in their learning logs (see Figure 8.5). Next, students work together to use fix-up strategies to figure out the meaning of their clunks. They record their definition and note in their learning logs the fix-up strategy or strategies they used to figure out the meaning. The first two fix-up strategies prompt students to use context clues. Fix-up strategies #3 and #4 direct students to examine the word, looking for word parts (i.e., morphology) or cognates in another language (Klingner et al., 2012).

1. Reread the sentence without the clunk, and look for key ideas to help you figure out the meaning of the word.

2. Reread the sentences before and after the clunk, looking for clues to determine the word meaning.

3. Break the clunk into parts (e.g., prefixes, suffixes, a known word part).

4. Look for a cognate that makes sense.

Students work together to figure out the meaning of the clunks they identify in their groups. This structure cues students to read the text more closely, use resources (e.g., lists of prefixes and suffixes), and pull from their personal reservoir of knowledge, including languages other than English. For instance, if a student in the group knows the meaning of the word, then he or she offers an explanation and together the group rereads the sentence to make sure the student-friendly definition makes sense in the context of the passage (see Figure 8.3).

Introducing Click and Clunk to Students   Teachers can introduce Click and Clunk by guiding students to think about themselves as skateboarders cruising down a sidewalk to the skate park (Klingner et al., 2012). Students can hear the click, click, click of the grooves as they ride their skateboards. Students may come off their skateboard when they lose their balance or try to do a trick, and clunk, they are stuck. They refine their technique and try again. If students come to a clunk when reading, then they refine their technique by using fix-up strategies.

Teachers introducing fix-up strategies may need to provide instruction beyond how to apply this component of CSR. Fix-up strategies #1 and #2 require students to read around the word. Depending on students' experiences using context clues, teachers may want to teach signal words and phrases that indicate how context supports word meanings. For instance, take the case of fourth graders interacting with a text on birds: *Shorebirds such as plovers are often found along sandy or rocky shorelines and in shallow waters.* A fourth-grade ELL in a CSR class identified the word *plover* as a clunk, but was unfamiliar with the term *such as* to indicate that an example was being provided. The teacher in this class realized that her ELLs needed additional instruction in common English language grammatical conventions and incorporated these features into her CSR and daily language arts instruction.

Students are taught content-specific prefixes, roots, and suffixes when learning to use fix-up strategy #3 (break the clunk into parts). Some students may also benefit from identifying compound words (*spokesperson; underdevelop*). Even when students are familiar with affixes and compound words, they may not be used to applying their knowledge as a way to figure out unknown words while they are reading. Thus, making these connections explicit helps students to gain access to knowledge that supports comprehension. Many teachers provide students with content-specific resources that can be used as quick references (e.g., lists of common science affixes). These resources can be contained in CSR student work folders or as table materials that can be shared by group members.

Fix-up strategy #4 (look for a cognate that makes sense) is useful when students speak a language other than English. A *cognate* is a word that looks the same and shares the same meaning as a word in another language. Thirty to forty percent of English words have a Spanish cognate (Colorín Colorado, 2007), and cognates exist in many other languages as well. For instance, the word *camouflage* has cognates in Spanish (camuflaje) and French (camouflage). Using cognates cues students to gain access to their knowledge of another language and to apply it to what they are learning.

Teachers must be aware that false cognates exist. For example, in the following sentence the word *globe* has a false cognate in Spanish (globo). *Globo* means balloon. When placed back into the sentence, "When Liza looked at the globe, she was surprised to see that Antarctica was so large," the false cognate is revealed because the definition of *balloon* does not make sense. Using cognates allows students who speak another language to use all available resources to facilitate comprehension.

After students have identified clunks on their own, they begin the process of using fix-up strategies to figure out the meaning of their clunks. In the following example Greg is the clunk expert—the student who guides the group to share clunks and use fix-up strategies. He offers procedural and conceptual explanations and checks for understanding (Klingner & Vaughn, 2000, pp. 87–88).

Pablo: My clunk is calcium.

Greg: Try to read sentences in the back and in the front to try to get a clue. Think if you see any sentences in the back or in the front that can help you. Did you get anything?

Pablo: No.

Greg: Okay, now I do, I get something. It is a tiny crystal-like mineral. Do you know what a mineral is?

Pablo: Yeah.

Greg: What is it?

Pablo: It's like a kind of vitamin.

BOX 8.3 /// **Click and Clunk**

What: Click and Clunk

Why: Learning to recognize when understanding breaks down and taking action to figure it out helps students comprehend text.

When: After reading a short section of text.

How:

• Identify words or ideas you do not know and write them in your learning log.

• Use fix-up strategies to figure out the meaning of clunks.

Greg: Okay, calcium is a type of element that is in the bones. And the bones need that. Calcium helps the bones in order to make them strong. Now do you understand what calcium is?

Pablo: Yes.

Greg: What is it again? One more time.

Pablo: It is a type of element that helps the bones grow.

Greg: Okay, good.

Pablo, an ELL with learning disabilities, might not have known what calcium meant when first reading the word, but he figured it out with his partner's help in the CSR structure. Furthermore, the other students benefit from rereading an important section of the text.

The goal of teaching students about Click and Clunk is to provide them with a set of tools to monitor their understanding as they read. Students working within a collaborative context help one another figure out the meaning of words or concepts that may impede understanding of the overall passage.

Get the Gist

Get the Gist, a practice that requires students to restate in their own words the main idea of a section of text, is the second strategy that occurs during reading. Generating the main idea is a task that most students are familiar with, yet more often than not, students are prompted to generate the main idea without knowing just how to perform this important skill (Pressley, 2006). Students using CSR are taught to write a brief gist (main idea) statement for each section of the reading. The gist statements are approximately 10 words long, a suggested length that pushes students to distill the most essential information and avoid adding unimportant details. Coming up with a gist requires higher level thinking and promotes students' memory for what they have learned.

As with the other CSR strategies, students benefit from interacting with each other. They agree on the most important "who" or "what" of a section, then write their own gists in their learning log. Students are encouraged to discuss the quality of each other's gists, and groups sometimes come up with a "super gist" that takes into account the best aspects of multiple gists. These student-led discussions often prompt students to reread because they must provide evidence from the text to support their ideas.

Introducing Get the Gist to Students Teachers introducing Get the Gist to students scaffold the process by breaking down gist writing into three steps.

BOX 8.4 /// **Get the Gist Example**

Pellagra was a disease found mostly in poor children, especially those living in orphanages or institutions. Many people believed that pellagra was passed from one person to another, such as through a cold or the flu. A doctor studying the cause of the disease, however, learned that children with pellagra ate almost no protein, such as meat, milk, or eggs. They were not catching pellagra; they were getting sick from not eating a healthy diet.

Most important "who" or "what:" pellagra
Most important information about the "who" or "what":

- A disease affecting mostly poor children
- People thought it was communicable
- Caused by poor diet

Possible gist: Pellagra is not contagious, but instead comes from eating poorly.

---

1. Identify the most important "who" or "what" of the section.

2. List the most important information about the "who" or "what."

3. Write a gist statement in about 10 words or less.

Students are given many opportunities to practice these steps on their own and in their small groups. A teacher can work with students to identify the most important "who" or "what" in a section. First, the teacher models the process by highlighting all of the places the most important "who" or "what" is mentioned in the text. This visual model demonstrates that the most important "who" or "what" is essential to the gist statement. Next, the teacher models how to identify the most important information. He or she may underline the essential aspects, ask students to offer key details, and encourage students to share with a partner the ideas that seem most important. Again, the visual modeling of underlining important details helps students clarify their understanding of the most important ideas. Finally, the teacher models and then provides practice in producing the gist statement. Box 8.4 is an example of whole-group practice in a science class.

As students become more proficient at gist writing, they no longer need to perform the intermediate step of listing the most important information. Students learn to agree on the most important "who" or "what" with their group members, write their own individual gists, and share and discuss. Students from Ms. Thompson's class are reading about clothes made from sustainable fabrics in the following lesson. Students in one small group are beginning to discuss the quality of the gists they have just written.

Diego (gist expert):   Is everyone finished?

Siena: I'm finished.

Diego: Are you done Henry?

Henry: Yeah.

Diego: Okay, who would like to share?

Siena: The companies are making earth-friendly fabrics out of waste products.

Diego: That's good. Okay, does anyone else have a different gist?

BOX 8.5 /// **Get the Gist**

What: Get the Gist

Why: Good readers process individual ideas and remember only the most important parts—the main ideas of what they read.

When: After identifying clunks and using fix-up strategies, students get the gist of a short section of text.

How:

• Name the "who" or "what" that the section is mostly about.

• Identify the most important information about the "who" or "what."

• Write a gist statement in about 10 words.

Henry: I said earth-friendly products are "in." So companies are making sustainable businesses.

Randy: Earth-friendly companies make clothes that protect our images.

Diego: Sustainable companies now make shirts out of farm waste such as chicken feathers or corn.

Diego: Okay, so most all of us are talking about the companies and most of us have the sustainable part. What about protecting our images? I don't think that's part of it.

Henry: Yeah, you're right. It's not protecting our image. It's protecting our environment. How about if I put. . .[discussion continues] (Adapted from classroom observation, April, 2009).

Wrap Up

Question generation and review are the two parts of the wrap-up. First, students write questions about what they read and share them with members of their group. Next, the teacher brings the class back together for a whole-class wrap-up. See Figure 8.6 for an example.

Question Generation   Students learn to write both straightforward and higher level questions. There are many ways to approach question generation. Teachers may teach students to write specific question types, such as those proposed by Rafael (1986) with question-answer relationships (QAR), or teachers may choose to present the type of information that is contained in questions and use question stems to scaffold question writing. The following describes how to use question stems to support the introduction of leveled questions. Question stems reinforce common language conventions and can spark ideas for question writing.

Questions that usually result in concrete fact-based responses often begin with *what, where, when,* or *how* (often, many). Question stems that help students come up with simple questions include the following.

• Who was it that _____?

• What is _____?

• When did _____ happen?

• Where did _____ happen?

• How many _____ were there?

AFTER READING: Wrap-Up
Questions: (write questions and answers)

Q: *How much ice has been lost in the North Pole?*
A: *The North Pole lost 65% of its ice cover in one year.*

Q: *What are the ways Climatologists study how much ice is melting?*
A: *Climatologists use different types of tools to study how much ice is melting. They use satellite images, first hand observations, and models.*

Q: *What would happen if all of the ice really does melt?*
A: *If all of the ice melts the sea level would rise and the animals living in the North Pole would not survive. The North Pole would not be the same.*

Review:
The temperatures in the North Pole are increasing and causing the thin and thick ice to melt. Scientists have made different predictions when the North Pole will be 100% ice free.

Figure 8.6. Questions a student has written during wrap-up. (From Klingner, J.K., Vaughn, S., Boardman, A.G., & Swanson, E. [2012]. *Now we get it! Boosting comprehension with collaborative strategic reading.* Copyright 2012 Jossey-Bass. This material is reproduced with permission of John Wiley & Sons, Inc.; adapted by permission.)

Other questions require students to make connections either to a student's own life or to the curriculum or combine information from various parts of the reading. These are often the most difficult to write and to answer. Question stems that require synthesis or combining information follow.

• What were some of the reasons for _____?

• What were some of the problems faced by _____?

• How was the problem of _____ solved?

• How are _____ and _____ different?

• How are _____ and _____ the same?

Question stems that require students to make connections or inferences follow.

• What would you do if you were _____?

• When do you think _____ could happen again?

• Where has _____ ever happened before?

• Why is _____ a good or a bad thing?

• Why do you think _____ happened?

Writing a variety of question types allows students to review the text and aids comprehension and memory. Students have eyes in the text as they reread and consider the text in order to come up with questions.

Introducing Question Generation Question types are taught separately at first. Teachers demonstrate how to write the question type with information about when to use it and why. Probe students to say why it is a particular question type. For instance, a student might respond, "This is a factual question because the question and the answer are found in one sentence in the text."

BOX 8.6 /// **Wrap Up: Question Generation**

What: Question generation

Why: Asking and answering questions requires students to summarize text, monitor understanding, integrate information from different parts of the text, remember what was read, and make connections that go beyond the text.

When: After reading a text

How:

• Think of questions and answers and write them in your learning log.

• Ask and answer questions with your group.

Next, teachers give students practice generating questions and answers. Writing answers is a key aspect of this strategy because it forces students to put additional thought into what they are asking. Students who write answers to their own questions are more likely to write specific and thoughtful high-quality questions.

After reading a short biography of Anne Frank, the following exchange occurred in an eighth-grade social studies class.

Pete: Why is this happening?

Elena: What?

Jack (question expert):   What's your question?

Pete: Why is this-? Okay. Wait.

Jack: I'll share mine. When did Anne Frank write her diary?

Students continue to ask and answer their questions, and Pete begins to write again.

Pete: Okay, I have mine now. Why is Anne Frank's book being translated into so many languages? (Adapted from classroom observation, January, 2010)

Not only was Pete now able to provide a thoughtful answer, but the group heard additional ideas when other students responded to his question.

Students can write more than one type of question at a time when they become familiar with question generation. Question generation also provides opportunities for differentiation. If some students are gaining proficiency with factual questions, then they can continue to generate questions and answers of that question type, whereas other students may be able to write questions that make connections or require inferential thinking. All students can participate and share in questions and answers. Teachers can ask some of the questions students have written as an exit ticket before leaving class, create a questioning game, or place students' questions on a quiz or assignment. These authentic applications are motivating for students and encourage them to write important questions about the text.

Review

Review is the final step in the CSR process. First, students write the most important ideas from the passage in their learning logs and take turns sharing and providing evidence within their small groups. Next, the teacher brings the class back together for a brief whole-class Wrap Up. Teachers

---

BOX 8.7 /// **Wrap Up: Review**

What: Review

Why: Reviewing the most important information helps students synthesize information and remember what they have read. Providing evidence for responses helps students to be more accountable and engaged readers.

When: After question generation

How:

• Write the most important ideas from the passage.

• Share with your group, providing evidence to support your ideas.

---

often choose to focus on wrapping up content learning and refining CSR strategy use during this time. Teachers can provide a variety of activities in a short period of time (5–10 minutes) to close the lesson.

Suggestions for content wrap-ups include reviewing key ideas with the class, creating a concept map connecting concepts with other topics in the curriculum, revisiting student predictions and checking for accuracy, playing a game with questions as a way to review content, having students write a longer summary of the text, and providing additional instruction or learning activities for important vocabulary terms.

For strategy-focused review activities, teachers can conduct a minilesson on one strategy. For instance, the teacher might ask groups to share gists from one section and reinforce information contained in high-quality gists. Teachers can have students circle their best gist and question. Those will be the ones the teachers will grade. Teachers may also have students reflect on their cooperative group work, identifying one thing they did well and one thing they need to work on next time.

Introducing Review   The Review Strategy is quick for students to learn. Writing the most important ideas is usually a straightforward task for students because they have done so much work to delve deeply into the text. In fact, teachers may need the most practice and refinement to maximize the learning during review. First, teachers need to leave time for review. Setting a timer and stopping the lesson with 5 or 10 minutes left in class is an important step to ensure that there is enough time to review. In addition, lesson planning as well as monitoring student work and discussions during class are key to review. For example, an eighth-grade language arts class was reading a section of Homer's *The Odyssey*. Students spent the class making meaning of the difficult text. They were observed in rich discussions around vocabulary and content and connecting this text to other ideas in their mythology unit. One of the unit goals included understanding how people are motivated to act. The teacher chose to focus the review on what might have motivated Odysseus. After using CSR to comprehend the text, students were able to engage with depth in a final teacher-led discussion that helped them understand high-level themes in *The Odyssey*.

FULL COLLABORATIVE STRATEGIC READING IMPLEMENTATION

Students are ready to engage in the regular use of the CSR reading process once they have learned the strategies and practiced pieces in cooperative learning groups. Use CSR one to three times each week so that students become familiar with the routine and apply the strategies on a regular basis. Some teachers reinforce strategy use with homework assignments, asking students to read and apply one or two strategies at a time at home.

Before Reading

Preview

- Teacher introduces the topic.
- Teacher preteaches vocabulary and/or proper nouns.
- Teacher builds background knowledge or connects to students' prior knowledge/content/curriculum.
- Students write brainstorms (what they already know about the topic) in their learning logs and share with group members.
- Students preview the passage.
- Students write predictions (what they will learn from the passage) in their learning logs and share with group members.
- Teacher sets the purpose for reading.

During Reading	

Click and Clunk	*Get the Gist*
<ul><li>Students identify words or ideas they do not understand and write them in their learning logs.</li><li>Students work together to use fix-up strategies to figure out the meanings of their clunks.</li><li>Students write clunks and definitions in their learning logs.</li></ul>	<ul><li>Students identify the most important "who" or "what" in the section and the most important information about the "who" or "what."</li><li>Students write their own gist in their learning log.</li><li>Students share gists and provide feedback to the group.</li></ul>

After Reading	

Questions and Answers	*Review*
<ul><li>Students write leveled questions (right there, think and search, author and you) and answers in their learning log.</li><li>Students share questions with their group.</li></ul>	<ul><li>Students write one or two of the most important ideas from the entire passage in their learning log.</li><li>Students share with their group and discuss why the ideas they have written are important.</li><li>Teacher leads whole-group wrap-up that reviews content and/or CSR strategies.</li></ul>

Group Work and Feedback

- Teacher assigns students to heterogeneous groups.
- Teacher provides feedback related to quality of CSR strategy use and content learning.
- Teacher promotes collaboration among students in small groups.
- Students have and use assigned roles during CSR.
- Students help each other while working in groups.

Teachers and students are active throughout the CSR process. The teacher leads the class during the Preview; facilitates group work during Click and Clunk, Get the Gist, and Question Generation; and guides the whole class again during Review. Teachers often benefit from having a checklist handy to guide them through the strategies. The CSR Checklist in Form 8.1 can be used as a guide by individual teachers or it can be used to facilitate an observation of a CSR lesson. Teachers can use student learning logs and the CSR checklist to inform their next steps.

The Teacher's Role During Collaborative Strategic Reading

The teacher's role in CSR occurs in three key areas—learning CSR, using cooperative learning, and deepening understanding. Of course, teachers know that there is never just one focus at a time in a classroom, and, thus, teachers are usually monitoring and providing feedback in several areas at once.

Learning Collaborative Strategic Reading   Teachers often focus on introducing and monitoring the process of CSR during the early stages of implementation. Do students know how to perform the various strategies? What additional practice is needed to help students apply CSR? Group feedback and minilessons may be warranted to refine practice. In addition, teachers may choose to pull a small group of students who are struggling with a particular component while the rest of the class works in their CSR groups. There may be a need to fine tune the use of a particular strategy even when students are proficient at CSR.

Using Cooperative Learning   Teachers may switch their focus to monitoring the use of cooperative group work skills as students learn the CSR strategies. Are students using their CSR roles? Are students writing their own individual responses for each strategy and then discussing with their group members? Are students grouped heterogeneously with peers who are supportive and work well together? What social skills do students need to develop (e.g., taking turns talking, politely disagreeing, helping each other)? Focusing on the expectations for group work and providing feedback to students goes a long way toward instilling strong group work behaviors in students.

Deepening Understanding   Teachers are able to focus more on the content of the reading and the quality of strategy application when students participate and work together. Teachers provide ongoing monitoring and feedback as students work in their groups. In addition, teachers may bring students together between sections of CSR to call their attention to difficult content or to improve the use of a particular strategy. One tip that has helped teachers is to make a point of listening first before asking a question or providing any feedback. Teachers can read learning logs and listen to student discussions before deciding what feedback is needed.

Teachers should also be aware that their comments during student-led group work can promote or hinder discussion among students. Some teacher behaviors such as interrupting or immediately evaluating can undermine the groups' sense of being in charge of their learning. Teachers are not only encouraged to provide informative feedback, but also foster collaboration as much as possible. For instance, if a student asks the teacher if his or her gist is correct, then the teacher could provide evaluative feedback, drawing attention to the teacher as the holder of correct information. Alternatively, the teacher can foster group collaboration by asking questions such as, "How is your gist similar to the gists of your group members?" Or, "Let's hear everyone's gist and decide together."

There is also a time to evaluate responses. Teachers use specific feedback when evaluating student work that provides information to students about what to do next. For instance, a group might determine that their gists were similar to one another, but the teacher notices that they had missed an important part of the section. The teacher might tell the group, "Your gists include important information about the first part of the section, but you are missing some key ideas that should be part of your gist. Reread this section again and work together to revise your gists to include the important information from the second part of the section." Feedback that is provided in the moment, as well as feedback provided to students on their learning logs, encourages high-quality strategy use and student learning.

CONCLUSION

Students using CSR become self-directed learners who stop at sections of text to monitor their understanding and talk to one another about their ideas and questions. They reread portions of the text as they work to improve their understanding, review and synthesize information, and write down key ideas and review statements. Furthermore, they use these strategies in a collaborative context, with each student assuming a specific role in the group.

Teachers may notice that CSR is comprised of reading comprehension strategies that have a long history in classrooms. Yet, as researchers have observed (e.g., Pressley, 2006), students are more often than not asked to perform strategies, such as writing a main idea statement, without ever being taught how to use them. CSR provides a model for teaching and applying a set of reading comprehension strategies that gives students specific and actionable steps for tackling difficult text across content areas.

REFERENCES

Boardman, A.G., Klingner, J.K., Boele, A., & Swanson, E. (2010). Teaching students with LD to use reading comprehension strategies: Using what students know to decide what to teach next. In T. Scruggs & M. Mastropieri (Eds.), *Advances in learning and behavioral disabilities: Literacy and learning* (Vol. 23, pp. 205–235). Greenwich, CT: JAI Press.

Bryant, D.P., Vaughn, S., Linan-Thompson, S., Ugel, N., Hamff, A., & Hougen, M. (2000). Reading outcomes for students with and without reading disabilities in general education middle-school content area classes. *Learning Disability Quarterly, 23*, 238–252.

Colorín Colorado. (2007). *Using cognates to develop comprehension in English.* Retrieved from http://www.colorincolorado.org/educators/background/cognates

Johnson, D.W., & Johnson, R. (1989). *Cooperation and competition: Theory and research.* Edina, MN: Interaction Book Company.

Kamil, M.L., Borman, G.D., Dole, J., Kral, C.C., Salinger, T., & Torgesen, J. (2008). *Improving adolescent literacy: Effective classroom and intervention practices: A practice guide* (NCEE# 2008-4027). Washington, DC: National Center for Education Evaluation and Regional Assistance, Institute of Education Sciences, U.S. Department of Education. Retrieved from http://ies.ed.gov/ncee/wwc/practiceguide.aspx?sid=8

Klingner, J.K., & Vaughn, S. (1996). Reciprocal teaching of reading comprehension strategies for students with learning disabilities who use English as a second language. *Elementary School Journal, 96*, 275–293.

Klingner, J.K., & Vaughn, S. (2000). The helping behaviors of fifth-graders while using collaborative strategic reading during ESL content classes. *TESOL Quarterly, 34*, 69–98.

Klingner, J.K., Vaughn, S., Boardman, A.G., & Swanson, E. (2012). *Now we get it! Boosting comprehension with collaborative strategic reading.* San Francisco, CA: Jossey-Bass.

Klingner, J.K., Vaughn, S., Dimino, J., Schumm, J.S., & Bryant, D. (2001). *Collaborative strategic reading: Strategies for improving comprehension.* Longmont, CO: Sopris West Educational Services.

Klingner, J.K., Vaughn, S., & Schumm, J.S. (1998). Collaborative strategic reading during social studies in heterogeneous fourth-grade classrooms. *Elementary School Journal, 99*, 3–21.

Palincsar, A.S., & Brown, A.L. (1984). The reciprocal teaching of comprehension-fostering and comprehension-monitoring activities. *Cognition and Instruction, 1*, 117–175.

Paris, A.H., Lipson, M.Y., & Wixson, K.K. (1983). Becoming a strategic reader. *Contemporary Educational Psychology, 8*, 293–316.

Paris, S., Wasik, B., & Turner, J. (1991). The development of strategic readers. In R. Barr, M. L. Kamil, P. Mosenthal, & P.D. Pearson (Eds.), *Handbook of reading research* (Vol. 2, pp. 609–640). White Plains, NY: Longman.

Pressley, M. (2006). *Reading instruction that works: The case for balanced teaching* (3rd ed.). New York, NY: Guilford Press.

Pressley, M., & Afflerbach, P. (1995). *Verbal protocols of reading: The nature of constructively responsive reading.* Mahwah, NJ: Lawrence Erlbaum Associates.

Raphael, T.E. (1986). Teaching question-answer relationships. *The Reading Teacher, 39*, 516–520.

Vaughn, S., Chard, D.J., Bryant, D.P., Coleman, M., Tyler, B., Linan-Thompson, S., & Kouzekanani, K. (2000). Fluency and comprehension interventions for third-grade students. *Remedial and Special Education, 21*, 325–335.

Vaughn, S., Klingner, J.K., Swanson, E.A., Boardman, A.G., Roberts, G., Mohammed, S.S., & Stillman-Spisak, S.J. (2011). Efficacy of collaborative strategic reading with middle school students. *American Educational Research Journal, 48*, 938–954.

9 | Using Self-Questioning, Summarizing, and Self-Monitoring to Increase Reading Comprehension

Sheila R. Alber-Morgan & Laurice M. Joseph

Today, more than ever before, students with disabilities can gain access to the general education curriculum and receive instruction in regular classrooms with their typically developing peers (Alber-Morgan, 2010). In fact, approximately 79% of high school students with disabilities were educated in general education classrooms, and 55% of those students spent more than 80% of their school day included (Swanson, 2008). Inclusive secondary classrooms place high demands on students with disabilities as they are expected to have mastered basic reading skills and comprehend information independently from content area texts. In other words, they should have already learned to read proficiently so they can now read to learn. Teaching students to read strategically has been demonstrated to be an evidence-based practice for improving reading comprehension of students with and without disabilities (Edmonds et al., 2009). Self-questioning, summarizing, and self-monitoring are among the most effective comprehension-fostering strategies for struggling adolescent readers (Faggella-Luby & Deshler, 2008). This chapter provides teachers with recommendations for teaching these comprehension strategies.

SELF-QUESTIONING STRATEGIES

Asking students questions that help them focus on essential information in the text is a common approach to teaching reading comprehension. Just as teachers ask students questions to guide and monitor their comprehension, students can learn how to self-question to achieve the same goal (Swanson & De La Paz, 1998). Several variations of self-questioning interventions have demonstrated positive effects for middle and high school students who struggle with reading (e.g., Clark, Deshler, Schumaker, Alley, & Warner, 1984; Crabtree, Alber-Morgan, & Konrad, 2010; Faggella-Luby, Schumaker, & Deshler, 2007). The following are examples of self-questioning strategies that have demonstrated positive effects for struggling readers.

Wong and Jones (1982) used expository texts and taught students a self-questioning strategy that guided them to underline the main idea of each paragraph in a reading passage, change the main idea to a paraphrased question (e.g., "How does crowding together in a school of herring protect them from their enemy?;" p. 233), and learn the answer to the question (e.g., "Crowding makes a school of herring look like a single, giant fish and scares away the enemy"; p. 233). Manset-Williamson, Dunn, and Hinshaw (2008) used the FIST strategy to increase reading comprehension of middle school students. FI is marked at the beginning of each paragraph in a reading passage and ST is marked at the end. The letters *FI* serve as a prompt for the students to read the first sentence and make up a question from that sentence. The letters *ST* marked at the end of the paragraph prompt the students to stop and see if the author answered his or her question.

Paraphrasing is another self-questioning strategy in which the students use the mnemonic RAP to monitor their reading comprehension (Schumaker, Denton, & Deshler, 1984). RAP stands for *R*ead a paragraph, *A*sk yourself the main idea and two details, and *P*ut the main idea and details in your own words. A variation of this strategy is RAP-Q. The Q stands for *Q*uestions. Specifically, the students write questions on index cards (based on what they paraphrased), write the answer on the back of the card, and use the index cards for studying.

The KWL strategy (Ogle, 1986) is a self-questioning strategy that also uses a mnemonic. KWL stands for *K*now (What do I already know about this topic?), *W*ant (What do I want to learn?), and *L*earn (What did I learn?). The KWL chart is a graphic organizer with three columns. Before reading, the students preview the text by examining the title, headings, and the first few sentences. Based on the preview, the students complete the K and W columns. As the students read, they look for the answers to the questions they wrote in the W column as well as additional important information. When they are finished reading, they write what they learned in the L column. After students complete the KWL chart, they can use their critical thinking skills to see if their what-I-know statements are accurate, determine whether they found the answers to the what-do-I-want-to-know questions, and decide what questions remain unanswered. An important benefit of the KWL strategy is that it helps to activate prior knowledge and provides a focus for reading resulting in increased reading comprehension.

The SQ3R, which stands for *S*urvey, *Q*uestion, *R*ead, *R*ecite, and *R*eview, is a more extensive self-questioning strategy for comprehending expository texts (Robinson, 1970). Students preview the text during the Survey step by examining the title, headings, pictures, captions, and the beginning and ending paragraphs. Students change the title and headings into questions in the Question step and also ask themselves what they already know about the subject. Students look for answers to the questions they generated in the first of the 3 Rs (Read). Students ask themselves questions about what they just read in the Recite step, highlighting and summarizing the information and taking notes. Finally, the Review step takes place over the course of several days. Students verbally rehearse the material during Review and use study strategies such as mnemonics, flash cards, and creating a study guide.

The previous strategies can be beneficial for helping struggling readers comprehend expository texts. Other self-questioning strategies were specifically developed for narrative texts, such as novels students read in American or World Literature class. For example, Clark et al. (1984) taught students to ask and answer "Wh" questions (e.g., "who," "what," "where," "when," "why") while reading and then mark each answer in the passage by placing a symbol on the answer (e.g., a clock face to answer a "when" question). In another example, the embedded story structure (ESS) routine was used for ninth graders with and without learning disabilities (Faggella-Luby et al., 2007). ESS included self-questioning, story structure analysis, and summary writing. The self-questioning component of ESS required students to ask themselves a series of questions related to critical story structure components (e.g., character, setting, conflict). Similar to Clark et al., the students used the words *who, what, when, where, which, how,* and *why* to help them remember the types of questions to ask.

Teachers can also use Bloom's Taxonomy (Bloom, 1956) to help more proficient readers develop higher level thinking questions. Bloom's Taxonomy, Revised (Anderson & Krathwohl, 2001), identified the following levels of learning from least to most advanced—remembering, understanding, applying, analyzing, evaluating, and creating. Students reading narrative fiction are provided a prompt showing each level and the kinds of questions to ask. Examples include,

> Who are the characters (Remembering)?" "How do the characters feel about each other (Understanding)?" "How can I connect this story to my life and experiences (Applying)?" "What literary device is used (Analyzing)?" "How has author perspective influenced the telling of this story (Evaluating)?" and "What does this story mean to me (Creating)?"(Buehl, 2009, p. 159)

Teachers should consider the student's level of functioning and the complexity of the strategy when determining the most appropriate self-questioning strategy to teach. In addition, teachers should consider including a summarization component.

SUMMARIZING STRATEGIES

Teaching students to summarize is a logical conclusion to a self-questioning procedure. As students read through each paragraph, questioning and paraphrasing the information as they go, they will have all of the information needed to write a summary. The ESS routine and SQ3R are examples of self-questioning interventions that include a summarizing component. Teaching students to summarize written text is an evidence-based practice for improving both reading comprehension skills and writing skills (Graham & Perin, 2007). Middle and high school students who learn to summarize text perform higher in immediate and delayed reading comprehension measures (Mateos, Martin, & Villalon, 2008; Rinehart, Stahl, & Erickson, 1986). The following are examples of summarization strategies teachers can select and modify for a range of diverse learners.

Paragraph shrinking is a simple strategy for teaching summary skills (McMaster, Fuchs, & Fuchs, 2006). The student stops reading at the end of each paragraph in a reading passage and states the main idea and two details. Then the student writes a summary of that paragraph using no more than 10 words. At the end of the passage, the student uses his or her 10-word summary sentences for each paragraph to write a summary of the entire selection.

Using the rule-governed summary is another approach to teaching summary writing (Rinehart et al., 1986). As students read through the text, they practice using the following rules: "(a) delete trivial information, (b) delete important but redundant information, (c) compose a word to replace either a list or individual components of an action, (d) select or create a topic sentence, and (e) relate the important supporting information" (Swanson & De La Paz, 1998, p. 212). The teacher guides the students through this strategy by providing direct instruction and practice with each rule. For example, the teacher must define and provide examples of trivial information and provide feedback to students as they work through identifying the information that is trivial and not trivial in a paragraph. Once students become proficient with applying these rules and summarizing one paragraph, they can move on to summarizing reading passages with multiple paragraphs.

The GIST strategy (Cunningham, 1982) stands for *Generating Interactions Between Reader and Text* and requires students to state the important information with a minimum number of words. Students answer "who," "what," "where," "why," and "how" questions as they read each paragraph in a passage to determine important information. The student reads the first paragraph and generates a summary of 20 words or less that answers those questions. The student reads the second paragraph and writes a 20-word summary that covers both paragraphs. The student reads the third paragraph and the 20-word summary will encompass the first three paragraphs. This process continues until the student reaches the end of the reading passage. Students should receive guided practice using newspaper articles when first learning this strategy. Newspaper articles are written in a predictable sequence enabling students to more easily answer the "who," "what," "when," "where," "why," and "how" questions. Once students are able to summarize newspaper articles in 20 words or less, they can make the transition to using the GIST strategy with content area textbooks.

If this summarizing strategy is too advanced for some students, then teachers can modify the procedures by guiding students to summarize at the sentence level first. Specifically, the student reads the first sentence and restates the main idea. Then the student reads the first two sentences and retells both sentences in 15 words or less. This procedure continues sentence by sentence until the student summarizes the whole paragraph in 15 words or less (Swanson & De La Paz, 1998). Students will need frequent feedback and guidance that can be gradually faded as they become more proficient.

Teaching Self-Questioning and Summarizing

Self-questioning and summarizing are both evidence-based practices for increasing reading comprehension. Several reading comprehension intervention packages demonstrated to be effective combine self-questioning with summarizing (e.g., Carr & Ogle, 1987; Faggella-Luby et al., 2007; Faggella-Luby & Wardwell, 2011). Students need to be able to synthesize a number of skills to effectively self-question and summarize, including previewing text, identifying text structure, making predictions, identifying important information, and paraphrasing. The following sections provide suggestions for teaching each of these skills.

Previewing   Teaching students to preview a reading passage enables them to identify important clues that will enhance their reading comprehension. Students can preview reading selections by examining the title, headings, key vocabulary words, beginning and ending sentences, and graphics. This will help students identify the topic and type of information they might find in the text. Previewing reading passages has been demonstrated to increase reading comprehension for middle and high school students (Burns, Dean, & Foley, 2004). Previewing also enables students to identify the text structure of the reading passage that is necessary for determining the types of questions to ask when self-questioning.

Teaching previewing involves providing students with written or verbal prompts to examine parts of the reading passage ("Look at the title and headings.") and to make predictions about what they might learn from the reading selection ("What is the topic?" "What do you think you'll find out about this topic?"). In addition, teachers should provide continuous feedback during early attempts at previewing and making predictions. The prompts can be gradually faded for independent previewing as students increase their previewing proficiency.

Teachers can initially provide even more support to students with more intensive instructional needs. For example, students can preview the reading selection by scanning it and underlining all of the vocabulary words they do not know. Then the teacher can preteach those vocabulary words prior to student reading. Previewing or preteaching vocabulary is an effective practice for increasing reading comprehension (e.g., Burns et al., 2004).

Making Predictions   In addition to making predictions during previewing, students can also make predictions throughout a reading passage. Making predictions provides students with direction and focus as they monitor whether their predictions turn out to be accurate. As students progress through a text, they can check the accuracy of their early predictions, revise their predictions or make new predictions, and continue checking for accuracy until they complete the reading passage. Nolan (1991) examined the effects of three comprehension interventions (vocabulary previewing, self-questioning only, and self-questioning combined with prediction) on the reading performance of middle school students. The poorest readers achieved the most dramatic increases in the combined self-questioning and prediction group. A simple way to implement this strategy is to provide embedded prompts in the reading passage for students to make predictions and check them (e.g., What do you think will happen next? Check your prediction). As with previewing, teachers can provide guided practice and continuous feedback when students begin learning to make predictions.

Using Text Structure to Identify Important Information   Students are better able to make predictions, generate appropriate questions, and construct an accurate summary when they can identify a text structure (Dymock, 2009). The types of questions generated when using a self-questioning strategy will depend on the text structure. The text structure of narrative fiction will have common story elements (e.g., characters, setting). Text structure in nonfiction includes description, sequence, compare and contrast, cause and effect, and problem and solution. Students may examine the format of the text and look for clue words in order to identify text structure. For example, a reading passage with descriptive text structure may include some of the following clue words: *characteristics, for example, to illustrate, such as.* After students can identify text structure, they may use a graphic organizer to help them self-question and summarize. Table 9.1 shows expository text structures with corresponding clue words, questions to ask, and the type of graphic organizer to use. After the students complete the graphic organizer, they may use that information to create a summary.

Table 9.1. Questions based on expository text structure

Text structure	Questions	Graphic organizer
Descriptive (Clue words: *characteristics, for example, to illustrate, such as*)	What is the main idea? What are the details?	Detail ← (Main idea) → Detail Detail Detail
Sequential (Clue words: *first, second, third, next, last, after, later, finally*)	What happened first? What happened second? What happened next? What happened last?	1. → 2. → 3. → 4.
Compare and contrast (Clue words: *similarly, but, likewise, on the other hand, whereas, however, conversely*)	What is being compared? How are these concepts alike? How are these concepts different?	Concept A Concept B different alike different
Cause and effect (Clue words: *if, then, because, since, as a result, therefore, consequently*)	What were the causes? What were the effects?	Causes → Effects
Problem and solution (Clue words: *dilemma, problem, answer*)	What is the problem? What is the solution?	Problem → Solution

Paraphrasing The ability to accurately paraphrase information in a reading passage is a good indicator of reading comprehension. Paraphrasing provides opportunities for students to connect the information in the reading passage to prior knowledge by using their own words (Kletzien, 2009). Because paraphrasing is a prerequisite skill to self-questioning and summarizing, students should be provided with direct instruction and practice with paraphrasing various types of reading passages. The teacher can model paraphrasing by thinking aloud and then providing guided practice with feedback until the student can independently paraphrase.

DIFFERENTIATING READING COMPREHENSION STRATEGIES

There are many variations of self-questioning and summarizing strategies, ranging from simple to advanced and requiring various levels of sophistication and independence. Highly structured strategies may be beneficial for students who struggle the most with strategic reading. Conversely, proficient readers will likely benefit from more challenging strategies. Students must generate questions on their own while reading a text in most of the self-questioning research. The ability to self-generate questions demonstrates a fairly sophisticated level of critical thinking that may be somewhat difficult for some struggling readers to independently accomplish, at least initially. Students who have difficulty generating their own questions will benefit from additional structure and support that is gradually faded. For example, the teacher could provide the students with a short list of questions to answer at predetermined stopping points marked in the text. Crabtree et al. (2010) used this procedure and demonstrated that high school seniors with learning disabilities substantially increased their reading comprehension. Specifically, Crabtree et al. provided the students with a series of five generic questions to answer at three predetermined stopping points marked in a story (e.g., What is the story about?). When the students reached each of the three stopping points marked in the text, they asked themselves the same generic questions and wrote the answer on a worksheet. At each stopping point they had an opportunity to revise their answers. After the students became proficient with the structured self-questioning procedures, the embedded stopping points were removed from the stories so the students had to decide when to stop and self-question. In addition, the prompts on the response sheet were faded to an abbreviated format. Even with faded prompts, the students continued to effectively self-question and maintain high levels of reading comprehension.

Creating materials that provide prompts that are gradually faded is an effective way to help students make the transition to independently generating questions. Form 9.1 shows an example of a structured self-questioning worksheet that includes the list of questions, signals to stop and self-question that correspond to the signals in the text, designated spaces to write and revise each subsequent response, and directions for summary writing. Form 9.2 shows how the prompts can be faded so the student can make the transition to producing self-generated questions. The questions are abbreviated to one word, and the student decides when to stop reading and self-question before writing the summary. The degree of guidance provided in Forms 9.1 and 9.2 can serve as a bridge to using the more advanced response sheet shown in Form 9.3.

Gradually fading structured prompts is one way to help students become more proficient with self-questioning and summarizing strategies. Students with disabilities may need additional accommodations that support their use of strategies that help them monitor their comprehension. For example, a student with severe writing difficulties can use an audio recording device or a speech recognition software program (e.g., Dragon Naturally Speaking) to ask and answer self-generated or teacher-generated questions while reading and identifying the main points to summarize the reading passage. After they have recorded their statements, they can listen to them and compare them to the contents in the text to see if they captured the meaning accurately and completely. They can then use the recordings as a study tool.

Students can also practice self-questioning and summarizing strategies with a peer or cooperative learning group. Incorporating peer-mediated instruction into comprehension strategies can provide additional support, feedback, and motivation for students as they practice the strategy. In addition, working with peers provides opportunities for students to practice using social skills, an important aspect of inclusive classrooms for diverse learners.

SELF-MONITORING

Self-monitoring is a self-management technique that involves observing and recording one's own behavior (Mace, Belfiore, & Hutchinson, 2001). Self-monitoring has been shown to be effective for individuals of all ages and abilities (Ganz, 2008). A review of the effects of self-monitoring on the reading performance of students with disabilities revealed that reading performance improved when students engaged in self-monitoring (Joseph & Eveleigh, 2011). In fact, greater reading outcomes were evident for students when reading comprehension strategies such as summarization strategies were coupled with self-monitoring than when the strategies were implemented without a self-monitoring component (Joseph & Eveleigh, 2011). Students can be taught to self-

Directions: Read the story. When you come to a stop sign in the story, stop, ask yourself the questions, and write the answers. Then write a summary from your notes in STOP 3.

	STOP 1	STOP 2	STOP 3
Who are the main characters?			
Where and when does the story take place?			
What is the problem?			
How are the characters trying to solve the problem?			
How do the characters feel?			
How does the story end?			

Summary

Directions: Read the story. Decide on three places to stop and ask yourself questions. Write your answers below.

	1	2	3
Who?			
Where? When?			
Problem?			
How?			
Feelings?			
Ending?			

Summary

Directions: Read the story. Stop at different places and ask yourself questions about the important story elements (characters, setting, plot, emotion, conflict, resolution)

Summary

monitor various types of behaviors related to reading comprehension, including accuracy, fluency, productivity, strategy use, and on-task behavior.

Self-Monitoring of Accuracy Self-monitoring reading comprehension accuracy involves recording occurrences when correct responses were made. For example, students record the number of correct responses to comprehension questions by placing the total number correct on a chart or plotting a point on a line graph. Another example would be recording elements of a story accurately on a form after students have read a story (see Form 9.4). Instructors may insert stopping points throughout the story for students who have difficulty recalling important details after they finish reading so that students can record important details while they read (e.g., Crabtree et al., 2010). Having students engage in self-monitoring accuracy of overt behaviors such as monitoring the accuracy of written responses to comprehension questions is straightforward and relatively simple. Having students self-monitor their covert reading behaviors during silent reading, such as checking for understanding of text, can be more challenging. Covert behaviors can be made overt, however, by having students record whether they understood what they read. For instance, checking for understanding during silent reading can occur by having students use the Click or Clunk technique (Klinger, Vaughn, & Schumm, 1998; Wright, 2001). After students have read each sentence, they ask themselves, "Did I understand that?" If the answer is yes, then the students say "click," and if the answer is no, then the students say "clunk." If the students say "clunk," then they can reread the sentence, and if that does not lead to a better understanding of the sentence, then they can seek assistance. To monitor the number of instances when students said "click" or "clunk," students can either place a checkmark or a counter beneath the click or clunk column on a worksheet or dry erase board.

Self-Monitoring Fluency Reading fluency (i.e., reading accurately, effortlessly, and with expression) is strongly related to comprehending text for primary grade students and moderately related to comprehending text for middle and high school students (Fuchs, Fuchs, Hosp, & Jenkins, 2001). Although fluency may not be sufficient for helping secondary students comprehend text, it is a necessary component because secondary students who read slowly face challenges keeping up with reading material and class demands (Woodruff, Schumaker, & Deshler, 2002). Many older struggling readers need to work on improving both their fluency and comprehension concurrently. Interestingly, fluency interventions (e.g., repeated readings) involving narrative texts had higher effects than those involving expository texts for improving secondary students' comprehension (Edmonds et al., 2009). The weaker effects for secondary-level expository texts suggests that these texts contain large amounts of challenging content (Swanson & Hoskyn, 2001) and require much sustained effort and application of strategies (Fuchs et al., 2001). Researchers have speculated that greater reading outcomes may be evident if fluency interventions are coupled with comprehension strategy instruction (Wexler, Vaughn, Edmonds, & Reutebuch, 2008). For instance, self-monitoring can be incorporated during silent reading so that students are made aware of when they are deriving meaning from text and know when they need to reread and get clarification (Whithear, 2011). Specifically, students can be taught to self-graph the number of times they had to reread the passage along with the number of correct responses to comprehension questions. In this way, students can readily evaluate the data and determine whether efforts directed at becoming more fluent at reading the passage aided them in comprehending the text better. Students are likely to be motivated to set new goals for increasing or maintaining their productivity when they examine a visual display of their performance on a graph (e.g., Stotz, Itoi, Konrad, & Alber-Morgan, 2008).

Self-Monitoring Productivity Self-monitoring reading comprehension productivity involves recording the amount of information students comprehended or attempted to comprehend in a given time period. For instance, during oral or written retells, students record on a chart the amount of words or sentences/main ideas they used to retell the passage (e.g., Mason, 2004). Another example would be to record the number of reading comprehension questions students completed relative to the number of questions assigned (e.g., Shimabukuro, Prater, Jenkins, &

Title of story: _____

Elements	Description	Check if completed
Main characters (people)		
Setting (places)		
Main idea (What was the story about?)		
Main events		
Conflict		
Resolution		

Smith, 1999). Students can then calculate a percentage of the number of questions completed and plot this percentage on a graph.

Self-Monitoring Strategy Use   Self-monitoring adherence to strategy procedures involves recording the instances when steps to executing a strategy have been followed. For example, Jitendra, Hoppes, and Xin (2000) taught middle school students with specific learning disabilities and serious emotional disturbance to self-monitor their use of a main idea summarization strategy by recording their adherence to procedures on a card. The students were asked to place a checkmark next to the following set of procedures if they completed them: "(a) read the paragraph, (b) used the prompt card to recall strategy steps, (c) applied the strategy to identify or construct the main idea of the passage, and (d) selected or wrote the main idea" (Jitendra et al., 2000, p. 131). The results demonstrated that students who received main idea summarization strategy instruction along with self-monitoring training procedures increased their comprehension significantly above their peers with disabilities who did not receive the training. In another study, Nelson and Manset-Williamson (2006) taught middle school students with reading disabilities to self-monitor their use of the following strategies: 1) setting goals, 2) activating prior knowledge, 3) predicting content to be read in the text, 4) identifying the main idea, and 5) retelling key parts of the text. Students self-monitored strategy use by placing a checkmark next to each strategy on a sheet after they used them. These researchers also incorporated strategy-valued feedback so that students could make the connection between using strategies and their improved reading comprehension performance. Explicit reading comprehension strategy instruction coupled with self-monitoring adherence to strategy steps is also effective for improving reading comprehension among students with behavior problems combined with attention-deficit/hyperactivity disorder (Rogevich & Perin, 2008).

Self-Monitoring On-Task Behavior   Self-monitoring on-task behavior involves recording the occurrences that one is engaged in while performing a task. For example, students may place a tally every 5 minutes if they are actually reading during a 30-minute silent reading period. Self-monitoring on-task behavior (sometimes referred to as *attention*) can be done in conjunction with self-monitoring performance (accuracy and productivity). To assist students with and without disabilities in inclusive classrooms, Rock (2005) taught students a mnemonic called ACT-REACT coupled with self-checks of both on-task behavior and performance at 5-minute intervals during sustained silent reading and during other independent seatwork activities. ACT-REACT stands for *A*rticulate your goals, *C*reate a work plan, *T*ake pictures, *R*eflect using self-talk, and *E*valuate your progress and ACT again. These students used a travel alarm clock with a snooze feature as their timing device to signal them to check if they were on task. The students recorded whether they were on task when the timer went off, and they recorded how many pages they read. They also compared their behavior with the behavior depicted in a photograph of them engaged in silent reading. These photographs were taken prior to self-monitoring so that students would have pictorial representations of themselves achieving their goals. The pictures were inserted into the recording sheets so that they could serve as visual prompts for the students. Students were taught to engage in self-talk at each 5-minute interval to explain why they were not on task and state how they could improve their behavior. Afterward, students were asked to evaluate their overall on-task behavior and their performance. For instance, students recorded on a sheet the percentage of time they were on task and the total number of pages they read. Results revealed that ACT-REACT plus self-checking was an effective strategy for helping students with and without disabilities increase their on-task behavior and productivity and maintain their accuracy levels in inclusive classrooms (Rock, 2005).

Teachers and students can select various types of signaling devices, depending on individual student needs, when monitoring on-task behaviors. For instance, a MotivAider, a pager-type device that can be clipped to a student's waistband and set to vibrate at intermittent or fixed time intervals, may be used when individualizing self-monitoring instruction. Teachers can use recorded intermittent tones for large groups of students to signal students to self-monitor their on-task behavior.

Researchers have examined the differential effects of self-monitoring on-task behavior and self-monitoring accuracy and productivity among diverse students with disabilities (e.g., Harris, Friedlander, Sadder, Frizzelle, & Graham, 2005; Rafferty & Raimondi, 2009). Findings have been relatively consistent indicating that self-monitoring on-task behavior results in better accuracy and productivity than no self-monitoring at all. When self-monitoring of on-task behavior is compared with self-monitoring accuracy and productivity, however, self-monitoring accuracy and productivity had greater effects on task engagement and reading achievement. Interestingly, students preferred to monitor their accuracy and productivity over their on-task behavior (Rafferty & Raimondi, 2009).

Students still benefit even if they do not self-monitor their performance or behavior accurately (Hallahan & Sapona, 1983). The act of self-monitoring helps students increase engagement and performance on tasks. The teacher can record students' behavior and performance and match the recordings with their students' recordings to promote accuracy in self-monitoring. The teacher can provide verbal praise when the recordings match. Discussions about discrepancies can occur when recordings do not match. The teacher can fade the frequency of the matching sessions when students meet a criterion level of correct matches and conduct them on a variable schedule until the students are able to accurately self-monitor on their own (e.g., Davies, Jones, & Rafoth, 2010).

TEACHING STUDENTS TO SELF-QUESTION, SUMMARIZE, AND SELF-MONITOR

Explicit instruction is the best way to learn to self-question, summarize, and self-monitor during reading. It is recommended that teachers provide instruction on self-questioning first, then summarizing, because self-questioning is conducive for creating a summary. Self-monitoring can be taught in conjunction with both strategies as a way to help students monitor their application of strategy use. The following instructional sequence can be applied when teaching these strategies—providing a rationale, modeling, providing guided practice with feedback, providing independent practice, and programming for generalization.

Providing a Rationale   The teacher should begin the lesson by stating a clear purpose(s) for using the strategy, including a discussion about the benefits of using the strategy. For example, the teacher describes the strategy and asks, "How do you think learning this strategy will help you?" and generates or guides students' responses such as, "I'll understand the chapter better," "I'll do better on my homework and tests," and "I might get better grades." The teacher can continue teaching the strategy using the following steps once students recognize the benefits and seem to be interested in learning the strategy.

Modeling   The teacher simultaneously verbalizes the process (think aloud) and demonstrates how to apply the strategy. The teacher can model self-questioning by reading a paragraph aloud and then modeling how to self-question. For example, "What is the main idea of this paragraph? Hmm, let's see, the paragraph is mostly about the feeding habits of whales. It says some eat microscopic animals and some eat very large animals. So, the main idea is different kinds of whales eat different kinds of food. Okay, which whales eat krill? Let me look back at the paragraph. It says here, 'Baleen whales eat mostly krill.' Let me write that down." After the teacher demonstrates self-questioning, she can model how to change the self-questioning responses into a summary paragraph.

The teacher can model self-monitoring by self-recording reading behaviors such as number of questions asked and number of strategy steps used. For example, teachers can demonstrate checking off each time a step of the strategy was completed by placing a checkmark on a card listing all of the steps. After the teacher models the strategies, he or she can provide guided practice with feedback.

Providing Guided Practice with Feedback   It is best to start with age-appropriate reading materials that are relatively short and easy when students are initially learning a strategy. This will allow students to practice the strategy with less demanding materials before allowing them to practice with more advanced grade-level textbooks. Teachers can prompt the students to demonstrate application of the strategy. Specifically, the teacher prompts the students to begin reading the text aloud and to ask and answer questions aloud. The teacher listens to the students' questions and answers and provides them with feedback. If the students are having difficulty generating questions or answering their questions, then the teacher can remodel the strategy. If students get stuck on any step, then the teacher can provide additional guidance for successful completion.

Independent Practice   Students apply the strategies on their own and are encouraged to seek teacher assistance when needed. Students can self-monitor their strategy use and signal the teacher for attention to obtain corrective feedback and reinforcement. Teachers can periodically collect students' self-recordings of strategy use and evaluate them for accuracy. Teachers can begin to program for generalization as students become more proficient at using the strategies independently.

Programming for Generalization   Cooper, Heron, and Heward (2007) identified several strategies designed to enable students to generalize or transfer skills across settings (e.g., different classrooms, home, library), situations (e.g., different teachers, small-group versus whole-class instruction), reading materials (e.g., different subject matter, different text genres), response modes (e.g., speaking, writing, keyboarding), and over time (i.e., maintenance). The following are ways teachers can program for generalization of reading comprehension strategies.

- *Aim for natural contingencies of reinforcement.* This strategy refers to using materials and procedures that motivate students to learn and continue using the strategy. Teachers can aim for natural contingencies of reinforcement by assessing students' preferences and selecting reading materials and topics that are highly interesting and personally meaningful to the students. Teachers can also increase motivation by providing choices of reading materials, assignments, and instructional arrangements (e.g., working with a peer or in a small group).

- *Teach enough examples.* The more examples taught, the greater degree of generalization (Cooper et al., 2007). Teaching many examples is not sufficient, however. Teachers must select examples that represent the range of situations the students are likely to encounter and the range of responses the students may have to make. Students should be provided with reading materials representing a range of topics and text structures when being taught paraphrasing and summarizing. Students should also practice the strategies using both verbal and written responses and in a variety of instructional arrangements.

- *Program common stimuli.* Programming common stimuli increases generalization by making the generalization setting (i.e., outside the classroom) as similar as possible to the teaching setting. Teachers can program common stimuli of self-questioning and summarizing strategies by creating a transportable prompt for the students to different settings. The prompt can be a laminated card taped in the student's binder that lists the steps for using the strategy. The students can refer to the strategy steps on the laminated card in all their content area classes, at home, or in the library.

CONCLUSION

Self-questioning, summarizing, and self-monitoring are three strategies that have been found to be effective for improving reading comprehension of students with and without disabilities in inclusive classroom settings. All of these strategies are often used together for the purposes of gaining meaning from text. Self-questioning is used to identify main ideas and make inferences about the content in a passage. The main ideas obtained from self-questioning can be used to create a summary of a passage. Students can self-monitor to determine if they are gaining meaning from the passage (e.g., recording the number of accurate main ideas they included in their summary). This chapter presented various self-questioning, summarizing, and self-monitoring techniques along with general procedures for how to teach the strategies. Secondary teachers in inclusive classrooms can differentiate instruction by making decisions about which techniques best match individual students' needs. Most important, students can learn to use these strategies independently in their future academic endeavors.

REFERENCES

Alber-Morgan, S. (2010). *Using RTI to teach literacy to diverse learners, K8: Strategies for the inclusive classroom.* Thousand Oaks, CA: Corwin.

Anderson, L.W., & Krathwohl, D.R. (Eds.). (2001). *A taxonomy for learning, teaching and assessing: A revision of Bloom's Taxonomy of educational objectives: Complete edition.* New York, NY: Longman.

Bloom B.S. (1956). *Taxonomy of Educational Objectives, Handbook I: The Cognitive Domain.* New York: David McKay Co Inc.

Buehl, D. (2009). *Self-questioning taxonomy: Classroom strategies for interactive learning* (3rd ed.). Newark, DE: International Reading Association.

Burns, M.K., Dean, J.D., & Foley, S. (2004). Preteaching unknown key words with incremental rehearsal to improve reading fluency and comprehension with children identified as reading disabled. *Journal of School Psychology, 42,* 303–314.

Carr, E., & Ogle, D. (1987). K-W-L-Plus: A strategy for comprehension and summarization. *Journal of Reading, 30,* 626–631.

Clark, F.L., Deshler, D.D., Schumaker, J.B., Alley, G.R., & Warner, M.M. (1984). Visual imagery and self-questioning: Strategies to improve comprehension of written material. *Journal of Learning Disabilities, 17,* 145–149.

Cooper, J.O., Heron, T.E., & Heward, W.L. (2007) *Applied behavior analysis* (2nd ed.) Upper Saddle River, NJ: Merrill/Prentice Hall.

Crabtree, T., Alber-Morgan, S.R., & Konrad, M. (2010). The effects of structured self-questioning on the reading comprehension of high school seniors with learning disabilities. *Education and Treatment of Children, 33,* 187–203.

Cunningham, J. (1982). Generating interactions between schemata and text. In J.A. Niles & L.A. Harris (Eds.), *New inquiries in reading research and instruction* (pp. 42–47). Washington, DC: National Reading Conference.

Davies, S.C., Jones, K.M., & Rafoth, M. (2010). Effects of a self-monitoring intervention on children with traumatic brain injury. *Journal of Applied School Psychology, 26,* 308–326.

Dymock, S. (2009). Teaching expository text structure awareness. In D. Lapp & D. Fisher (Eds.), *Essential readings on comprehension* (pp. 62–68). Newark, DE: International Reading Association.

Edmonds, M.S., Vaughn, S., Wexler, J., Reutebuch, C., Cable, A., Taqckett, K.K., & Schnakenberg, J. W. (2009). A synthesis of reading interventions and effects on reading comprehension outcomes for older struggling readers. *Review of Educational Research, 79,* 262–300.

Faggella-Luby, M.N., & Deshler, D.D. (2008). Reading comprehension in adolescents with LD: What we need to learn. *Learning Disabilities Research and Practice, 23,* 70–78.

Faggella-Luby, M.N., Schumaker, J.S., & Deshler, D.D. (2007). Embedded learning strategy instruction: Story structure, pedagogy in heterogeneous secondary literature classes. *Learning Disability Quarterly, 30,* 131–147.

Faggella-Luby, M., & Wardwell, M. (2011). RtI in middle school: Findings and practical implications of a tier-2 reading comprehension study. *Learning Disability Quarterly, 34,* 35–49.

Fuchs, L.S., Fuchs, D., Hosp, M.K., & Jenkins, J.R. (2001). Oral reading fluency as an indicator of reading competence: A theoretical, empirical, and historical analysis. *Scientific Studies of Reading, 5,* 239–256.

Ganz, J.B. (2008). Self-monitoring across age and ability levels: Teaching students to implement their own positive behavioral interventions. *Preventing School Failure, 53,* 39–48.

Graham, S., & Perin, D. (2007). *Writing next: Effective strategies to improve writing of adolescents in middle and high school.* Washington, DC: Alliance for Excellence in Education.

Hallahan, D.P., & Sapona, R. (1983). Self-monitoring of attention with learning disabled children: Past, present, and current issues. *Journal of Learning Disabilities, 16,* 616–620.

Harris, K.R., Friedlander, B.D., Sadder, B., Frizzelle, R., & Graham, S. (2005). Self-monitoring of academic performance: Effects among students with ADHD in the general education classroom. *Journal of Special Education, 39,* 145–156.

Heward, W.L. (2006). *Exceptional children: An introduction to special education* (8th ed.). Columbus, OH: Pearson.

Jitendra, A.K., Hoppes, M.K., & Xin, Y.P. (2000). Enhancing main idea comprehension for students with learning problems: The role of summarization strategy and self-monitoring instruction. *Journal of Special Education, 34*(3), 127–139.

Joseph, L.M., & Eveleigh, E. (2011). A review of the effects of self-monitoring on the reading performance of students with disabilities. *Journal of Special Education, 45,* 43–53.

Kletzien, S.B. (2009). Paraphrasing: An effective comprehension strategy. *The Reading Teacher, 63*, 73–77.

Klinger, J.K., Vaughn, S., & Schumm, J.S. (1998). Collaborative strategic reading during social studies in heterogeneous fourth-grade classrooms. *Elementary School Journal, 99*, 3–22.

Mace, F.C., Belfiore, P.J., & Hutchinson, J.M. (2001). Operant theory and research on self-regulation. In B.J. Zimmerman & D.H. Schunk (Eds.), *Self-regulated learning and academic achievement: Theoretical perspectives* (2nd ed.; pp. 39–65). Mahwah, NJ: Lawrence Erlbaum Associates.

Manset-Williamson, G., Dunn, M., & Hinshaw, R. (2008). The impact of self-questioning strategy use on the text-reader assisted comprehension of students with reading disabilities. *International Journal of Special Education, 23*, 123–135.

Mason, L.H. (2004). Explicit self-regulated strategy development versus reciprocal questioning: Effects on expository reading comprehension among struggling readers. *Journal of Educational Psychology, 96*, 283–296.

Mateos, M., Martin, E., & Villalon, R. (2008). Reading and writing to learn in secondary education: Online processing activity and written products in summarizing and synthesizing tasks. *Reading and Writing: An Interdisciplinary Journal, 21*, 675–697.

McMaster, K.L., Fuchs, D., & Fuchs, L.S. (2006). Research on peer-assisted learning strategies: The promise and limitations of peer-mediated instruction. *Reading and Writing Quarterly, 22*, 5–25.

Nelson, J.M., & Manset-Williamson, G. (2006). The impact of explicit, self-regulatory reading comprehension strategy instruction on the reading-specific self-efficacy, attributions, and affect of students with reading disabilities. *Learning Disability Quarterly, 29*, 213–230.

Nolan, T.E. (1991). Self-questioning and prediction: Combining metacognitive strategies. *Journal of Reading, 35*, 132–138.

Ogle, D.M. (1986). K-W-L: A teaching model that develops active reading of expository text. *The Reading Teacher, 39*, 564–570.

Rafferty, L.A., & Raimondi, S.L. (2009). Self-monitoring of attention versus self-monitoring of performance: Examining the differential effects among students with emotional disturbance engaged in independent math practice. *Journal of Behavioral Education, 18*, 279–299.

Reichrath, E., de Witte, L.P., & Winkens, I. (2010). Interventions in general education for students with disabilities: A systematic review. *International Journal of Education, 14*, 563–580.

Rinehart, S.D., Stahl, S.A., & Erickson, L.G. (1986). Some effects of summarization training on reading and studying. *Reading Research Quarterly, 21*, 422–438.

Robinson, F.P. (1970). *Effective study* (4th ed.). New York, NY: Harper & Row.

Rock, M.L. (2005). Use of strategic self-monitoring to enhance academic engagement, productivity, and accuracy of students with and without exceptionalities. *Journal of Positive Behavior Interventions, 7*, 3–17.

Rogevich, M.E., & Perin, D. (2008). Effects on science summarization of a reading comprehension intervention for adolescents with behavior and attention disorders. *Exceptional Children, 74*, 135–154.

Schumaker, J.B., Denton, P.H., & Deshler, D.D. (1984). *The paraphrasing strategy.* Lawrence, KS: University of Kansas.

Shimabukuro, S.M., Prater, M.A., Jenkins, A., & Smith, P.E. (1999). The effects of self-monitoring of academic performance on students with learning disabilities and ADD/ADHD. *Education and Treatment of Children, 22*, 397–414.

Stotz, K.E., Itoi, M., Konrad, M., & Alber-Morgan, S.R. (2008). Effects of self-graphing on written expression of fourth grade students with high incidence disabilities. *Journal of Behavioral Education, 17*, 172–186.

Swanson, C.B. (2008). *Special education in America: The state of students with disabilities in the nation's high schools.* Retrieved from http://www.edweek.org/media/eperc_specialeducationinamerica.pdf

Swanson, H.L., & Hoskyn, M. (2001). Instructing adolescents with learning disabilities: A component and composite analysis. *Learning Disabilities Research and Practice, 16*, 109–120.

Swanson, P.N., & De La Paz, S. (1998). Teaching effective comprehension strategies to students with learning and reading disabilities. *Intervention in School and Clinic, 33*, 209–218.

Wexler, J., Vaughn, S., Edmonds, M., & Reutebuch, C.K. (2008). A synthesis of fluency interventions for secondary struggling readers. *Reading and Writing: An Interdisciplinary Journal, 21*, 317–347.

Whithear, J. (2011). A review of fluency research and practices for struggling readers in secondary school. *Literacy Learning in the Middle Years, 19*, 18–28.

Wong, B.Y.L., & Jones, W. (1982). Increasing metacomprehension in learning disabled and normally achieving students through self-questioning training. *Learning Disability Quarterly, 5*, 228–240.

Woodruff, S., Schumaker, J.B. & Deshler, D. (2002). *The effects of an intensive reading intervention on the decoding skills of high school students with reading deficits* (Report No. RR-15). Washington DC: Special Education Programs. (ERIC Document Reproduction Service No. ED469293)

Wright, J. (2001). *The savvy teacher's guide: Reading interventions that work.* Retrieved from http://www.interventioncentral.org

10 || Multicomponent Interventions for Improving Content Learning

Asha K. Jitendra and Meenakshi Gajria

T his chapter explains multicomponent strategies and reviews research on the importance of multicomponent interventions for improving content learning. It also describes some multicomponent interventions that can be implemented in small groups or in heterogeneous classrooms with instructional grouping that facilitates cooperative learning or partner learning. Finally, it describes issues to consider and ways to help teachers effectively present or use these interventions in their classrooms.

STRATEGY KNOWLEDGE AND MULTICOMPONENT INTERVENTIONS

Many students who struggle with reading evidence problems with comprehension that may be directly related to deficits in word recognition skills and require effective interventions to remediate decoding deficits. Poor readers who demonstrate slow, inaccurate reading, as well as students with adequate decoding skills but who primarily have difficulty in understanding text, require direct instruction in constructing meaning. Although reading comprehension depends on several student-related factors such as vocabulary, background knowledge, motivation, and self-perception, it is the lack of mastery and use of strategic knowledge that distinguishes poor and skilled readers (see Gersten, Fuchs, Williams, & Baker, 2001; Palincsar & Brown, 1984; Pressley, Goodchild, Fleet, Zajchowski, & Evans, 1989). Unlike skills that indicate routinization, strategies allude to reflective use. It is well recognized that comprehension strategies to construct meaning should help "readers enhance their understanding, overcome difficulties in comprehending text, and compensate for weak or imperfect knowledge related to the text" (Shanahan et al., 2010, p. 10). Therefore, "a good strategy involves multiple cognitive subroutines. As an example, generating questions about a text is a strategy that relies on searching the text, combining information, evaluating the worth of the question, and then judging whether one could answer the question" (Johnson-Glenberg, 2000, p. 772). Research suggests that implementing the subroutines can result in improved comprehension (Rosenshine, Meister, & Chapman, 1996). Furthermore, reading comprehension is strongly correlated with cognitive and metacognitive strategies (Soprer, Brunstein, & Kieschke, 2009; see Stanovich & Cunningham, 1991).

Reading is a multilevel interactive process that not only involves integrating new and existing knowledge, but also flexibly using strategies to "foster, monitor, regulate, and maintain comprehension" (Alfassi, 2004, p. 171). As such, the difficulties that struggling readers and students with reading disabilities experience with regard to knowing strategies, choosing appropriate strategies (as well as knowing how, when, and why to apply comprehension strategies), and monitoring strategies points to the relevance of explicit instruction in multiple strategies to foster reflective reading (Gajria, Jitendra, Sood, & Sacks, 2007). A synthesis of reading comprehension instruction for students with reading difficulties shows the promise of multiple strategies for affecting "transfer to more generalized measures of reading achievement" (Gersten et al., 2001, p. 307)

Although cognitive strategies such as recognizing text structure, cognitive mapping, questioning, identifying main ideas, and summarization in isolation are known to be effective, some researchers have incorporated them into multicomponent strategy packages to determine the benefits of the combined strategies for improving students' text comprehension skills. According to Shanahan et al., "Multiple-strategy instruction might be more complicated initially, but it familiarizes students with using the strategies together from the very beginning, providing a more authentic, strategic reading experience" (2010, p. 13). Skilled reading involves interacting with the content and coordinating the application of multiple strategies in a way that learning becomes deliberate, self-directed, and self-regulated. Multiple strategy instruction requires helping students coordinate the use of a repertoire of strategies, which may involve reading the text, asking questions, drawing connections, finding main ideas, clarifying meaning, rereading, and paraphrasing or summarizing key information (see Jitendra, Burgess, & Gajria, 2011). One well-researched multicomponent strategy package is reciprocal teaching and its variants, such as collaborative strategic reading (see Chapter 8) and POSSE (*P*redict, *O*rganize, *S*earch, *S*ummarize, *E*valuate). The SQ3R (*S*urvey, *Q*uestion, *R*ead, *R*ecite, *R*eview) is another multicomponent strategy approach and involves verbal rehearsal strategies. The multipass strategy is an adaptation of SQ3R. Transactional strategy instruction (Pressley et al., 1992) and concept-oriented reading instruction (e.g., Guthrie et al., 1998) are other multicomponent interventions that have not been addressed and are beyond the scope of this chapter.

RECIPROCAL TEACHING

Reciprocal teaching (Palincsar & Brown, 1984) is one of the most comprehensive and validated multiple strategy instruction packages. The theoretical framework for reciprocal teaching is based on Vygotsky's (1978) notions about social construction of knowledge and the importance of interactive dialogue for learning. Reciprocal teaching was designed for children with adequate decoding skills but who had difficulties comprehending age-appropriate text. The approach, which is suitable for use before, during, and after reading, includes comprehension-fostering activities to promote acquisition of specific knowledge as well as comprehension-monitoring activities to facilitate self-monitoring and self-regulation necessary for independent learning. The core features of reciprocal teaching involve 1) instruction and practice in applying four comprehension-fostering and comprehension-monitoring strategies (i.e., prediction, clarification, question generation, summarization) to comprehend novel text, 2) interactive teacher–student dialogue as the basis for learning and applying the four strategies, and 3) scaffolded instruction in the use of the strategies during which the teacher fades modeling of the strategies and students assume responsibility. In the early work of Palincsar and Brown (1984) and other studies of reciprocal teaching (e.g., Labercane & Battle, 1987), the teacher initially modeled (expert scaffolding) and had students practice the strategies in small groups during the dialogues, with a gradual shift in responsibility to the students in leading a discussion of the text and understanding why, when, and where the four strategies are applied to understand new text. In later studies by Palincsar and colleagues (Palincsar, Brown, & Martin, 1987; Palincsar, David, Winn, & Stevens, 1991) and other researchers (e.g., Alfassi, 1998; Bruce & Chan, 1991; Hart & Speece, 1998; Lederer, 2000; Lysynchuk, Pressley, & Vye, 1990), students received direct instruction in each of the four strategies in separate lessons before beginning the dialogues (see Appendix A for a sample script on explicit teaching of questioning prior to reciprocal teaching dialogue). Explicit instruction on the four strategies was deemed important in scaffolding instruction for poor readers, students with learning disabilities, and English language learners (ELLs).

Rosenshine and Meister (1994) reviewed studies on reciprocal teaching and found it to be effective in improving student comprehension of text. Treatment effects were higher for experimenter-developed comprehension tests, however, than standardized tests used to evaluate the impact of reciprocal teaching in these studies. The seminal study by Palincsar and Brown (1984) provided the foundation for the value of reciprocal teaching in promoting self-directed and flexible use of the four strategies via scaffolded instruction and collaboration. Palincsar and Brown taught junior high school students with comprehension problems either in pairs (Study 1) or in whole classes (Study 2) to apply the four strategies to comprehend text. The authors summarized the effectiveness of reciprocal teaching in terms of improvement not only in students' dialogues, but also increased pretest-to-posttest comprehension on comprehension tests, including a standardized reading comprehension measure. Furthermore, students retained the effects of the learned strategies for 8 weeks following the end of the 20-day intervention and demonstrated generalization to a classroom setting, with students meeting or surpassing the average performance of their peers without comprehension problems. The effects of reciprocal teaching were evident when implemented by researchers or teachers.

Several studies since the seminal work of Palincsar and Brown (1984) have examined the impact of reciprocal teaching in different settings and geographic areas for elementary through postsecondary students with reading comprehension problems (Alfassi, 1998; Bruce & Chan, 1991; Hart & Speece, 1998; Labercane & Battle, 1987; Le Fevre, Moore, & Wilkinson, 2003; Lysynchuk et al., 1990; Palincsar et al., 1987). The benefits of reciprocal teaching were unequivocal, with the exception of one early investigation of reciprocal teaching conducted in Canada with middle school students with learning disabilities (Labercane & Battle, 1987). The authors reported no significant intervention effect for the 10 students trained in the four strategies (i.e., summarizing, questioning, clarifying, predicting) within the framework of reciprocal teaching dialogue compared with a second group of 10 students who did not receive such instruction (Labercane & Battle, 1987). The question generation strategy on the reciprocal teaching framework in this study was supplemented by Raphael's (1982) question-answer relationship (QAR) procedure, an effective strategy for both answering and generating questions. The QAR strategy helps students engage in text meaning searches using two sources—text and background knowledge and experiences—to determine "right there," "think and search," and "on my own" QARs. The reciprocal teaching intervention included a total of 28 lessons taught over a 14-week period. Although reciprocal teaching lessons for the first 4 weeks were presented to all 10 students, the class was then divided into two small groups to better foster interaction among group members. Therefore, one plausible reason for the reported failure of reciprocal teaching with students with learning disabilities is that they may not have benefited from conventional reciprocal teaching, given that peer interactions in the group process may not have elicited the information needed for less knowledgeable students to learn from more knowledgeable peers because all students in the study experienced significant reading problems (functioning at least three grades below grade level). Another possibility is that the standardized reading comprehension test used to evaluate the impact of reciprocal teaching placed considerable demands on students with learning disabilities (e.g., required different strategies than the ones in reciprocal teaching) and was less sensitive to intervention to mask the intervention effect.

In contrast, Bruce and Chan's (1991) work with seven fifth- and sixth-grade students in a primary school in New South Wales, Australia, demonstrated the importance of explicit strategy instruction before beginning reciprocal teaching dialogue along with transenvironmental programming. Students were provided with explicit instruction to apply the four strategies (i.e., predicting, clarifying, questioning, summarizing) they learned in the resource room to similar tasks in their homeroom reading and social studies classes. Results of a multiple baseline across settings design showed that these students, who had significant comprehension deficits with percentile rankings from 4 to 33 on a standardized test, dramatically improved from baseline to intervention (65% and 44% improvements for fifth- and sixth-grade students, respectively) on experimenter-developed comprehension tests and maintained their improved performance 4 weeks following the last reciprocal teaching session. Furthermore, strategy generalization to the two settings was seen for all students but was more pronounced for students who had relatively high initial word recognition and comprehension scores. The cumulative effect of opportunities to use and master the strategies seemed to promote strategy generalization.

Several later studies conducted with students with comprehension problems all demonstrated the positive effects of reciprocal teaching (e.g., Alfassi, 1998; Hart & Speece, 1998; Lovett et al., 1996; Lysynchuk et al., 1990). Providing explicit instruction in the four strategies prior to reciprocal teaching dialogues common across these studies may have accounted for the benefits accrued from reciprocal teaching. All four studies demonstrated the effectiveness of reciprocal teaching on experimenter-developed comprehension or strategy acquisition tests, and two studies also showed intervention effect on a standardized test (Hart & Speece, 1998; Lysynchuk et al., 1990). The comparison groups in these studies consisted of small-group no-strategy instruction (Lysynchuk et al., 1990), traditional classroom reading instruction (Alfassi, 1998), cooperative group reading instruction (Hart & Speece, 1998), and alternate treatment (study skills) control (Lovett et al., 1996). The reciprocal teaching group membership in two studies ranged from two to five English-speaking Canadian students in fourth to seventh grade (Lysynchuk et al., 1990) to six to eight postsecondary students from a large Mid-Atlantic metropolitan area (Hart & Speece, 1998). In contrast, the reciprocal teaching instructional groups in two other studies were relatively large. Alfassi (1998) included a reciprocal teaching group of 10–11 freshman high school students enrolled in remedial reading classes, and Lovett et al. (1996) included about 15 students per group of seventh- and eighth-grade students. Reciprocal teaching intervention was provided for 10, 13, 20, and 25 days in Hart and Speece (1998), Lysynchuk et al. (1990), Alfassi (1998), and Lovett et al. (1996) studies, respectively.

Lederer (2000) taught upper elementary students (grades four through six), including 25 students with learning disabilities, in mixed ability-level groups (four to five students) to apply the four strategies in reciprocal teaching to comprehend social studies text. Students in the reciprocal teaching group outperformed students in the control group, who received strictly teacher-directed instruction with little interaction between students or with the teacher on their ability to answer short questions, ability to generate questions, and ability to compose summaries. Lederer, however, did not report the effects of reciprocal teaching on the reading comprehension of students with learning disabilities to determine the extent to which these students were responsive to reciprocal teaching intervention conducted in heterogeneous classrooms.

Le Fevre et al. (2003) used a heterogeneous mix of students (poor decoders and poor comprehenders or adequate decoders and poor comprehenders) and explored the effectiveness of modified reciprocal teaching on the comprehension of students with decoding skills deficits and comprehension problems in an urban school in Auckland, New Zealand. Students who were poor decoders scored at least 2 years below grade level on both decoding and comprehension standardized tests at the start of the study. Given that previous research with reciprocal teaching did not include readers with severe decoding skill deficits (except for students with learning disabilities in Labercane & Battle, 1987), Le Fevre et al. designed "tape-assisted reciprocal teaching using high interest, age-appropriate texts with students who had poor decoding and comprehension abilities" to enable "more heterogeneous reading ability groups to operate" (p. 40). In the first study of two multiple baseline across participants design studies, students who were adequate decoders but poor comprehenders benefited from both conventional reciprocal teaching and tape-assisted reciprocal teaching, whereas students who were poor decoders demonstrated improved comprehension using tape-assisted reciprocal teaching but not conventional reciprocal teaching. The second study, which involved only tape-assisted reciprocal teaching corroborated the findings of the first study, with improved comprehension scores on both experimenter-developed and standardized tests as well as transfer to a recall task for all students. Furthermore, students maintained the strategy effects (10 weeks later) at a level higher than baseline performance. The authors concluded that "assisted reciprocal teaching may be seen as a form of 'cognitive bootstrapping' to enable poor readers to escape the cycle of reading failure and engage more meaningfully in the process of reading" (p. 38).

Takala (2006) extended the research on reciprocal teaching to fourth- and sixth-grade special education students in mainstream classes (natural science and history) and students with specific language impairment (SLI) in Finland. Results suggested that the benefits of explicit strategy instruction before reciprocal teaching dialogues were more robust for special education students in mainstream classes than for students with SLI on experimenter-designed tests of comprehension.

Reciprocal teaching has also been used with ELLs; however, the effects of reciprocal teaching for these students are mixed. Although Cotterall (1990) reported no significant effects for postsecondary ELL students following reciprocal teaching intervention, two studies (Fung, Wilkinson, & Moore, 2003; Klingner & Vaughn, 1996) of reciprocal teaching intervention demonstrated improved comprehension on experimenter-designed and standardized tests for middle school participants. The success of these two studies may be attributed to encouraging or formally requiring participants to use their first language (Spanish or Taiwanese) to increase their understanding of important content.

In addition to the previous studies that used conventional reciprocal teaching (e.g., Palincsar & Brown, 1984; Labercane & Battle, 1987), explicit strategy instruction before reciprocal teaching dialogues (e.g., Alfassi, 1998; Lysynchuk et al., 1990), or enhanced reciprocal teaching (i.e., tape-assisted reciprocal teaching; Le Fevre et al., 2003), several variations of reciprocal teaching have been implemented with considerable success. One successful adaptation of reciprocal teaching is Collaborative Strategic Reading (CSR), which consists of four strategies—Preview, Click and Clunk, Get the Gist, and Review (see Chapter 8). Students using CSR learn to apply these strategies in different phases of reading. Students are taught to use the Preview strategy before they begin reading by connecting the topic with what is already known and predicting what will be learned about the topic. Students learn to monitor their comprehension during reading, use fix-up strategies to decipher unknown words or phrases (Click and Clunk), and identify the most important ideas in the text to Get the Gist. Students generate questions and review key ideas learned during the Review strategy.

Explicitly teaching text structure (i.e., the logical relationship of ideas about a topic) to students with learning disabilities within the framework of reciprocal teaching is another successful adaptation of reciprocal teaching (Englert & Mariage, 1991). The varied text structures (e.g., description, sequence, compare and contrast, problem and solution, cause and effect) in expository texts make comprehension of unfamiliar content difficult, particularly for students with learning disabilities. Instruction in identifying the underlying text structure and using it to visually represent key ideas in a passage has been shown to promote students' reading comprehension (Gersten et al., 2001). Englert and Mariage used the reciprocal teaching model to combine text structure mapping with instruction in an integrated set of comprehension strategies cued by the POSSE acronym in their work with upper elementary students with learning disabilities. POSSE strategies include *P*redicting ideas based on prior knowledge, *O*rganizing ideas using the text structure, *S*earching/*S*ummarizing main ideas within the text structure, and *E*valuating comprehension. Researchers designed cue cards and strategy sheets to scaffold instruction and provide guided practice (see Figure 10.1 for a partially completed strategy sheet). This combined intervention led students using the POSSE strategy to outperform students who received traditional instruction in the same text on all comprehension measures, total free recall of ideas, recall of main ideas, overall organization of recalls, and strategy knowledge.

Summary of Reciprocal Teaching

Overall, research supports using reciprocal teaching across grade levels to promote reading comprehension of expository text for students with comprehension difficulties, including students with learning disabilities. Improvements in reading comprehension were documented on both experimenter-developed comprehension measures and standardized tests (Fung et al., 2003; Hart & Speece, 1998; Klingner & Vaughn, 1996; Palincsar & Brown, 1984). Maintenance and general-

POSSE

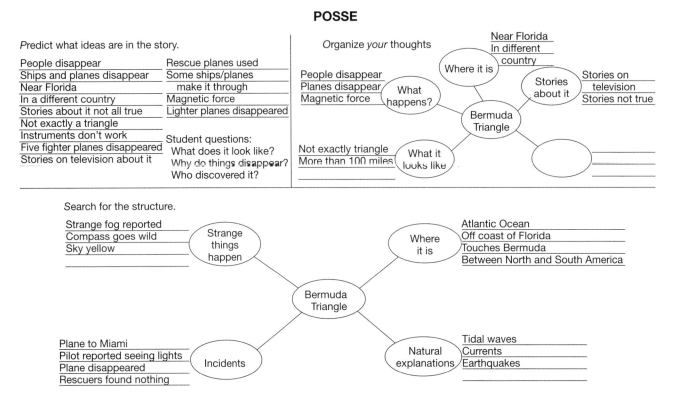

Summarize. Summarize the main idea in your own words. Ask a "teacher" question about the main idea.

Evaluate. Compare. Clarify. Predict.

Figure 10.1. Partially completed POSSE strategy sheet. (From Englert, C.S. & Mariage, T.V. [1991]. Making students partners in the comprehension process: Organizing the reading "posse." *Learning Disability Quarterly, 14*[2], p. 129. LEARNING DISABILITY QUARTERLY by COUNCIL FOR EXCEPTIONAL CHILDREN ; COUNCIL FOR LEARNING DISABILITIES Copyright 2012 Reproduced with permission of SAGE PUBLICATIONS INC. JOURNALS in the format Republish in a textbook and "other" book via Copyright Clearance Center.)

ization outcomes were also positive (Bruce & Chan, 1991; Palincsar & Brown, 1984). Despite the overwhelming support of reciprocal teaching, this instructional model presents several difficulties with regard to implementation in real-world classrooms. For example, teachers may not be familiar with reciprocal teaching or may find it challenging to implement the scaffolding technique in assisting students to develop responsibility for the strategic behavior (Fuchs et al., 2001). Evidence of difficulties in implementing reciprocal teaching is based on an observational study that examined teachers' implementation of reciprocal teaching in two elementary schools over a 3-year period (Hacker & Tenent, 2002). Teachers encountered several obstacles related to each of the core features of reciprocal teaching. With regard to strategy use in reciprocal teaching groups, although teachers employed questioning and summarizing strategies most often, the focus was on superficial levels of the text. Furthermore, teachers effectively used the predicting strategy with narrative text; however, the strategy did not lend itself to expository text. In contrast, teachers seldom used the clarification strategy. Teachers reported that even though students learned the strategies through explicit instruction in the first few weeks, a breakdown occurred in the application of the strategies. Stimulating meaningful dialogue within the student reciprocal teaching groups also was problematic and limited due to students' poor discourse skills. Some students assigned as group leaders lacked the motivation to lead, resulting in other group members becoming disengaged in the learning process. As many reciprocal teaching groups continued to need extensive teacher support in using the strategies even after 2 months of implementation, teachers provided greater scaffolding of the collaborative processes essential for interactive dialogue. In summary, the need to build in considerable time and effort for both teacher and student training for effective application of the reciprocal teaching model was seen as crucial.

Guidelines for Implementing Reciprocal Teaching   The work of Palincsar and colleagues (Palincsar & Brown, 1984; Palincsar, David, & Brown, 1989) provided explicit guidelines for implementing reciprocal teaching. The first step in implementing reciprocal teaching is engaging students in a discussion of difficulties experienced in understanding text and introducing them to questioning, summarizing, clarifying, and predicting as helpful strategies for understanding and remembering what is read in different content areas. Palincsar et al. (1987) pointed out that the four strategies were not designed to limit the choice of strategies, but to illustrate the significance of using multiple comprehension strategies before, during, and after reading segments of text. Recommendations for practice include 25 class sessions of 40 minutes each to teach reciprocal teaching, with the first five sessions emphasizing direct instruction in each of the strategies, one strategy per session (Palincsar et al., 1989). The teacher would use think alouds and a simple text to model the application of each strategy (see Appendix A for explicit teaching of questioning prior to reciprocal teaching dialogue). The fifth session would entail a review of all four strategies, with the teacher modeling the combined use of the strategies applied to a short passage. The teacher can assign students to reciprocal teaching groups, preferably six students with different reading abilities (good, adequate, and poor comprehenders) per group. Furthermore, reading partners or peer dyads can be formed within groups.

Once students learn the four strategies, they can then take turns assuming the role of the teacher in their reciprocal teaching groups. In a typical reciprocal teaching session, the student assigned to act as the teacher/leader reads aloud a segment (about four paragraphs) of the text. Next, the student leader can engage the other students in generating questions about the text read, clarifying difficult words or expressions, summarizing what has been read so far, and making predictions for the upcoming section of the text (see Appendix B for a sample dialogue in a reciprocal teaching group conducted with eighth graders). An adaptation of the reciprocal teaching model requires all students to silently read a segment of the text and write two questions, a summary, and a prediction, and note any item that needs clarification (Soprer et al., 2009). Students can do this individually or with a reading partner before the text is read aloud and discussed. This sequence of a student leader reading the text, engaging the group in a meaningful dialogue about the text, and applying the four strategies is then repeated with remaining sections of the text.

Teachers can play a prominent role in implementing reciprocal teaching in the early sessions by providing explanations, prompting thought-provoking rather than literal questions, modeling strategies, and monitoring the progress of the leader and students' participation in each group. Over time, students gradually assume increasing responsibility for leading discussions and applying the strategies. The extensive practice with different texts and continued teacher feedback serves to help students internalize the cognitive subroutines and strategies so that they can apply them independently to understand the material and self-regulate their comprehension (Pressley & McCormick, 1995).

Palincsar (1986) noted that although rich meaningful dialogue is critical to strategic processing of text in the reciprocal teaching model, it is also an area of concern. Groups may be constrained in their application of the strategies and discussion of text due to ineffective interaction skills. In such cases, teachers would need to directly address group discourse skills and instruct students in how to listen, take turns, reach consensus, and provide feedback. An evaluation of group performance may indicate that teachers need to continue scaffolding instruction for an extended period, including explicit modeling of the strategies and providing guidance with group interaction skills. Teachers will eventually need to fade the scaffolding to allow students to gain ownership of the strategies and effectively process text to monitor and promote their comprehension.

SQ3R

SQ3R (Robinson, 1941) is one of the oldest multiple component strategy packages for expository texts to prepare students to read strategically and help them organize, elaborate, and rehearse information from text to promote reading comprehension and recall. SQ3R is comprised of the following steps: *S*urvey headings and subheadings to gain an overview of the reading passage, *Q*uestion—change headings and subheadings to questions to set a purpose for reading, *R*ead the passage/text to answer questions, *R*ecite the important information and write brief notes about key ideas, *R*eview the main points and try to recall them, checking to see if correct. Recitation or verbal rehearsal of the information is a key component of SQ3R because it provides students with immediate feedback related to understanding the material, directs them to segments of the text that need additional study, and helps them remember important information from texts.

Adams, Carnine, and Gersten (1982) examined the effectiveness of systematic instruction (SI) in study strategies on the comprehension and recall of social studies text. Typically achieving fifth-grade students with adequate decoding skills were taught the following steps: 1) preview the passage by reading headings and subheadings, 2) recite the subheadings, 3) ask questions based on subheadings, 4) read to find important details under the subheading, 5) reread the subheading and recite important details, and 6) after Steps 2–5 are repeated for each subheading, reread the subheading and recite important details. Adams et al. focused on multiple repetitions of the subheadings so that the subheadings would serve as a retrieval cue. Results indicated that in comparison with an independent study with feedback (ISF) group (using the same social studies materials as the SI group) and a no-instruction group, students in the SI group did significantly better on factual, short-answer comprehension tests and maintained their performance 10 days after training. No significant differences were noted in retell or free recall of the passages. The authors questioned the usefulness of free retells as a comprehension measure for lengthy texts (800-word passages) and for elementary-age students, given the problems in deciphering their retells and the presence of incomplete idea units in their recall.

Alexander (1985) replicated the previous study and worked with three 11-year-old students with learning disabilities with grade-level decoding skills but poor comprehension to apply the study strategies package developed by Adams et al. (1982). Materials included 200-word third–grade-level expository passages that were modified to contain suitable subheadings. Explicit instruction in the strategies increased students' oral retelling of the passage, and the effect was maintained. Although these results are encouraging, they are inconsistent with the findings of Adams et al. (1982), possibly due to the difference in the instructional materials. McCormick and Cooper (1991) taught secondary students with learning disabilities diagnosed with reading deficits to apply SQ3R to history texts. SQ3R did not affect reading comprehension outcome assessed via oral recall of history text across three experiments. Consistent with prior work (Adams et al., 1982; Alexander, 1985), the percentages of retelling were strongly related to the length of the text read, with higher percentages of recall noted for shorter rather than longer passages.

The multipass strategy (Schumaker, Deshler, Alley, Warner, & Denton, 1982) is a successful adaptation of the SQ3R strategy package for independently extracting information from reading content area texts. Multipass requires three passes of the material by having students engage in three substrategies—survey, size-up, and sort-out. Students use the survey substrategy to familiarize themselves with the main ideas and organization of the chapter by focusing on subheadings, illustrations, and reading the chapter summary. Students use the size-up substrategy to gain specific information from the text without completely reading the text by focusing on end-of-chapter questions to determine what is important and then skimming the text to find answers. Students use the sort-out substrategy to test themselves on questions and other important material in the text. Schumaker et al. used principles of direct instruction, including teacher modeling, verbal rehearsing of strategy, and guided practice in controlled and grade-level materials, and documented significant gains in reading comprehension for secondary students with learning disabilities on both instructional and grade-level expository texts.

BOX 10.1 /// Sample Prompt Sheet for Teaching SQ3R

1. *Survey.* First survey the material/passage to get an overall idea of the subject matter. Look over the title, sub-headings, diagrams, captions, and graphs. Read the overview and summary, if provided, to get the general idea and see how the information is organized.

2. *Question.* Turn each subheading into a question. Authors often use subheadings that capture important information or main ideas. You can write the question on a sticky note and place it in the passage. You can use different colored sticky notes to differentiate information (e.g., yellow for vocabulary or definitions of terms, blue for larger text units). The subheading "Kinds of rocks" can be changed to "How many different kinds of rocks are there?" or "What are the characteristics of the different kinds of rocks?"

3. *Read.* Read the passage to answer the question that you generated. Find important details to elaborate on your answer. Reading to answer a question helps you to focus on what is important in the passage.

4. *Recite.* Stop and test yourself before moving to the next section. Try to recite the question and the answer to yourself. If you cannot remember everything, then go back and reread the section and try once again to answer the question. Write down the main points of your answer. You may want to use a two-column note system, with the question in the left column and the answer in the right column.

Repeat Steps 2, 3, and 4 for each of the subheadings until you have read the entire passage.

5. *Review.* When you have finished the assignment, spend a few minutes reviewing what you read. Ask yourself the questions you created from the subheadings and try to recall the major points. Check your responses by looking at your notes. Repeating the question and answer to yourself will help you remember the material.

Check your work by answering the following questions.

- Did you note the title of the passage?
- Have you generated a question for each of the subheadings?
- Did you write brief answers for each question?
- Can you recall the answers to yourself?

Summary of SQ3R

Overall, research results on SQ3R and its adaptations indicate that explicit instruction can be successfully used to teach complex strategies with multiple components to students with deficits in reading comprehension, including students with learning disabilities. Also, training in SQ3R is effective in promoting reading comprehension and recall of expository text materials.

Guidelines for Teaching SQ3R   Given that SQ3R is a complex, integrated set of strategies, direct instruction in the specific strategies and extensive practice in the combined use of the strategies is essential. In the studies reviewed, direct instruction was provided individually or in small groups, and the amount of instruction time varied from a minimum of 3 hours (Adams et al., 1982) to 11 hours (Schumaker et al., 1982). Using SQ3R assumes that students have the requisite skills, specifically transforming subheadings into questions, finding main ideas, locating details, taking notes, organizing ideas, and condensing all the information accessed in the process of applying the strategies to review text. In addition, knowing text structure may help students generate better questions that target important information. As students may lack some of these skills, teachers should assess for these prerequisites to effectively plan instruction.

Teachers can scaffold instruction in the first few training sessions (about 30–40 minutes each session) by inserting additional subheadings to divide longer passages into smaller segments.

Explicit instruction in framing questions is important because generating questions is one of the most important components of SQ3R and multipass. Teachers should use short expository passages and model question generation by asking meaningful questions that address the main points in a section of the text. Teachers can provide sample question starters and provide feedback as students practice framing questions so they can move beyond developing factual questions only. Once students have learned question asking, teachers can describe the different components of SQ3R, discuss benefits of using the system, model each step, and provide guided practice with feedback. Teachers should provide students with a prompt sheet that lists components of SQ3R so that students do not feel overwhelmed and lose interest in the assignment.

CONCLUSION

Reciprocal teaching and SQ3R are similar because they both integrate multiple strategies before, during, and after reading and positively influence reading comprehension. Systematic instruction and extensive practice in reciprocal teaching and SQ3R is extremely beneficial as it helps students to extract meaning as well as organize and remember information from reading content area texts. Findings from research studies on both reciprocal teaching and SQ3R provide direction for how teachers can implement effective strategy instruction for students with adequate word decoding skills that experience problems in comprehending information.

- *Provide explicit instruction in learning the multicomponent strategy package.* Teach each of the strategy components in isolation prior to introducing students to the application of the integrated set of strategies. Salient features of effective strategy instruction include teacher modeling using think alouds, followed by student verbal rehearsal, extended guided practice with different materials, and immediate, corrective feedback (Jitendra & Gajria, 2011). It is only when students have acquired declarative knowledge of the strategy (what it is), procedural knowledge (how to apply it), and conditional knowledge (when to use it and why) that they can monitor and self-regulate their comprehension processes. Combine "small-group activities with whole-class instruction to make the collaborative learning process easier for students as well as for the teacher" (Soprer et al., 2009, pp. 273–274).

- *Ensure commitment of time and resources.* Instruction in the comprehensive set of strategies requires a commitment of time and mental energy on the part of teachers and students. Teachers must recognize that some students will need extended scaffolding to coordinate the use of multiple strategies and assume responsibility for their own learning. Also, students should be convinced that the benefits of reciprocal teaching or SQ3R outweigh the amount of time and effort needed for effective strategy use.

- *Carefully consider the selection of instructional materials.* The text may need to be modified when first learning the strategies to allow students to apply a specific strategy. Also, the text should be at the students' instructional reading level rather than their grade level to preclude difficulty with word identification or vocabulary knowledge. Children should eventually be provided systematic practice in applying the learned strategy on grade-level materials, a variety of authentic texts that they will encounter in school, to assure transfer of the strategy.

In conclusion, reciprocal teaching and SQ3R are comprehensive strategies proven effective for increasing higher order comprehension skills and recall of expository text for students with learning difficulties. These multicomponent interventions can be used to differentiate instruction in general education classes to promote independent studying in the content areas, particularly science and social studies.

REFERENCES

Adams, A., Carnine, D., & Gersten, R. (1982). Instructional strategies for studying content area texts in the intermediate grades. *Reading Research Quarterly, 18,* 27–55.

Alexander, D.F. (1985). The effect of study skill training on learning disabled students' retelling of expository material. *Journal of Applied Behavior Analysis, 18,* 263–267.

Alfassi, M. (1998). Reading for meaning: The efficacy of reciprocal teaching in fostering reading comprehension in high school students in remedial reading classes. *American Educational Research Journal, 35,* 309–332.

Alfassi, M. (2004). Reading to learn: Effects of combined strategy instruction on high school students. *Journal of Educational Research, 97,* 171–184.

Bruce, M.E., & Chan, L.K.S. (1991). Reciprocal teaching and transenvironmental programming: A program to facilitate the reading comprehension of students with reading difficulties. *Remedial and Special Education, 12,* 44–54.

Cotterall, S. (1990). Reciprocal teaching: A problem-solving approach to reading. *Guidelines, 12,* 2.

Englert, C.S., & Mariage, T.V. (1991). Making students partners in the comprehension process: Organizing the reading "POSSE." *Learning Disability Quarterly, 14,* 123–138.

Fuchs, D., Fuchs, L.S., Thompson, A., Svenson, E., Yen, L., Al Otaiba, S., . . . Saenz, L. (2001). Peer-assisted learning strategies in reading: Extensions for kindergarten, first grade, and high school. *Remedial and Special Education, 22,* 15–21.

Fung, I.Y.Y., Wilkinson, I.A.G., & Moore, D.W. (2003). L-1-assisted reciprocal teaching to improve ESL students' comprehension of English expository text. *Learning and Instruction, 13,* 1–31.

Gajria, M., Jitendra, A.K., Sood, S., & Sacks, G. (2007). Improving comprehension of expository text in students with LD: A research synthesis. *Journal of Learning Disabilities, 40,* 210–225.

Gersten, R., Fuchs, L.S., Williams, J.P., & Baker, S. (2001). Teaching reading comprehension strategies to students with learning disabilities: A review of research. *Review of Educational Research, 71,* 279–320.

Gunning, T.G. (2012). *Building literacy in secondary content area classrooms.* Upper Saddle River, NJ: Pearson Education, Inc..

Guthrie, J.T., Van Meter, P., Hancock, G.R., Alao, S., Anerson, E., & McCann, A. (1998). Does concept-oriented reading instruction increase strategy use and conceptual learning from text? *Journal of Educational Psychology, 90,* 261–278.

Hacker, D.J., & Tenent, A. (2002). Implementing reciprocal teaching in the classroom: Overcoming obstacles and making modifications. *Journal of Educational Psychology, 94,* 699–718.

Hart, E.R., & Speece, D.L. (1998). Reciprocal teaching goes to college: Effects of postsecondary students at risk for academic failure. *Journal of Educational Psychology, 90,* 670–681.

Jitendra, A.K., Burgess, C., & Gajria, M. (2011). Improving expository text comprehension of students with learning disabilities using cognitive strategy instruction: The quality of evidence. *Exceptional Children, 77*(2), 135–160.

Jitendra, A.K., & Gajria, M. (2011). Main idea and summarization instruction to improve reading comprehension. In R.E. O'Connor & P.F. Vadasy (Eds.), *The handbook of reading interventions* (pp.198–219). New York: Guilford Press.

Johnson-Glenberg, M.C. (2000). Training reading comprehension in adequate decoders/poor comprehenders: Verbal versus visual strategies. *Journal of Educational Psychology, 92,* 772–782.

Klingner, J.K., & Vaughn, S. (1996). Reciprocal teaching of reading comprehension strategies for students with learning disabilities who use English as a second language. *Elementary School Journal, 96,* 275–293.

Labercane, G., & Battle, J. (1987). Cognitive processing strategies, self-esteem, and reading comprehension of learning disabled students. *B.C. Journal of Special Education, 11*(2), 167–185.

Lederer, J.M. (2000). Reciprocal teaching of social studies in inclusive elementary classrooms. *Journal of Learning Disabilities, 33,* 91–106.

Le Fevre, D.M., Moore, D.W., & Wilkinson, I.A.G. (2003). Tape-assisted reciprocal teaching: Cognitive bootstrapping for poor decoders. *British Journal of Educational Psychology, 73,* 37–58.

Lovett, M.W., Borden, S.L., Warren-Chaplin, P.M., Lacerenza, L., Deluca, T., & Giovinazzo, R. (1996). Text comprehension training for disabled readers: An evaluation of reciprocal teaching and text analysis training programs. *Brain and Language, 54,* 447–480.

Lysynchuk, L.M., Pressley, M., & Vye, N.J. (1990). Reciprocal teaching improves standardized reading-comprehension performance in poor comprehenders. *Elementary School Journal, 90,* 469–484.

McCormick, S., & Cooper, J.O. (1991). Can SQ3R facilitate learning disabled students' literal comprehension of expository text? Three experiments. *Reading Psychology, 12,* 239–271.

Moss, J., & Wilson, G. (1998). *Profiles in American history: Civil Rights movement to the present.* Detroit, MI: UXL.

Palincsar, A.S. (1986). The role of dialogue in providing scaffolded instruction. *Educational Psychologist, 21,* 73–98.

Palincsar, A.S. (1987, April). *Collaborating for collaborative learning of text comprehension.* Paper presented at the Annual Meeting of the American Educational Research Association, Washington, DC.

Palincsar, A.S., & Brown, A.L. (1984). Reciprocal teaching of comprehension-fostering and comprehension-monitoring activities. *Cognition and Instruction, 1,* 117–175.

Palincsar, A., Brown, A.L., & Martin, S.M. (1987). Peer interaction in reading comprehension instruction. *Educational Psychologist, 22,* 231–253.

Palincsar, A.S., David, Y.M., & Brown, A.L. (1989). *Using reciprocal teaching in the classroom: A guide for teachers.* Unpublished manual.

Palincsar, A., David, Y., Winn, J., & Stevens, D. (1991). Enhancing the content of strategy instruction. *Remedial and Special Education, 12,* 43–53.

Pressley, M., El Dinary, P., Gaskings, I., Schuder, T., Bergman, J.L., Almasi, J., . . . & Brown, R. (1992). Beyond direct explanation: Transactional instruction of reading comprehension strategies. *Elementary School Journal, 92,* 513–555.

Pressley, M., Goodchild, F., Fleet, J., Zajchowski, R., & Evans, E.D. (1989). The challenges of classroom strategy instruction. *Elementary School Journal, 89,* 301–335.

Pressley, M., & McCormick, C.B. (1995). *Advanced educational psychology for educators, researchers, and policymakers.* New York, NY: HarperCollins.

Raphael, T. (1982). Question-answering strategies for children. *The Reading Teacher, 36,* 186–190.

Robinson, F.P. (1941). *Diagnostic and remedial techniques for effective study.* New York: Harper and Brothers.

Rosenshine, B., & Meister, C. (1994). Reciprocal teaching: A review of the research. *Review of Educational Research, 64,* 479–450.

Roshenshine, B., Meister, C., & Chapman, S. (1996). Teaching students to generate questions: A review of the intervention studies. *Review of Educational Research, 66,* 181–221.

Schumaker, J.B., Deshler, D.D., Alley, G.R., Warner, M.M., & Denton, P.H. (1982). Multipass: A learning strategy for improving reading comprehension. *Learning Disability Quarterly, 5,* 295–304.

Shanahan, T., Callison, K., Carriere, C., Duke, N.K., Pearson, P.D., Schatschneider, C., & Torgesen, J. (2010). *Improving reading comprehension in kindergarten through 3rd grade: A practice guide* (NCEE 2010-4038). Retrieved from http://whatworks.ed.gov/publications/practiceguides

Soprer, N., Brunstein, J.C., & Kieschke, U. (2009). Improving students' reading comprehension skills: Effects of strategy instruction and reciprocal teaching. *Learning and Instruction, 19,* 272–286.

Stanovich, K.E., & Cunningham, A.E. (1991). Reading as constrained reasoning. In R.J. Sternberg & P.A. Frensch (Eds.), *Complex problem solving: Principles and mechanisms* (pp. 3–60). Mahwah, NJ: Lawrence Erlbaum Associates.

Takala, M. (2006). The effects of reciprocal teaching on reading comprehension in mainstream and special (SLI) education. *Scandinavian Journal of Educational Research, 50,* 559–576.

Vygotsky, L.S. (1978). *Mind in society: The development of higher psychological processes* (M. Cole, V. John-Steiner, S. Scribner, & E. Souberman, Eds. and trans.). Cambridge, MA: Harvard University Press.

APPENDIX A

This script excerpt from Palincsar (1987) demonstrates the explicit teaching of questioning before the reciprocal teaching dialogue.

"Questions play an important part in our lives. Much of our class discussion is focused on answering questions. What are some other occasions or situations when questions are important?"
Elicit responses from the students that might include the following.

- Reading assignments usually require us to answer questions at the end of a story.

- Tests usually require us to answer a series of questions.

- We need to ask questions when we need more information about something.

"Let's practice asking some questions for situations when we might need more information. For example, suppose you want to see the movie, 'The Empire Strikes Back,' however, you do not know when the movie begins. You might call the theater and ask "What time does the movie, "The Empire Strikes Back" begin?'

"One of the activities we will be doing for the next couple of weeks is learning to ask good questions about material we have read. We will focus on asking questions about important information rather than about unimportant, trivial, or detailed information. There are several reasons why we will learn to ask questions while reading. (List italicized phrases on the chalkboard.)

(a) It is a way in which we can test ourselves to make sure we understand what we have read.

(b) It is a good way to focus on important information in a passage.

(c) It is possible with a little practice that we can become skilled enough at questioning that we can predict the kinds of questions we might be asked on a test. This would be very useful while studying.

"Let's begin by talking about the words that are used to ask questions. What are some of the words that we use to begin questioning sentences?" (List responses on the chalkboard.)

Who	What
When	Where
Why	How

"Let's practice by asking questions about the following sentences. At first you will be given the question word; however, later you will be asked to think of your question words. Look at the first sentence on your papers. 'The falcon is a female hunting bird.' Ask a question word about the information in this sentence that begins with the word 'what'."

1. The falcon is a female hunting bird.

   WHAT is a falcon? or What is the name of a female hunting bird? What does a falcon do? (Accept any appropriate responses.)

"Ask a question about the information in Sentence 2. Begin your question with the word 'who'."

2. In medieval times, in Europe, only members of a royal family could own falcons.

   WHO could own falcons in medieval times?

"Ask a question about the third sentence that begins with the word *why.*"

3. The falcon bathes in shallow streams to control bird lice that live in her feathers.

   WHY does the falcon need to bathe?

Script excerpted from Palincsar, A.S. (1987, April). *Collaborating for collaborative learning of text comprehension.* Paper presented at the Annual Meeting of the American Educational Research Association, Washington, DC; reprinted by permission.

4. A falcon prefers to hunt for its prey in open areas.

    WHERE do falcons hunt?

5. In the 1950s the falcon populations in North America and Central Europe dropped suddenly.

    WHEN was there a decline in the falcon population?

6. The falcon hunts by swooping down on her prey and grabbing it with her sharp talons.

    HOW does the falcon catch her prey?

"For further practice, make up questions for each of the following sentences (7–11). This time, however, no question words are given." (You may continue to complete these items as a whole-class discussion or give the students the opportunity to complete them independently by writing down their responses. Discuss their questions and accept any question that captures the main idea of the sentence and is posed clearly.)

7. Although animals do not have language as we do, they do communicate with each other by signals of some kind.

8. Scientists study animal communication through experiments and observations.

9. Because snakes are totally deaf, it is the movement of the snake charmer that charms the snake, not the music the snake charmer plays.

10. Some ants give off a special alarm odor that warns nearby ants of danger.

11. The sounds made by bats, moths, and whales are too high for humans to hear.

"Now that you are successful making up questions, we will discuss selecting the most important information in the paragraph about which to ask a question. Look at number 12 on your papers. Number 12 is a short paragraph. There are three questions after the paragraph. One of these questions is better than the other two because it is about the most important information in the paragraph. Let's first read the paragraph."

12. Deaths from snakebites have been cut down in recent years by the use of antivenins—medicines that work against the snake poisons. There are now few deaths from snakebites in the United States and Canada.

"Let's read the three questions that follow this paragraph and try to decide which question asks about the most important information." (Read through all three choices.)

_____ a. Why do snakes bite people?

"This is not a good main idea question. Can anyone tell us why?" (This is not a good main idea question because the question is not answered in the paragraph. This question would make a good prediction, however, because it shows that you are thinking about what kinds of information might come next in the story.)

_____ b. In what countries do few people die from snakebites?

"This is what we could call a detail question. Although the answer is in the paragraph, it is not about the most important information in the paragraph."

_____ c. Why do fewer people die from snakebites these days?

"This question is the best because to answer it you must discuss the antivenin or medicine, which is the main topic of the paragraph."

"Let's try another example. Read paragraph 13 and the three questions that follow it. Put a checkmark next to the best question. Remember that the best question should be clear and should be about the most important information in the paragraph. Be ready to discuss your choice." Once students have selected the best response, discuss each question and why it is/is not the best choice.

13. Contrary to what some people believe, snakes do not sting with their tongues. Their tongues are used to sharpen their sense of smell. The snake picks up tiny particles of matter in the air with his tongue and puts them in two tiny holes at the bottom of his nostrils so that he can smell better.

    _____ a. How many holes does a snake have at the bottom of his nostrils? (detail question)

    _____ b. What does a snake use his tongue for? (main idea question since paragraph discusses how a snake uses his tongue for smelling rather than for stinging)

    _____ c. Why do people use the expression, "He speaks with forked tongue"? (question not answered in the text)

APPENDIX B

The following is a script of a reciprocal teaching lesson based on a reading about Eleanor Roosevelt from *Profiles in American History: Civil Rights Movement to the Present* (Moss & Wilson, 1998) taken from Gunning (2012, pp. 164–166).

(Lead-in question)

Adam (student discussion leader):   My question is, what was Eleanor Roosevelt's childhood like?

Carmen: She was rich. And her family was famous.

(Clarification Request)

Reginald: The book says that her family was one of the original "400" aristocratic families in the United States. That needs to be clarified. I don't know who these 400 people were. And I'm not sure what *aristocratic* means.

Charles: *Aristocratic* means high class. I think maybe 400 is referring to the top 400 people in the United States. Maybe the richest 400?

Teacher: You are on the right track. I'm not sure myself how the 400 were chosen. That's something for us to research.

Adam: Eleanor Roosevelt did come from a wealthy family, but she had some problems. What were they?

Janine: Her mother was cold. She wasn't a very warm person. I mean she probably never hugged Eleanor.

Alicia: And she criticized her. Her mother told her she was awkward and too serious. She called her "Granny."

Charles: And her father was almost never home.

Carmen: Not even on Christmas.

Teacher: Good observation. What problem did Eleanor's father have?

Paula: He drank. He was an alcoholic. What a family. It just goes to show that money isn't everything.

Adam: But the family wasn't all bad. What good things did they teach Eleanor?

Carmen: They taught her to be kind. The father gave money to crippled kids. And Eleanor was sent to soup kitchens to help out.

Teacher: Good answer. Can you summarize this section of the chapter, Adam?

(Summary)

Adam: This section says that Eleanor Roosevelt's family was rich and famous, but they had problems. The mother was cold and critical, and the father drank too much and was hardly ever around. Still, he taught Eleanor to help others.

Teacher: That's an excellent summary, Adam. You've given us the highlights of this section.

(Prediction)

Teacher: What do you predict will happen next?

Adam: I think the next section will tell us how Eleanor Roosevelt overcame some of the difficulties of her childhood and how she happened to meet and marry Franklin Roosevelt.

Teacher: Does anyone have a different prediction? Okay. Let's read the next section to see how our prediction works out. Who would like to be the leader for this section?

11 Integrating Technology in Content Area Classrooms to Support Reading Comprehension

Joseph John Morgan, Randall Boone, and Kyle Higgins

Struggling readers often have difficulty gaining access to content area text due to deficits in three main areas: 1) word identification, 2) vocabulary, and 3) comprehension of the material read (Bryant, Ugel, Thompson, & Hamff, 1999). In addition, struggling readers tend to have a lack of experience with the topic of content area lessons and have a difficult time making connections between their own experiences and the information being presented by the author (Bryant et al., 1999; National Joint Committee on Learning Disabilities [NJCLD], 2008). Interventions and adaptations designed to target these areas of the reading comprehension process have been found to be effective for struggling readers (Roberts, Torgesen, Boardman, & Scammacca, 2008).

Although students with disabilities may have difficulty in all areas of reading, targeted intervention and support in vocabulary instruction and comprehension strategies have shown a significant effect on the academic achievement of this population (Bryant et al., 2000; Roberts et al., 2008). Direct and explicit instruction of the word, as well as its definition and importance to the topic, are highly effective ways to increase knowledge of vocabulary and to teach struggling readers specific vocabulary terms (Roberts et al., 2008). Students should be provided opportunities to generalize and contextually use the word as frequently as possible after they have learned it in order to ensure mastery (NJCLD, 2008).

Adapting the material and guiding the learning process have been identified as effective strategies to aid in a student's comprehension of content area material and support mastery of content area material (Higgins, Boone, & Lovitt, 2002; NJCLD, 2008; Scruggs, Mastropieri, & Okolo, 2008). Adapted material focuses on the essential information from content and eliminates much of the extraneous information (Abadiano & Turner, 2002). Using adapted materials allows the content to become accessible to a wider range of students in the classroom environment (Higgins et al., 2002). Using organizational frameworks and graphic organizers to assist students in structuring their thinking while reading content area material is another strategy found to be effective in developing comprehension skills (NJCLD, 2008; Scruggs et al., 2008). Graphic organizers help students identify where they are in the reading process, what the essential ideas are, and how they connect with other information learned.

Understanding reading adaptations and interventions is important in the content areas because the textbook is the primary instructional tool utilized for students to gain information (Boone & Higgins, 2007a; Bryant et al., 1999; Higgins et al., 2002; Mastropieri, Scruggs, & Graetz, 2003; NJCLD, 2008). Struggling readers tend to have difficulty gaining access to information presented in a textbook for a variety of reasons. The textbooks often are written with a structure and coherence that does not make sense to struggling readers, are written at a grade level that is within the students' frustration level, and contain pictures and graphics that are distracting from the content (Bryant et al., 1999; Higgins et al., 2002; Mastropieri et al., 2003). Strategies, accommodations, and adaptations to gain access to and use the textbook are essential for student success in content area classrooms.

TECHNOLOGY-BASED APPLICATIONS TO
SUPPORT CONTENT AREA READING COMPREHENSION

Integrating technology is one strategy to address the needs of struggling readers in content area classrooms. Using technology in classroom instruction has shown clear evidence for increasing the academic achievement of struggling learners in content area classroom environments as well as increasing motivation to gain access to additional materials (Anderson-Inman & Horney, 2007; Boon, Fore, Blankenship, & Chalk, 2008; Jerome & Barbetta, 2005; Kennedy, 2011). It is important to remember that the textbook remains the main source of instruction in content area classrooms at the secondary level when thinking about incorporating technology into content area instruction (Boone & Higgins, 2007a; Bryant et al., 1999; Higgins et al., 2002; Mastropieri et al., 2003; NJCLD, 2008). Therefore, technology accommodations and supports incorporated into content area instruction tend to focus on providing access to the textbook. This includes adapting text and placing it into digital format, using technological devices to support understanding of material, adapting software to support content area instruction, and developing appropriate background knowledge to provide a contextual reference point.

Planning to Incorporate Technology for Content Area Reading Comprehension

Using technology to support instruction can take time and preplanning in order to 1) connect to the learning standards and objectives of the content area course, 2) ensure that students will learn the essential information as determined by the instructor, and 3) meet the needs of struggling readers in the classroom environment (Anderson-Inman & Horney, 2007; Cowan, 2008; Higgins et al., 2002). Teachers can increase the likelihood that incorporating technology into instruction will be successful if they create specific and purposeful lessons plans that make connections between the content area standards and the technology integration.

Using Technology that Supports Student Mastery of the Objective   Integrating technology into content area instruction holds promise for increasing the reading comprehension of struggling readers. It is important, however, that teachers understand how to connect technology to the mastery of the objective in the classroom setting (Cowan, 2008). The informational box contains a step-by-step process that teachers should follow when making the decision to include technology in classroom instruction.

Teachers should begin the planning process by considering the requirements of the content area curricula (e.g., the standards set by the state, the scope and sequence of the textbook). Teachers should identify places in the content area curricula where 1) struggling readers might have difficulty gaining access to the material and 2) technology might be a logical fit to support student comprehension (Cowan, 2008). Teachers who want to incorporate technology should ensure that the technology is aligned to the objective for the rest of the class. For example, if the objective of an algebra class is to graph points on a line and determine the slope, then a graphing calculator would be a logical choice for technology integration; using a piece of software designed to practice basic math skills in a repetitive format would not. Student learning is enhanced if there is a clear connection between the integration of technology and the instructional objective of the course. Simply integrating technology for technology's sake does not assist in learning the material. Any technology selected should 1) support student understanding of a topic and 2) connect to the instructional standards and objectives.

Cowan (2008), drawing on an early paradigm for considering technology use in education (Taylor, 1980), suggested that technology can be used in three main ways to support classroom instruction—as a tutor, as a tool, and as a tutee. When technology is serving in the role of a tutor, students are generally practicing repeatable skills to assist them in generalization and memorization (Cowan, 2008). For example, technology might serve as a tutor in a math class for students to practice their basic math skills or in an elementary social studies class when students are memoriz-

---

BOX 11.1 /// **Steps in Planning to Integrate Technology into Classroom Instruction**

1. Consider the academic curricular standards and expectations and determine if there is a logical place to integrate technology to support student learning.

2. Consider the academic levels of students in the classroom in order to determine their needs for accommodations and adaptations.

3. Determine what role technology will serve (tutor, tool, or tutee); this decision should be based on the instructional objective and student needs.

4. Identify technology resources available (and needed, if applicable) to support student learning.

5. Write a detailed plan for how students should gain access to and use the technology, and teach this plan to students prior to use.

6. Assess students frequently to ensure they are learning the necessary material.

7. Make adjustments to the technology integration based on student assessment data.

---

ing the names of the 50 states. Technology serves as a tool when it assists the student in completing a specified task. A technology tool might assist a student in writing a history essay by allowing him or her to complete research and write the final paper or in a science class by graphing the data found during a science lab. Finally, technology serves as a tutee when a student programs the computer to do a particular task (Cowan, 2008). Technology serves as a tutee when a student creates a computer program to follow the stock market for an economics class or creates a multimedia simulation of a frog dissection for a biology class.

Once instructional components have been identified that could be enhanced by the use of technology, teachers must make a plan for student access to resources and how the technology will be used in the classroom environment (Cowan, 2008). Teachers should determine the amount and types of technology available to them for classroom instruction. An explicit teaching plan with detailed instructions should be developed once resources have been identified and secured—both to guide the teacher's instruction and support the student's use of technology (Cowan, 2008; Higgins et al., 2002). Expectations of student learning and use of technology to support comprehension should be clearly explained to students prior to use.

Student Mastery of the Technology After planning technology integration that supports both student needs and the curricular agenda, teachers must ensure that students adequately know how to use the technology designed to support their learning. If students are not familiar with the technology being introduced, then they may spend more time focusing on the basics of the technology and not enough on gaining comprehension of content area materials. Therefore, prior to introducing the technology, teachers should allow students to explore the technology that will be used to aid in content area comprehension. Students should be shown the main characteristics of the technology, including buttons (either physical or digital), basic functions of the technology, and the structure of information. Teachers should assess students in their knowledge of the piece of technology and explicitly reteach the components of the technology if students do not show mastery on the assessment.

After teaching about the structure of the technology being integrated into classroom instruction, teachers should provide an overview of the instructional pedagogy used within the technological application. A preview of the structure of technological content, the steps that students will follow to gather the necessary information, and the assessment checks for the students should all be considered. This will help students structure their own learning process and will also provide a structure for understanding if they are learning the material.

Incorporating Adapted Texts into Content Area Instruction

Because the textbook remains the main component of instruction for content area classrooms, it becomes important for educators to find ways to accommodate struggling readers within these environments (Boone & Higgins, 2007a; Bryant et al., 1999; Higgins et al., 2002; Mastropieri et al., 2003; NJCLD, 2008). Using adapted textbooks is one accommodation that has been shown to be effective for struggling readers (e.g., books on e-readers, open-source books, digital text) (Anderson-Inman & Horney, 2007; Cavanaugh, 2011; Higgins et al., 2002). Using adapted texts in content area classrooms has had a positive effect on student achievement, primarily because the texts provide accessibility options that are not found in the traditional textbook (Anderson-Inman & Horney, 2007; Higgins et al., 2002). Common features of adapted texts include: 1) text-to-speech capabilities, 2) media that is related to the material being presented, 3) shortened material that focuses on important concepts, 4) focus and support on key vocabulary, 5) summarizations of the key information, and 6) the option to change the pace of instruction (Higgins et al., 2002). In addition, using technology in reading has been linked to increased student motivation to read the material (Maynard, 2010).

Anderson-Inman and Horney (2007) identified 11 main ways that text can be adapted to serve struggling students in academic instruction.

1.   Presentational, which is focused on altering the physical layout of the text

2.   Navigational, which addresses the reader's ability to link within the text or to outside supports

3.   Translational, which provides alternative language to describe content

4.   Explanatory, which provides additional information to clarify a point

5.   Illustrative, which provides examples of the content being presented

6.   Summarizing, which highlights the main points for the reader to ensure understanding

7.   Enrichment, which provides additional and extended information to students

8.   Instructional, which provides prompts and questions to support reader understanding during the reading process

9.   Notational, which provides the reader with the opportunity to take notes during reading

10. Collaborative, which allows the reader to connect with other readers to discuss information

11. Evaluational, which allows the reader to assess his or her understanding of the material

Different types of adapted text will support struggling readers in various ways. Content area teachers should first assess their students' reading needs when making the decision to incorporate an adapted text into classroom instruction and use those data to inform the type of adapted text chosen for instruction. Table 11.1 contains a questionnaire that teachers can use in order to determine what type of accommodations a student with specific deficits might need in an accommodated text.

Teachers have several options when it comes to incorporating adapted text into content area instruction, including using e-book readers and open-source textbooks and creating adapted texts. Teachers should consider the following when deciding whether to use a specific adapted text: 1) the needs of the student, 2) the resources available for acquiring adapted textbooks, 3) the technology available in the classroom, and 4) the amount of time to commit to using adapted texts. Table 11.2 contains a summary of the different options for digital text as well as suggested uses and the amount of time needed for implementation.

Table 11.1. Determining the type of accommodations students may need

If a student has reading comprehension problems related to. . .	He or she may need. . .
Issues reading the font due to size or color	Presentational adaptations
Reading passages that are too long or navigating back and forth between sections in a traditional textbook	Navigational adaptations
The language of the text (either native language issue or the academic level of the text is too high)	Translational adaptations
Lack of background knowledge or experience or understanding the concepts being presented	Explanatory or illustrative adaptations
Connecting ideas as they are reading or putting the information together after reading a passage	Summarizing, instructional, notational, or collaborative adaptations
Discussing the information read (either through oral or written language)	Collaborative adaptations
Monitoring their learning and ensuring they have learned the appropriate material	Summarizing or evaluational adaptations

E-book Readers   E-book readers have become a popular method for acquiring information from text. E-book readers provide text in digital format that can be read from a variety of different mobile devices. Users can click on a variety of hyperlinks that provide additional information about concepts or vocabulary, initiate accessibility features such as text-to-speech, highlight important information and take notes while reading, and easily navigate between different parts of the book.

E-books are available from a variety of sources (Edyburn, 2011). Free e-books can be downloaded from the Internet, including Project Gutenberg (http://www.gutenberg.org) and the University of Pennsylvania (http://onlinebooks.library.upenn.edu). These e-book files can be read on a computer or retrieved or translated to a format that is compatible to an e-book reader. In addition, local libraries often have a collection of e-books that are available for checkout. E-books can also be downloaded from the "bookstores" of different electronic devices (e.g., Kindle store on Amazon.com, iBook store for iPad, Barnes and Noble store for the Nook). Many books within these stores are available for free as well as for purchase, including some textbooks.

Table 11.2. Types of adapted digital texts

Adapted digital text option	Suggested uses	Financial resources	Time
E-book readers	Use during reading because e-book readers often have accessibility functions (e.g., text-to-speech) and academic supports (e.g., hyperlinked vocabulary words and notes functions).	Teachers would need to purchase the reader itself and the books (although sometimes they are free).	Limited amount of time
Open-source textbooks	Use before, during, and after reading because open-source textbooks often provide introductory activities to build background knowledge, support for students during the reading of the material, and after-reading support through summaries and assessment questions.	Many open-source textbooks are free for educators or cost a nominal subscription fee.	Limited amount of time
Adapted digital texts	Use before, during, and after reading because adapted digital texts are created by the teacher and focus on the content students should be learning during the class period. Adapted digital texts provide accommodations and adaptations designed for a particular classroom.	Adapted digital texts have little to no cost, depending on the software used to create the text.	Large amount of time for teacher planning

Cavanaugh (2011) suggested that teachers should plan lessons that teach the structure of an e-book before implementing its use within the classroom environment to ensure that students understand the features of the device and how to navigate the text within the e-book. Ensuring mastery of the e-book device itself allows students to focus on comprehending the material instead of how to use the technology.

Instructors must consider the accessibility of the reader when deciding to use an e-book. The Americans with Disabilities Act (ADA) of 1990 (PL 101-336) and Section 508 of the Rehabilitation Act of 1973 (PL 93-112) require that the technology used within educational environments meet standards of accessibility wherein people with disabilities can adequately use the technology at equal levels to their typical peers. It is important for teachers to familiarize themselves with the accessibility features of e-book readers, the needs of the students in their classroom environments, and the legal requirements of technology integration prior to securing technology to use as a part of instruction.

There are some limitations to using e-book readers to support content area comprehension. First, many of the texts that are available for download are adapted to meet only presentational, navigational, and translational needs (e.g., the font can be varied, users can easily move back and forth between parts of the text, text-to-speech can be used). The content is not modified, explained, or illustrated in a different manner than the traditional textbook, however. Although the modifications for presentation, navigation, and translation are important for some struggling readers, students who are reading well below grade level may still have difficulty gaining access to the text independently.

Open-Source Textbooks   Open-source textbooks are available in a variety of formats (e.g., text, downloadable digital file, hypertext online) that can be revised and edited by the instructor of the course to meet the needs of students in the classroom (Shelstad, 2011). Many open-source textbooks are available for free or a small fee and are available in a variety of settings and formats. Open-source textbook publishing operates from a philosophy that users should have the right to 1) reuse content for instructional purposes, 2) revise content to be up to date and reflect current thought on a topic or idea, 3) remix content to meet the needs of students in a specific classroom, and 4) redistribute edited content to other users via the Internet so they can review, critique, and strengthen information (Shelstad, 2011). Users can easily see who wrote the material for the open-source textbook, who has edited it, and can track changes that have occurred with the content. Open-source textbooks often also address the organization and structure of learning by providing students with an advance organizer that provides 1) the objective of the section they are about to read, 2) the vocabulary that they need to know to gain access to the material, 3) summaries of each lesson, and 4) assessment questions they can ask themselves in order to ensure mastery.

Open-source textbooks can provide students with a variety of additional resources to support their understanding of the concepts and materials. Users will find links throughout many open-source textbooks that make explanatory, illustrative, and enrichment accommodations. For example, a lesson might introduce the topic of the scientific method in a text. After describing the scientific method, the authors of the open-source textbook might embed a hyperlink to an online video that shows an example of how someone might use all the parts of the scientific method. In addition, the authors might create hyperlinks to specific vocabulary words that are important for students to know in order to gain access to the material. Providing resources ensures that students have a complete understanding of the concept being introduced and allows them to accommodate their own learning and knowledge. Rose and Meyer (2002) contended that the principle of universal design for learning requires multiple means of representation of content.

It is important for teachers who are deciding whether to supplement content area instruction with an open-source textbook to ensure that the presentation of the material supports the instruction happening in the classroom environment. Open-source textbooks are available from a variety of web sites and can often be downloaded to an e-book reader (see Table 11.3). Finally, accessibility should also be considered to ensure that all students will be able to learn equally from the

Table 11.3.   Open-source textbooks

Open-source textbook	Web site
CK-12 Flexbooks	http://www.ck12.org/flexbook
Connexions	http://cnx.org
Curriki	http://www.curriki.org
Flat World Knowledge	http://www.flatworldknowledge.com
Open Text Book	http://www.opentextbook.org
Wikibooks	http://en.wikibooks.org

technology provided. The National Instructional Materials Accessibility Standards is a technical file format standard that has been developed by the National Center on Accessible Instructional Materials (see http://aim.cast.org) to help standardize the file format for publishers to provide to people with disabilities. Individuals with certain specific disabilities (e.g., significant sensory disabilities) as outlined in the Chaffee Amendment of 1996 (PL 104-197) are eligible for free access through an "authorized entity" (e.g., a disability support organization, educational service group) to almost any published text, including textbooks.

Creating Adapted Texts   Both e-books and open-source textbooks provide text in a digital format to students. Digital text in these formats, however, are not always individualized and may not meet the instructional needs of the students. A teacher may make the decision to create his or her own adapted text in order to provide accessible information in a way that is closely aligned with classroom instruction. Teacher-created adapted digital texts contain many of the same components of an e-book reader and open-source textbook, including hypertext to provide additional information, graphics and charts to support student understanding, and links to connect the reader to outside resources to support student understanding of the concepts (Higgins et al., 2002).

Creating an adapted digital text is a labor-intensive task, primarily in the planning stages. The majority of time is spent in the early stages of planning to ensure that the adapted digital text will: 1) meet the instructional objective of the teacher, 2) meet the needs of the student, and 3) function appropriately within the classroom setting (Higgins et al., 2002). Higgins et al. suggested that teachers should review a variety of academic resources that are already available (e.g., instructional software, web sites or resources that provide the additional information, modifications to the existing textbook) prior to creating an adapted digital text.

Once teachers decide to use an adapted digital text, they should review the content from the traditional textbook, as well as grade-level content standards, to determine the essential information to include in the adapted version of the text (Higgins et al., 2002). Essential information includes material that: 1) will be used in subsequent lessons to teach additional information, 2) will be used in subsequent grade levels or courses, and 3) will be assessed (either on standardized assessments or summative assessments used in class). After identifying essential information, teachers creating an adapted digital text should then determine the types of accommodations or modifications that might be needed for struggling readers in the content area, including hyperlinked vocabulary words, guiding questions, interactive notetaking, or graphic organizers to assist in structuring the student's learning (Higgins et al., 2002). The teachers should also determine if additional resources (e.g., audio files, sample videos, illustrations) should be included. After all of these instructional decisions have been made, the teachers can then begin creating the content for the adapted digital text.

A variety of options are available for teachers to create adapted digital text. One of the easiest ways is to type the content into a standard word processing document and then save the file as HTML, which is the basic file format for all web browsers. This is easily read by web development software, making it easily loadable to the Internet for use. Options for web development software include basic cut-and-paste editors that provide a "what you see is what you get" interface, on the easier end, content management systems, and professional web design software for more ad-

Table 11.4.　Tools for creating adapted digital text

Word processors	Microsoft Word http://www.microsoftstore.com Pages http://www.apple.com	These productivity tools allow the user to save content, both text and graphical, as an HTML, which can be processed by a browser into a web page.
Web development	Dreamweaver http://www.adobe.com Google Sites http://www.sites.google.com Drupal http://www.drupal.org	Content development tools for the Internet vary widely, from dedicated commercial software (e.g., Dreamweaver) to free online options (e.g., Google Sites). Content management systems (e.g., Drupal) offer highly sophisticated options for implementing larger web sites within an organization or group of user/developers.
Mobile devices	Live Code http://www.runrev.com GameSalad http://www.gamesalad.com	Although digital text development may not be the primary focus of the application programming interfaces indicated here, both provide the opportunity for creating text-based content for students.
Multimedia text authoring	iBooks Author http://www.apple.com	New tools complete with authoring templates similar to those found in presentation software are specifically designed to create digital textbooks.

vanced users. Teachers could also use application programming interface software that uses natural, intuitive language in its programming code to create adapted digital texts for many popular mobile devices such as smartphones and tablet computers. Finally, an adapted digital text could be formatted to work on an e-book reader or other mobile device using conversion software. Free as well as paid versions of conversion software are available online. Teachers should consider the resources available to them and their students when determining what platform to use to create an adapted digital text. Table 11.4 outlines several digital tools for creating adapted digital text.

Teachers also must consider copyright regulations when making adapted versions of textbooks. There are no specific rules on creating adapted digital text, and teachers are encouraged to work with their school district to determine appropriate use of copyright within the classroom environment (Higgins et al., 2002).

Handheld Devices　　Mobile handheld devices (e.g., iPod touch, iPhone, iPad, tablet computers) also can be used for reading digital text. In addition, they can be used to develop student vocabulary (Kennedy, 2011). Kennedy created a series of podcasts designed to explicitly teach social studies vocabulary to students with and without disabilities in general education classroom settings. The podcasts incorporated audio and graphic representations of the vocabulary words being taught in the classroom environment, as well as evidence-based practices related to vocabulary instruction. Students reviewed these podcasts and then completed an assessment. Kennedy found that struggling students who used podcasts that included direct instruction outperformed all other students in their mastery of the vocabulary on the end-of-week assessments. Creating vocabulary podcasts can free up classroom instructional time as students download and review them independently without direct teacher support.

Handheld devices also can assist students during reading to gain access to the pronunciation and definition of unknown words. Because unknown vocabulary inhibits reading comprehension (Scruggs et al., 2008), it is important that students have the ability to look up the word in order to ensure strong contextual understanding of the material. Many handheld devices contain internal dictionaries or have dictionary applications available for download. Students could use handheld devices during content area instruction to look up additional resources or information to clarify the content being discussed. Students could independently gain access to videos, graphics, and alternative presentations of material being discussed in the content area.

Finally, applications on handheld devices can support and extend content area comprehension. Many educational applications are available for download (both free and for minimal cost) on several handheld devices and smartphones. For example, several applications relate to the study of U.S. history, including the presidents of the United States, major events within U.S. history, and games related to topics often covered in U.S. history classrooms. In addition, several textbook publishing companies have applications for download that review and extend information found in the textbook.

Software

Educational software is commonly used within classroom environments to support student comprehension of content area instruction (Boon et al., 2008; Boone & Higgins, 2007b; Higgins, Boone, & Williams, 2000; Jerome & Barbetta, 2005). Software publishing companies have produced a large amount of educational software to teach students specific concepts and skills, assist students in extending their learning, and help students organize their thoughts while participating in content area instruction. Researchers have found that using software to organize student understanding of grade-level texts (e.g., Inspiration software) can increase student understanding of the material on posttest measures when compared with traditional textbook instruction (Boon, Burke, Fore, & Hagan-Burke, 2006b; Boon, Burke, Fore, & Spencer, 2006a). Jerome and Barbetta found that students who used software that actively engaged them in a social studies classroom significantly increased scores on a posttest measure. Along with active gains in academic achievement as a result of software use, students have also reported being more motivated to learn the material and more excited about instruction (Boon, Fore, & Rasheed, 2007).

Although the successful incorporation of educational software into content area instruction for students with disabilities may lead to higher academic achievement and motivation, it is important for teachers to be critical consumers of educational software (Boone & Higgins, 2007b; Higgins et al., 2000; Marino & Tsurusaki, 2011). Not all educational software programs have been adequately assessed using formative and summative evaluations to ensure that they are effective, especially when it comes to specific populations of students (e.g., those with disabilities, English language learners, struggling readers) (Boone & Higgins, 2007b). Educators should consider a variety of questions when determining whether software would be an effective intervention for struggling learners, including 1) the students the software was designed for, 2) the content and itsappropriateness for learning objectives, 3) the presentation of material and if it meets universal design criteria, and 4) the ease of use (Boone & Higgins, 2007b). Teachers also should consider whether the students in a content area classroom would be interested in using the software and whether the type of instruction used meets the needs of struggling learners (Marino & Tsurusaki, 2011). Teachers can evaluate software and critically review its effectiveness to ensure that the technology supports student learning and mastery of the material.

Background Knowledge-Building Activities

Background knowledge is essential for reading comprehension because it helps students make connections to previously learned materials and their personal experiences to comprehend the new information being presented (Gill, 2008; Lacina, 2008). Struggling readers often lack the background knowledge and the ability to activate necessary background knowledge needed to read content area texts with comprehension (Gersten, Fuchs, Williams, & Baker, 2001). Therefore, it is important for content area teachers to create opportunities for struggling readers to build background knowledge before reading. Virtual field trips (VFTs) and WebQuests are two options for building background knowledge using technology.

Virtual Field Trips Klemm and Tuthill (2003) defined a *VFT* as a visit to a distant location using technological devices (e.g., Internet, mobile device, video). VFTs typically contain text or audio/video files that orient the user to the material being presented and then provide users with an opportunity to explore the location through multimedia opportunities (Frick, Ruppert, & Ballard, 2010). VFTs allow students to learn information about a concept or topic with which they have little knowledge or experience. For example, students in a science class might take a VFT to

Table 11.5. Virtual field trip web sites

Virtual field trip topic	Web site
Blackwell's Best	http://www.vickiblackwell.com/vft.html
History Tech: 15 Awesome Interactive Virtual Field Trips	http://historytech.wordpress.com/2011/04/26/15-awesome-interactive-virtual-field-trips
Public Broadcasting Service	http://www.pbs.org
Simple K12: Virtual Field Trips	http://www.simplek12.com/virtualfieldtrips
The Teacher's Guide: Virtual Tours and Field Trips	http://www.theteachersguide.com/virtualtours.html
Tramline	http://www.tramline.com/trips.htm
Utah Education Network	http://www.uen.org/tours

a desert location to see the types of plants and animals that live there. Creating background knowledge increases the likelihood that students will have a conceptual reference point to focus on while reading about the topic, thereby increasing their comprehension of the material.

Teachers can either participate in VFTs that have been developed by outside agencies or create their own for use in classroom instruction (Klemm & Tuthill, 2003; Lacina, 2008; Smedley & Higgins, 2005). Several VFTs have been created and are available on the Internet or via a mobile device that would be appropriate to incorporate into content area instruction. For example, Frick et al. (2010) created a series of VFT applications available for download that allow students to experience different geographical locales (e.g., salt marshes, swamp forests, cove forests). Table 11.5 provides a list of VFTs that are available for use in content area classrooms.

Teachers can also create their own VFTs for students in the content area. Smedley and Higgins (2005) suggested that creating a VFT allows teachers to focus students on the information that will be important to the unit of study and ensure that the information presented is relevant. Teachers can use a digital camera (either video or still) in an everyday location in order to create a VFT. Teachers use the camera to walk students through the key elements of the location or topic that they will be reading about (Smedley & Higgins, 2005). The video file can then be saved on a computer, on individual CDs, or on external hard drives for students to view before reading the material in class. The teacher can then think about the important things he or she would like to convey through the VFT and create a storyboard or concept map for how that information should be presented (Mongan-Rellis, n.d.).

Teachers should consider the background knowledge a student must have prior to reading the material before incorporating a VFT into content area instruction. The teacher should then review the VFT to make sure that the background material needed is addressed. In addition, the teacher should ensure that the VFT includes accessibility features, including text that can be read by a screen reader, hyperlinked information for additional information, and descriptions of pictures or charts that are included. Teachers should consider including a graphic organizer with detailed instructions on what students should focus on throughout the VFT, thereby scaffolding the students' learning and ensuring they experience the appropriate material.

WebQuests A *WebQuest* is defined as a directed Internet-based resource search to find information or answer a specific question (Skylar, Higgins, & Boone, 2007). Students participating in a WebQuest review a series of web sites preselected by the teacher in order to gather information, solve a problem, or answer a specific question (Skylar et al., 2007). The WebQuest should be structured to include the: 1) introduction, 2) task, 3) resources, 4) process, and 5) evaluation (Lacina, 2008). Because WebQuests are on the Internet, students can click additional hyperlinks to gain access to related information, seek alternative resources to help them in their understanding, and review information that is often presented in a variety of formats (e.g., text, audio, video) (Skylar et al., 2007).

Although there are many benefits to using a WebQuest to build background knowledge, there may be a few drawbacks for struggling readers. The first is that WebQuests are founded on

Table 11.6. Content accessibility tools

Constraints	Google Custom Search Engine http://www.google.com/cse	This tool allows teachers to preselect web sites to limit the number and content of sites that a particular search term would produce.
	TrackStar http://trackstar.4teachers.org	Web sites can be linked in a specific sequence for students to follow using this tool.
Affordances	Awesome Highlighter http://www.awesomehighlighter.com	An annotated facsimile of any web page can be created with this online tool. Annotations include highlighted text and sticky notes.
	Readability http://www.readability.com	Web pages that are cluttered with nonessential information or advertisements can be stripped of those unwanted elements using this tool.

an inquiry-based learning approach in which students make their own connections between pieces of information (Skylar et al., 2007). Struggling readers may have difficulty gaining access to the information that is presented on the web site without additional support and may not make the appropriate connections between pieces of information. In addition, WebQuests can take a large amount of time to develop and to implement in the classroom environment (Skylar et al., 2007).

Skylar et al. (2007) suggested that developing a WebQuest study guide using hypertext might aid struggling students in structuring the needed information. These study guides should include the components of effective instruction for struggling readers, including 1) an advance organizer to orient students to the task, 2) introduction to the objective of the WebQuest, 3) use of a graphic organizer to structure information, 4) provision of partial responses to the graphic organizer so that students can simply complete the thoughts, 5) a list of needed vocabulary words, and 6) explicit instructions on what the student should be doing at each step of the activity. The information reviewed by struggling readers has structure and organization with these supports, thereby assisting the appropriate development of background information to support student understanding.

CONTENT ACCESSIBILITY ON THE INTERNET

Brunvand and Abadeh (2010) suggested several online web-support technologies that can help students locate and understand digital content from the Internet. Instructional design of specific content lessons can include customized search engines and special-focus browser tab configurations that provide appropriate constraints when students are seeking information within the larger Internet milieu. There are also tools that allow the addition of instructional affordances such as annotations, highlighting, and readability improvement (see Table 11.6).

CONCLUSION

Appropriate technology use can increase academic achievement and student motivation to learn (Anderson-Inman & Horney, 2007; Boon et al., 2008; Jerome & Barbetta, 2005; Kennedy, 2011). Technology can be an effective curricular adaption in content area classrooms to improve the vocabulary development of struggling readers, provide access to text materials being used in the classroom environment, build background knowledge related to unknown concepts and ideas, and assist in structuring student thinking about a topic to ensure that they are understanding the overarching concepts and structures of the topic being discussed. Teachers can utilize technology to provide access to content area materials that students never have had before with appropriate planning, direct and explicit instruction on the use of technology, and careful monitoring and assessment of student learning (Cowan, 2008). Because comprehending content area material is essential for success in postsecondary measures (e.g., graduation, entry into institutions of higher education, job acquisition), general and special education teachers must determine ways to provide access to materials for struggling learners to set them up for success in their future endeavors (NJCLD, 2008). Technology as an adaptation or accommodation provides access and prepares students to be active participants in an increasingly global society that is bridged by digital communication.

REFERENCES

Abadiano, H.R., & Turner, J. (2002). Reading expository text: The challenges of students with learning disabilities. *The Northeastern Educational Research Association Journal, 38,* 49–55.

Americans with Disabilities Act (ADA) of 1990, PL 101-336, 42 U.S.C. §§ 12101 *et seq.*

Anderson-Inman, L., & Horney, M.A. (2007). Supported etext: Assistive technology through text transformations. *Reading Research Quarterly, 42,* 153–160.

Boon, R.T., Burke, M.D., Fore, C., & Hagan-Burke, S. (2006b). Improving student content knowledge in inclusive social studies classrooms using technology-based cognitive organizers: A systematic replication. *Learning Disabilities: A Contemporary Journal, 4*(1), 1–17.

Boon, R.T., Burke, M.D., Fore, C., & Spencer, V.G. (2006a). The impact of cognitive organizers technology-based practices on student success in secondary social studies classrooms. *Journal of Special Education Technology, 21*(1), 5–15.

Boon, R., Fore, C., Blankenship, T., & Chalk, J. (2008). Technology-based practices in social studies instruction for students with disabilities: A review of the literature. *Journal of Special Education Technology, 22*(4), 41–56.

Boon, R.T., Fore, C., & Rasheed, S. (2007). Students' attitudes and perceptions toward technology-based applications and guided notes instruction in high school world history classrooms. *Reading Improvement, 44,* 23–31.

Boone, R., & Higgins, K. (2007a). The role of instructional design in assistive technology research and development. *Reading Research Quarterly, 42,* 134–139.

Boone, R., & Higgins, K. (2007b). The software checklist: Evaluating educational software for use by students with disabilities. *Technology in Action, 3*(1), 1–16.

Brunvand, S., & Abadeh, H. (2010). Making online learning accessible: Using technology to declutter the web. *Intervention in School and Clinic, 45*(5), 304–311.

Bryant, D.P., Ugel, N., Thompson, S., & Hamff, A. (1999). Instructional strategies for content-area reading instruction. *Intervention in School and Clinic, 34,* 293–302.

Bryant, D.P., Vaughn, S., Linan-Thompson, S., Ugel, N., Hamff, A., & Hougen, M. (2000). Reading outcomes for students with and without reading disabilities in general education middle-school content area classes. *Learning Disability Quarterly, 23,* 238–252.

Cavanaugh, T.W. (2011, February 9). *Getting to know a digital textbook.* Retrieved from http://www.techlearning.com/article/getting-to-know-a-digital-textbook/47632

Chaffee Amendment of 1996, PL 104-197, 17 U.S.C. §§ 121 *et seq.*

Cowan, J.E. (2008). Strategies for planning technology-enhanced learning experiences. *Journal of Educational Strategies, Issues, and Ideas, 82,* 55–59.

Edyburn, D. (2011). A brief introduction to eBook readers. *Special Education Technology Practice, 13*(2), 19–21.

Frick, J., Ruppert, E., & Ballard, B. (2010). *Salt marsh virtual field trip* [iPod application]. Retrieved from the iTunes App Store.

Gersten, R., Fuchs, L.S., Williams, J.P., & Baker, S. (2001). Teaching reading comprehension strategies to students with learning disabilities: A review of research. *Review of Educational Research, 71,* 279–320.

Gill, S.R. (2008). The comprehension matrix: A tool for designing comprehension instruction. *The Reading Teacher, 6,* 106–113.

Higgins, K., Boone, R., & Lovitt, T.C. (2002). Adapting challenging textbooks to improve content area learning. In M.A. Shinn, H.M. Walker, & G. Stoner (Eds.), *Interventions for academic and behavioral problems II: Preventive and remedial approaches* (pp. 755–790). Bethesda, MD: National Association of School Psychologists.

Higgins, K., Boone, R., & Williams, D.L. (2000). Evaluating educational software for special education. *Intervention in School and Clinic, 36,* 109–115.

Jerome, A., & Barbetta, P.M. (2005). The effect of active student responding during computer-assisted instruction on social studies learning by students with learning disabilities. *Journal of Special Education Technology, 20*(3), 13–23.

Kennedy, M.J. (2011). *Effects of content acquisition podcasts on vocabulary performance of secondary students with and without learning disabilities* (Doctoral dissertation). Retrieved from Proquest. (3458221)

Klemm, E.B., & Tuthill, G. (2003). Virtual field trips: Best practices. *International Journal of Instructional Media, 30,* 177–193.

Lacina, J. (2008). Technologically based teacher resources for designing comprehension lessons. In C.C. Block & S.R. Parris (Eds.), *Comprehension instruction: Research-based best practices* (pp. 362–377). New York, NY: Guilford Press.

Marino, M.T., & Tsurusaki, B.K. (2011). Selecting software for students with learning and other disabilities. *The Science Teacher, 78*(3), 70–72.

Mastropieri, M.A., Scruggs, T.E., & Graetz, J.E. (2003). Reading comprehension instruction for secondary students: Challenges for struggling students and teachers. *Learning Disability Quarterly, 26,* 103–116.

Maynard, S. (2010). The impact of e-books on young children's reading habits. *Publishing Research Quarterly, 26,* 236–248.

Mongan-Rellis, H. (n.d.). *Virtual field trips.* Retrieved from www.duluth.umn.edu/~hrallis/guides/Virtual FieldTrips.html.

National Joint Committee on Learning Disabilities. (2008). Adolescent literacy and older students with learning disabilities. *Learning Disability Quarterly, 31,* 211–218.

Rehabilitation Act of 1973, PL 93-112, 29 U.S.C. §§ 701 *et seq.*

Roberts, G., Torgesen, J.K., Boardman, A., & Scammacca, N. (2008). Evidence-based strategies for reading instruction of older students with learning disabilities. *Learning Disabilities Research and Practice, 23,* 63–69.

Rose, D., & Meyer, A. (2002). *Teaching every student in the digital age: Universal design for learning.* Alexandria, VA: Association for Supervision and Curriculum Development.

Scruggs, T.E., Mastropieri, M.A., & Okolo, C.M. (2008). Science and social studies for students with disabilities. *Focus on Exceptional Children, 41*(2), 1–24.

Shelstad, J. (2011). How flat world knowledge is transforming college textbook publishing. *Publishing Research Quarterly, 27,* 254–258.

Skylar, A.A., Higgins, K., & Boone, R. (2007). Strategies for adapting WebQuests for students with learning disabilities. *Intervention in School and Clinic, 43,* 20–28.

Smedley, T.M., & Higgins, K. (2005). Virtual technology: Bringing the world into the special education classroom. *Intervention in School and Clinic, 41,* 114–119.

Taylor, R.P. (1980). Introduction. In R.P. Taylor (Ed.), *The computer in school: Tutor, tool, tutee* (pp. 1–10). New York, NY: Teachers College Press.

Index

Note: *b* indicates boxes, *f* indicates figures, *t* indicates tables.

Effective Instruction for Middle School Students with Reading Difficulties
The Reading Teacher's Sourcebook

By Carolyn A. Denton, Ph.D., Sharon Vaughn, Ph.D.,
Jade Wexler, Ph.D., Deanna Bryan, & Deborah Reed, Ph.D.

"A valuable resource for middle schools striving to meet reading standards."—*LINDA H. MASON, PH.D., THE PENNSYLVANIA STATE UNIVERSITY*

"An outstanding book that every reading teacher should have."—*ROBERT REID, PH.D., UNIVERSITY OF NEBRASKA*

US$49.95 | Stock #: BA-72438 | 2012
328 pages | 8 ½ x 11 | layflat paperback |
ISBN 978-1-59857-243-8

YOU'LL LEARN TO:

- select and administer assessments for comprehension, fluency, and word recognition
- use assessment results to plan individualized instruction
- apply research-supported instructional practices within a schoolwide RTI framework
- set manageable short-term learning goals with students
- give appropriate positive and corrective feedback

INCLUDES 20+ SAMPLE LESSONS

that model successful instruction step by step, with suggested teacher scripts, checklists for planning instruction, tips on generalization, and more.